THE
PATTERN LIFE

TEACHINGS OF
THE ORDER OF CHRISTIAN MYSTICS

THE PATTERN LIFE

Teachings of The Order of Christian Mystics

The "Curtiss Books" freely available at

WWW.ORDEROFCHRISTIANMYSTICS.CO.ZA

THE MASTER JESUS

Of course there were no pictures of the Master made during His Earthlife. All the pictures now in existence are but the various artists' conceptions. This picture was precipitated for the author directly from the invisible. The discarnate artist stated that the radiance of the Master was so glorious that it almost blinded him.

This sketch was the best he could do under the circumstances. When it was finished he precipitated it into the physical for our use. The face is sensitive and kind without being effeminate; strong, positive and masculine without being stern.

The Pattern Life

Transcribed by
HARRIETTE AUGUSTA CURTISS
and
F. HOMER CURTISS, B.S., M.D.
Founders of
THE ORDER OF CHRISTIAN MYSTICS
and
AUTHORS OF THE "CURTISS BOOKS"

2013 EDITION

REPUBLISHED FOR THE ORDER BY
MOUNT LINDEN PUBLISHING
JOHANNESBURG, SOUTH AFRICA
ISBN: 978-1-920483-24-1

Dedication

This edition is lovingly dedicated to the Memory

of the Founders of

The Order of Christian Mystics

Pyrahmos and Rahmea

and to

The Teacher of the Order

who on earth was called

Helena Petrovna Blavatsky

"Ministers of Christ and Stewards of the Mysteries of God."
1 Corinthians 4 vs. 1

TABLE OF CONTENTS

PREFACE

The life of Jesus has been studied from many angles
and has been given many interpretations, but never, as far
as we know, from the scientific standpoint of its analogy
with other expressions of life, and especially in connection
with the astronomical events in the heavens. It is from this
standpoint that we shall attempt to treat it.

Modern scientific research in atomic physics, also in
psychical research, has shown that the world which we
contact with our physical senses is not the only world.
Worlds have been proven to exist composed of substances
and forces whose rates of vibration are far too high for
our sense-organs to register. The external phenomena
which our senses report are, therefore, but the physical
and materialized manifestations of causes generated in the
super-physical worlds which can be contacted only by our
psychic and spiritual senses. And it is with these super
physical worlds, and their relation to the material world
and man, that all scriptures largely deal.

The archetype or ideal of all manifested forms must
have pre-existed in the super-physical realms as a pattern
ideal, etheric double or model, or there would be nothing
to guide the forces of Nature to produce symmetrical and
thoroughly organized forms.

As we have pointed out elsewhere: "This doctrine of
the pre-existence of all things before their physical manifestation is illustrated in many biblical passages. Not only
was 'every plant of the field *before* it was in the earth, and
every herb *before* it grew' (*Genesis, ii*, 5), but, 'Verily,
verily I say unto you, *Before* Abraham was, I am.' 'And
now, O Father, glorify thou me with thine own self with
the glory *which I had* with thee *before* the world was.'

(*St. John, xvii, 5*). And this same doctrine is the basis of all great religions and is implicit in most philosophies."[1]

We must remember that anything which changes, as all material things do, does not belong to the Realms of the Eternal, but to the realms of the temporal and transitory. The Eternal Reality is therefore found only in the super physical realms, where the prototypes or pattern-ideals exist, and not in their imperfect physical materialization. Therefore Reality does not depend upon having "spatio-temporal location" as some materialistically minded modern philosophers claim.

The only things upon which we can rely absolutely are therefore the spiritual pattern-ideals as the only true expressions of the one Reality, God. For God manifests as an objectively existing Cosmic Power, an independently existing Reality, which is directly presented and revealed to some extent, within the normal range of our perceptual experience. Hence, His existence, and something of what He is, has been discovered and made known. As St. Paul tells us, to understand the truth about the manifested universe: "We look not at the things which are seen, but at the things which are not seen: for the things which are seen are temporal; but the things which are not seen are eternal." (*II Corinthians, iv, 4*).[2]

The universe, therefore, sprang into physical manifestation not out of nothing nor by accident, but because of the creative ideals originated in the Consciousness and formulated by the Mind, and projected into manifestation by the Will of the Creator (Father), and then taken up, cherished, nourished and brought forth by the feminine aspect of the Creator (the Divine Mother).

---

[1] See *Why Are We Here?*, Curtiss, 3, 4.

[2] The theory that there exists the expression of Cosmic Energy called Life, which has certain vital and psychical qualities which, by contracting or materializing the universal into the particular, are the responsible cause of all diversified forms, and hence are competent to produce Reality, is called *Hylozoism*. It provides for a kind of Monism which includes both material and immaterial Reality.

The fact that the pre-existing etheric patterns of all forms are invisible is no proof that such patterns are only imaginary or are only mental concepts, and have no actual existence. The air we breathe, an odor, a colorless gas or an atom is invisible, yet they all actually exist and affect our lives. A field of force, such as surrounds the ends of a magnet, has both form and extension, yet it is invisible. We are so accustomed to think of matter as being something that is coarsely molecular, that we fail to remember that it is also atomic, etheric and radionic, and that a large part of the universe is invisible to our unaided sight.

Since all forms of life originate from eggs — or modified eggs, such as seeds, spores, etc. — which at first are identical in substance and structure, there must be a pre-existing pattern for their detailed and specific unfoldment. For, as the great naturalist, Louis Agassiz, rightly says: "Nature is the work of thought, the product of intelligence, carried out *according to plan*, therefore is premeditated!"[3] He is also correct in saying that: "All things had their origin in Spirit."[4] For the *involution* of the pattern must have preceded its *evolution* in matter or there would have been no pattern to unfold into an organized form.

It therefore follows logically that since man is the most highly evolved form in Nature, he also must have a super physical archetype or pattern which the forces of Nature are trying to unfold and materialize in ever greater perfection through the slow, upward processes of evolution.[5]

But man is far more than an animal body. The Real Self of man is a Spiritual Being striving to manifest temporarily through a human animal body. Since this truth is obvious, it is the spiritual archetype or invisible pattern that he is seeking to manifest on earth. And it is the stages in the unfoldment of this spiritual pattern which we shall

---

[3] *Methods of Study*, 14.
[4] *Principles of Zoology*, 154.
[5] For details see *The Truth About Evolution and the Bible*, Curtiss.

endeavor to show is exemplified in the successive incidents recorded in the life-story of Jesus. Even though we are told by standard authorities that: "It is now recognized that the Gospels are in no sense 'lives' of Jesus, and do not provide the material for a 'life,' merely a portrait,"[6] it is that "portrait" which we shall endeavor to clarify and enlarge.

Symbolically interpreted, the Gospel story relates to the individualized Ray of the Cosmic Christ which is latent in each human heart. In the events of Jesus' life we see this Christ-consciousness conceived, come to birth, grow in power, overcome the lower nature, master all its forces and make them willing servants, and finally triumph over death itself.

In this volume we do not intend to present a new theology or a new exegesis of the old theology, but merely to point out that the events related in the *Gospel* story were not first enacted in the life of Jesus, but have recurred cyclicly since the beginning of time. This was well known to the early church historian St. Augustine. He plainly tells us that: "The thing itself which is now called the Christian religion, really was known to the ancients, nor was it wanting *from the beginning of the human race*, until the time when Christ came in the flesh, from whence true religion, *which had previously existed*, began to be called Christian; and this in our days is the Christian religion, not as having been wanting in former times, but as having in later times received this name."[7] "There is a striking passage in the homily known as II. Clement, chapter xiv. . . . 'And the books of the apostles plainly declare that the Church existeth *not now for the first time*, but *hath been from the beginning*.'"[7]

That the essence of the teachings did not originate with Jesus is no reflection on Him; in fact, it proves that He was a true expression of the ageless cosmic truths as to the relation of God to man. And in spite of its many historical

[6] *Encyclopedia Britannica*, 13th Ed., Vol. I, 310.
[7] *Opera Augustini*, i,12. *Studies in Mystical Religion*, Jones, 80.

inaccuracies, and even flat contradictions,[8] the story is essentially and spiritually true when properly interpreted. Instead of following the usual orthodox interpretation of this age-old story, our spiritual interpretation seeks to illumine it by pointing out its spiritual meaning, and to apply it to our daily progress in spiritual unfoldment.

We hope that this symbolic and spiritual interpretation[9] will do much to counteract the destructive effects of, and help to rescue the Master's teachings from, the historical, materialistic, so-called "rational" or "higher criticism." For those materialists and higher critics who refuse to believe that God reveals Himself to man periodically, it will be impossible for them to explain the persistence through the ages of the universal traditions relating to a Virgin Mother and her immaculately conceived Son—which are found in nearly all religions—until they are willing to admit that there is a divine element of universal truth, and the same truth, in all religions, however overlaid by ignorance and distorted by superstition they may be.

We also wish to point out that by getting the *cosmic concept* of the teachings we can look through and beyond the letter of the *Gospels* and discover in them the cosmic laws governing the manifestation of Christhood through the human personality. Thus we may learn better how to manifest that spark of Christhood which is latent in every human heart. For by seeking to know the cosmic concept back of Jesus' teachings we can enter more and more into His thought and life and begin to demonstrate it in our own lives. For it is a psychological law that we react to and tend to express, even unconsciously, whatever ideas engage our active interest and focus our attention. And by knowing more of what He thought and meant we can train our minds to think somewhat after the fashion of His thought, and thus attune our minds more responsively to His mind. Thus will our minds tend to shape our lives more closely after His *Pattern Life*.

[8] See *Appendix* D.
[9] See *Appendix* B.

And because we see the universal, cosmic Law of Manifestation thus expressed in the story of Jesus' life, we claim that His life is the *Pattern Life* which the Spiritual Selves of all humanity must ultimately follow until they too can manifest the Divine through the human. They will thus prove that they are truly Sons and Daughters of God, the universal Father of all.

Because of the *Gospels'* many inaccuracies and contradictions,[10] many intellectuals and the worldy-wise have ridiculed the *Bible*. They say it is so inaccurate that it is wholly unreliable. And so they have deprived themselves of its spiritual message for the inspiration, comfort and guidance of their personal lives. But while we must necessarily accept the proven facts discovered by the higher critics as to the historical accuracy of certain names, places and dates, the actual sequence of events, and the objective reality of the miracles and other phenomena as related in the story, we shall nevertheless endeavor to discount, explain and *refute their well-meant conclusions*. Such considerations as they bring forward do not materially affect our thesis.

And that thesis is that the events in the life-story of Jesus—as a manifestation of the Spiritual Sun—follow the same steps or stages of unfoldment, and in the same order, as are followed by the physical Sun manifesting in Nature, as it makes its annual circuit through the twelve signs of the zodiac. While the incidents thus out pictured in the zodiac do not point to any one isolated historical event, however important and sacred that event may be considered by a particular people, religion or sect, they do point to the ever-recurring, periodic expressions of the Law of Manifestation of the Creator alike in Nature and humanity.

With this cosmic concept of the *Gospel* story in mind, we are not disturbed either by the ridicule of the *Gospels* by the agnostics and infidels, or even by either present or

---

[10] See *Appendix* D.

future discoveries of the scholars. In fact, we can turn the tables on them and laugh at them for their lack of spiritual understanding of a deeply religious book. We can join the Psalmist when he says: "He that sitteth in the heavens (or in the cosmic concept or higher, spiritual understanding) shall laugh; the Lord shall have them in derision." (*Psalms, ii*, 4).

The sequence of solar events set forth herein is called *the Universal Solar Myth* because these events take place continually in a regular cyclic manner among the stars in heaven. And the record of these cyclic events has been preserved and handed down age after age in many languages and religions, so that all who were capable of more fully understanding it, and were ready to accept its higher implications, might have an esoteric and symbolic explanation of the fundamental Law of Manifestation of God, both in the Cosmos and in man.

With this cosmic concept in mind we can see a new significance in the well-known passage: "The heavens declare the glory of God; and the firmament sheweth his handiwork. Day unto day uttereth speech, and night unto night sheweth knowledge." (*Psalms, xix*, 1,2).

The object in publishing this volume is three-fold. First and foremost, to apply the spiritual meaning of the universal incidents of *The Pattern Life* to help us to master and make the best use of the similar incidents in our own lives. Second, to refute the destructive conclusions of the Higher Critics, and eliminate further controversy over the many historical inaccuracies and flat contradictions in the *Gospels*. And thirdly, to recapture and revive the interest of that great company of still spiritually hungry, and therefore dissatisfied and unhappy, Souls who have turned away from the help, comfort and Soul-satisfaction the *Gospels* can give, because of a lack of understanding of those very inaccuracies and contradictions.

Since the various incidents and their interpretation overlap so closely, we trust that we will be pardoned for a certain amount of repetition. But we trust that such repetition will serve to fix our interpretation more firmly in the mind of the thoughtful reader.

No doubt some literalists will criticise our symbolic, universal and spiritual interpretation of the *Gospel* story in an effort to discredit our thesis, and we welcome all enlightening and constructive criticism.[11] But unless they can give a more satisfactory explanation of the historical inaccuracies and flat contradictions discussed herein, criticism of other matters is beside the point.

---

[11] We are inclined to agree with Prof. Arthur Drews when he says that: "Whoever, though not a specialist, invades the province of any science, and ventures to express an opinion opposed to its official representatives, must be prepared to be rejected by them with anger, to be accused of a lack of scholarship, 'dilettantism,' or 'want of method,' and to be treated as a complete ignoramus. This has been the experience of all up to now who, while not theologians, have expressed themselves on the subject of an historical Jesus. . . . He has been accused of 'lack of historical training,' 'bias,' 'incapacity for any real historical way of thinking,' etc." *The Christ Myth*, Drews, 13.

INTRODUCTION

THE UNIVERSAL SOLAR MYTH

BASIC PRINCIPLES

"There is no religion higher than Truth." *Ancient Aphorism*

"We maintain that, instead of the life story of Jesus' and other Saviors' being a mere personification of the natural phenomena occurring during the Sun's cycle of the year, both are exemplifications of one and the same universal law, i.e. the Law of Cyclic Manifestation. In other words, because the Sun is the Light Bearer and self-sacrificing Savior in Nature, it exemplifies the same unfoldment in the physical life of the universe that every divine Light Bearer or Savior of man exemplifies in the unfoldment of man's spiritual life." *The Key of Destiny*, Curtiss, 119.

There is but one Law of Manifestation, for the basic law is one, not many. This law is that all manifestation comes from above downward, from within outward and from center to circumference. And this law applies not only to the life-forms in Nature, but to life and consciousness on *all* planes.

Following this law our physical Sun radiates its life-giving forces from the center to the circumference of our solar system. In other words, it is the focal point through which the One Life of the Cosmos is poured forth to supply all the physical life-forms in Nature.

Since everywhere in Nature we see plan, purpose, design and the will-to-manifest—from the organization of cosmic systems down to the beautifully executed organization of the tiniest insect or the electrons in the atom—it is now generally accepted that there must be a supreme Cosmic

Intelligence or Great Architect—commonly called God—whose consciousness is so vast that it embraces all that we know of the manifested cosmos, which in turn is but the result of His Will-to-manifest. The projection of this Divine Will produces the cosmic force which causes all manifestation.

The universe has no explanation or meaning without postulating a Cosmic Intelligence, a cosmic power and a cosmic substance which together are able to create and preserve it until its inherent purpose toward a predetermined end is accomplished. In fact, no one whose mind can run the gamut from micro-millimeters to light-years, who can recognize a universe in both an atom and a solar system, who can recognize a manifestation of consciousness in the amoeba as well as in the inspirations of genius and the ecstasies of a mystic, can fail to recognize the workings of a Cosmic Intelligence back of all manifestation.

This primordial, universal cosmic force is called *Fohat* in Eastern Philosophy, and in Christian terminology is called the Cosmic Christ-force. All manifestations of life are therefore animated by greater or lesser currents of this One Life of the Cosmos.

It is called the Christ-force because it is the "only begotten son of the Father," or the primordial outgoing current of the Cosmic Life-force sent down into all the myriad forms in the manifested universe to animate them with the current of life necessary to enable them to unfold their pattern-form and fulfill their destined place in the Grand Plan of the Cosmos. Some aspect of this Divine Life-force must therefore be present as the energy of every atom and everything brought forth on earth.

Since we have seen that the Sun is the source of all physical light, life and force to all Nature, its Cosmic Life-force we call the Cosmic Christ-force to our solar system. Hence it may rightly be regarded as the Sun of God to the material universe.

It is a fundamental postulate in the philosophy of Cosmic

Soul Science that the spiritual Sun—the radiant source of
the Cosmic Christ-force stands—in a similar relation to
mankind as the physical Sun does to the physical universe,
namely, the source of all light, life and spiritual power to
all humanity.

Since the Law of Manifestation is One, the method
by which spiritual light, life and power is radiated by the
Spiritual Sun will naturally be exemplified by the physical
Sun, its material offspring. And since this same method
of radiation is exemplified in the events of Jesus' life, it
is from this cosmic standpoint that we shall interpret this
miraculous story, rather than from the literal, materialistic
and historical. It will thus be seen that every event, however miraculous and seemingly impossible, is positively
true as an inner spiritual experience in the life of every
Soul whose spiritual development has reached the stage
where the Annunciation has been made and the Christ-
consciousness (cosmic consciousness) has begun to unfold
and the Path to Christhood has been entered.

It is necessary to grasp this cosmic concept of Jesus'
life to understand fully its significance as the universal
Pattern Life for all mankind. For in it we find practically
the same list of events as in the life story of nearly every
Savior and Redeemer presented by former religions down
through the ages.

These events—from the miraculous birth from a virgin,
the flight, the baptism, the crucifixion, the rock tomb, the
descent into the nether regions, the resurrection and the
appearance afterward—all find a parallel in the lives of the
other Saviors or Lightbringers, all of whom held the same
exalted place in the minds and hearts of their worshippers
as Jesus holds among Christians.

If these events were found in but one or two instances
they might be attributed to coincidence. But since they are
found *in each case*, there must be some profound reason,
some fundamental law, back of these strange events which
are so astonishingly repeated in the same order.

This uniformity, far from belittling Jesus or representing Him as "just another Savior," in reality exalts Him, for it proves that *He was a divine personification* of the Law of God—the Law of Manifestation—to man, as is so plainly written in the heavens for our learning by the annual Cycle of the Sun as it passes through the 12 signs of the zodiac. Each event follows the same *Pattern Life*, the one in the physical world, the other in the spiritual world. Since the Law of Manifestation is one, it finds expression in and governs all worlds.

The presence in the *Bible* of the universal cosmic symbolism established by the Cycle of the Sun, is proof either of directly inspired writing, such as St. Paul refers to as coming through direct revelation (*Galatians*, i, 12-13), or else that the writers had been initiated into the Mystery Schools to which Jesus referred when He told His disciples that: "Unto you it is given to know the mysteries of the kingdom of God: but unto them that are without (*i.e.*, uninitiated), all these things are done in parables," (*St. Mark, iv*, 11). In either case the symbolism used shows the comprehension of the definite and universal stages of unfoldment governed by the Law of Manifestation and outpictured by the events in the universal story of the *Pattern Life* of its exponent in all great religions age after age.

We therefore know that the events in the life-story of Jesus contain a far deeper meaning and significance than appears on the surface. In fact, when properly interpreted they reveal the mystery of all manifestation, from the physical Sun in the solar system to the Son of God in the heart of man. But to understand this mystery we must grasp the cosmic concept of it. We are warned against being satisfied with the literal meaning of the words. "Who also hath made us able ministers of the New Testament: not of the letter, but of the spirit: for the letter killeth, but the spirit giveth life."[1]

The learned Fathers of the early Christian church taught

---

[1] *II Corinthians, III, 6.*

that we should make little of events themselves in comparison with the truths they conveyed. One of the greatest of these authorities, Frater Origen (185-254 A.D.), held that in most cases the allegorical and mystical interpretations are used to explain the spiritual meaning of actual facts. But in other cases they were *the only interpretations* to be accepted. As St. Paul tells us: "The natural man receiveth not the things of the Spirit of God: for they are foolishness unto him: neither can he know them, because they are spiritually discerned." (*I Corinthians, ii*, 14).

We shall therefore regard each incident in the life of Jesus as being a symbol or parable which contains an inner universal meaning applicable to the stages of unfoldment of the Christ-consciousness in the heart of each of us. "But without a parable spoke he not unto them."[2]

In simple words, our thesis is that just as the successive events in the passage of the Sun through the heavens govern the expressions of physical life in Nature, so in a corresponding manner, and following the same Law of Manifestation, the successive events in the life of Jesus exemplify the expression of the spiritual life in man.

We therefore repeat that the various events of the Sun in manifesting through the twelve signs of the zodiac during the cycle of the year are in reality an expression of the Divine Life-force—the Cosmic Christ-force—as individualized and embodied in the Sun, manifesting through the physical events of Nature. It is only natural then that when the cyclic period arrives for the renewed manifestation of the Spiritual Sun to humanity—individualized and embodied in the appearance on Earth of a spiritual Lightbringer, a Divine Being, an Avatar or Son of God—the events of His life should follow the same order as the events of the physical Sun in passing through the twelve signs of the zodiac. This cosmic outpouring takes place not only around us in the heavens (the macro-

---

[2] *St. Mark, IV*, 34.

cosmos), but also within us (the microcosmos). It is a drama in which the whole cosmos takes part.

In earlier ages these events were usually outpictured in the religious dramas of the various Mystery Schools of antiquity. Recent archeological discoveries have revealed the complete program of these events as witnessed by the people of Babylon more than 4000 years ago. Instead of being recorded on manuscripts or papyri which could fade or be altered, these records were made in cuneiform writing on baked clay tablets, so they have come down to us unaltered. Hence there can be no argument as to their accuracy or their priority thousands of years before the Christian era. Also the Chinese Trigrams show that they had a well-developed science of the stars 20,000 years B.C.

It is this regular cycle of events, repeated in a definite order, that is called "The Universal Solar Myth" or the life-story of the Mythic Christ, and which we find exemplified in the apparent histories of all great spiritual teachers or Lightbringers. It is also exemplified as the Mystic Christ in each heart in the spiritual events through which each Soul passes after the birth of the Christ-consciousness takes place in the heart until the final illumination and Mastery is achieved. This identity of events results not because each Teacher adopts or plagiarizes the legends of previous Teachers or because he copies the events of the Sun-cycle, but because *both are expressions of the same Divine Life-force*—the Cosmic Christ-force—of the Spiritual Sun, the one in the physical universe in terms of physical life, light and warmth, and the other to humanity in terms of spiritual Life, Light and Love.

Since all religions are based upon the manifestation of a Lightbringer whose life exemplifies the events of the Universal Solar Myth, the actual astronomical events[3] in the heavens give us a solid and scientific basis to guide our study as we take up the detailed explanation and

---

[3] For details see *Appendix* A.

spiritual interpretation of each event in the following chapters. With the aid of a star-map[4] it will be easy to follow the path of the Sun through the zodiac and note the marvelous succession of events.

Altho in the following chapters we shall clearly and irrefutably show that the events of the cosmic Sun-cycle are fully depicted in the life-story of Jesus, those who seek in that story of many contradictions only the literal interpretation of historical events as applied to the life of a single personality, will find only the outer garments; only the grave clothes and an empty tomb. But if their inner spiritual ears are open they can hear the Angel of the Tomb say to all who will listen and are ready to understand: "Why seek ye the living among the dead? He is not here, but is risen."

That these teachings are far older than the Christian era is testified to by St. Paul when he exhorted the Colossians (*i*, 23) to: "Be not moved away from the hope of the Gospel, which ye have heard, and *which was preached to every creature* which is under heaven; whereof I Paul am made a minister."

Lest the uniform coincidence of the events in the *Pattern Life* with those of the cycle of the Sun lead some to conclude that Jesus was just another mythological character, we can assure them that in spite of the coincidence, our years of research have corroborated our original belief—and that of Christendom—that Jesus of Nazareth was undoubtedly a physically historical personality.[4] Around Him the events of the Sun-cycle gradually gathered, just as they did around other historical characters such as Gotama, Cyrus, Alexander, Aesculapius, Appolonius, Confucius and many others.

As Mrs. Annie Besant very properly says: "The historical Christ, then, is a glorious Being belonging to the great spiritual hierarchy that guides the spiritual evolution

---

[4] In spite of such books as *The Christ Myth, Pagan Christs, Jesus, a Myth, Christianity and Mythology, Paganism in Our Christianity*, etc.

of humanity. . . . Round this glorious figure gathered the myths which united Him to the long array of His predecessors, the myths telling in allegory the story of all such lives, as they symbolize the work of the Logos in the Kosmos and the higher evolution of the human Soul."[5]

---

[5] *Esoteric Christianity*, Besant 139-40.
NOTE. It is hoped that the student will refer frequently to the astronomical events listed in *Appendix A* as to the order of those events as the details are interpreted in the following chapters. Follow them also on the star map in the *Appendix*.

CHAPTER I

INTERPRETATION OF THE GOSPELS

"Who that has understanding will suppose that the
first and second and third day, and the evening and the
morning, were without sun and moon and stars, or that
the first day was without sky?.... I do not suppose that
anyone doubts that these things are said figuratively
by means of a history which is external and is not
literally told. . . . Those who are not wholly blind can
collect countless such instances recorded as if they
had happened, but which *did not literally* happen." *De
Principiis*, Origen, IV, iii, 1.

"In the narrative of events which have happened, we
enquire whether all things are to be accepted only in a
figurative sense or whether they are also to be asserted
and defended as literal occurrences." *De Genesis and
Lit.*, St. Augustine, XI, 2.

The sacred scriptures of all religions have one and the
same general three-fold aim, *i.e.*, (a) a description of the
relation of God to man and the universe: (b) the *process* by
which the individual may become aware of the Ray of God
within himself; and (c) the *changes* which must necessarily
take place in the personality as a result of that realization.
These changes include changes in the animal instincts, in
the mind and in the heart, as the correlation is made between the Christ within and the universal Cosmic Christ.

All these miraculous changes are uniformly described
in terms of such physical objects and incidents as are
well known and easily understood by the people to whom
they are given. This applies to all scriptures whether de-
scribing the events of a war between the Kurus and the

Pandavas, as related in the sacred gospel of the Hindus—
The Bhagavad Gita—or to the events in the life of a carpenter's son, as related in the Christian *Gospels*. "There
is one body, and one Spirit . . . .one Lord, one faith, one
baptism, one God and Father of all, who is above all, and
through all and *in you all*."[1]

In each case the allegorical nature of the tale and the
mystical nature of the forces operating are well known to
all but the unenlightened and materially minded multitude. And it is to enlighten and inspire this multitude that
priests, preachers and teachers who understand the inner
meaning of the allegory are needed. "And he gave some
to be apostles; and some prophets; and some evangelists;
and some pastors and teachers; for the perfecting of the
saints, for the work of the ministry, for the edifying of the
body of Christ: till we all come in the unity of faith, and
of the knowledge of the Son of God, unto a perfect man,
unto the measure of the stature of the fullness of Christ;
that we henceforth be no more children, tossed to and fro,
and carried about by every wind of doctrine, by the sleight
of men, and cunning craftiness, whereby they lie in wait
to deceive; but speaking the truth in love, may grow up
into him in all things; which is the head, even Christ."
(Ephesians, iv, 11-15).

Therefore, the universal esoteric or spiritual interpretation, instead of the literal, is just as necessary for the
Christian scriptures as for any other. For the worship of a
mere symbol without a realization of its true meaning, of
that which it symbolizes, is mere fetish-worship.

In studying the life of Jesus as set forth in the *Gospels*
it is therefore wise to consider carefully all the circumstances, and in the order in which they are related, which
gather around His miraculous birth and life. Such a
study makes plain that the events are purposely intended
to be of a miraculous character. And those who try to
ignore or explain away the miraculous elements in re-

---

[1] *Ephesians, IV*, 4-6.

ligion, and refuse to admit their super-physical character, empty it of its chief and essential contents.

Miraculous means something which while true, is extremely exceptional; something performed according to a law which we do not understand, and whose real meaning can be grasped directly only by the higher or super physical consciousness. To reach the lower consciousness of the everyday life its inner meaning can be grasped only through an understanding of its spiritual symbology or significance. For, like most events in our lives which profoundly affect our inner trend of thought and action, they are the result of some mysterious cause of action. This is usually expressed symbolically to us in the depths of our consciousness in dream, vision or strongly compelling impression, which only later takes form and is expressed in a far more imperfect, limited and commonplace way in our lives.

While there will naturally be differences in the expression of the same truths, according to the different types of minds, schools of thought, and stages of civilization, nevertheless they should agree in the main facts. The differences should lead, not to conflict and antagonism or to the conceit that only one can be right and all the others wrong and "heathenish," but to a careful study and interpretation of all the facts in the light of their universal symbology.

It is therefore useless for *Bible* critics merely to prove that there is no authentic *external contemporaneous* historical proof[2] that Jesus lived at the time indicated or

---

[2] The foremost Hebrew historian, Josephus, has much to say about John the Baptist (*Antiquities of the Jews*, Book XVIII, Chapter V), about Pilate and a false Messiah who led the Samaritans up Mt. Gerizim to find the sacred vessels Moses is said to have buried there, also about a false prophet, Thuedas, and about the Essenes, but nothing about Jesus, except a few lines (Book XVIII, Chapter III) which scholars now universally admit was a medieval interpolation. Among other writers of the period Tacitus gives only a few lines to the persecution of the Christians: "Who had their denomination from Christus," but nothing about Jesus. Plutarch does not mention Him. And Philo, who is said to have been a friend of St Luke and to have met St Peter and St Paul in Rome makes no mention of Jesus. Among other authorities of the time who fail to mention Jesus are Pliny the younger, Seneca, Diogenes Laeritius, Pausanias, and many authorities on the Talmud. etc.

actually passed through the miraculous events related, without their giving an adequate explanation for the survival of such a story. For it requires far more than the mere example of an historical life to revolutionize the thought of the whole western world and produce such lasting results.

Only some higher power, actual currents of spiritual force eternally broadcasted from centers of spiritual truth in the spiritual realms, could sustain the early Christians in their terrible sufferings as they calmly walked to the stake, faced the wild beasts or boldly met the horrors of the Inquisition. It was this Christ-force which actually brought light to the eyes and smiles to the lips of the martyrs during their torture and cruel death. This same power comes as a benison from on high to the countless millions who have received comfort and surcease from suffering by contemplating those sublime ideals.

We must admit the dual nature of the mind—higher or spiritual and lower or rational—and recognize that the higher mind is intuitive and godlike in nature, while the lower mind is but its rational, imperfect and limited reflection in the human personality. During moments of inspiration the higher mind can and does penetrate into and respond to the Cosmic Consciousness or Divine Mind above. It is thus able to transmit Its eternal truths to the lower human consciousness. Thus only can the marvellous results of such a miraculous story be explained.

As we have outlined in the *Introduction*, there are three lines of internal evidence inherent in the *Gospel* story which prove its essential and universal truth when symbolically and spiritually interpreted, no matter how conflicting the evidence may be from literal or historical standpoint. Firstly, the events of the entire story are outpictured in the signs of the zodiac. Secondly, the same order of events is followed in the life-stories of all previous Saviors and Lightbringers, such as Agni, Krishna, Horus, Herakles, Dionysus, Apollo, Mithras, Osiris, etc. And thirdly, this same order of events is experienced in the spiritual unfoldment of every Soul who has been spiritually awakened and has begun the long climb up the Mount of Attainment to Christhood. The stories all deal with facts, and the same facts, but facts of the inner spiritual life. They are all symbols of realities, but the realities are not of the outer objective life. They are actual facts, but of Soul unfoldment, even though physical and astronomical events are used to illustrate and explain the universal symbology and the laws involved in the process of that unfoldment.

The symbolical and mystical interpretation is therefore the only unassailable and completely satisfying explanation of *The Pattern Life*, both in the *Gospel* story and as applied to the stages of unfoldment of the Christ-consciousness within each heart and life.

It is this symbolical and mystical interpretation[3] which we will endeavor to present and explain in some detail in this volume. For a mere recital of facts or of historical events is of little value unless it broadens our minds, expands our consciousness and gives us a greater understanding of the miracle of our incarnation in the flesh and of our mission here in the material world.[4] And so must it be with the events in the life-story of Jesus. Unless we can apply the lessons of these events to our own experiences and react to them they will have little effect on our lives.

As to the record of these events, modern scholars tell us that even the earliest manuscripts now in existence are only late copies of the originals, for no originals of the entire first and second centuries are known. Most of them are said to have been destroyed after the canon was

---

[3] See *Appendix B*.
[4] For details see *Why Are We Here?*, Curtiss.

fixed at the Synod of Damascus in 382 A.D., which canon was ratified by several later Synods.

It is probable that the four *Gospels* were not written by the disciples whose names they bear, for all the titles are prefaced by the qualifying words: "The Gospel *according to*" as though to signify that they were written either from memory or from notes taken from the disciples' talks, or from traditions.

But even the original manuscripts were written many years after the events. As we have pointed out elsewhere: "Since *The Encyclopedia Britannica*[5] tells us that, 'the first piece of Christian literature (*I Thessalonians*) which has an independent existence and to which we can fix a date. . . .was written some *twenty years after* the crucifixion,' (about 50 A.D.) and the first of the four *Gospels* (*St. Mark*) was written fifteen years later than that (about 65 A.D.), how can we be sure that the writers correctly reported the circumstances after so great a lapse of time and without any documentary evidence or records?. . . . The only records are those written from memory thirty-five and even *ninety years after* the events are supposed to have taken place!" Also our King James version omits many passages found in the earliest manuscripts.

"We hold, nevertheless, that those records were not pious fictions, but were allegories written, not through 'automatic writing' or any form of subjective mediumship, but by Disciples who were trained, independent Seers (Gnostics or 'knowers'), inspired by the Master Himself after His withdrawal to the higher realms, just as other sacred scriptures in other ages were inspired and given to mankind in the same way."[6] In fact, this is one fulfillment of the promise of the descent of the Holy Ghost "whom the Father will send in my name, he shall teach you all things, and bring all things to your remem-

---

[5] *Vol. XV*, 348, 11th Edition.

[6] See lesson, *The Lord Jesus Christ*, Curtiss, I, 1.

brance, whatsoever I have said unto you," *i.e.*, that they might have a permanent record of His teaching.

It is a significant fact that all religions are founded upon a multiplicity of miracles and psychic phenomena, or physical manifestations of unseen intelligences and super-physical forces. That this is as true of the Christian religion as of all others is further evidence of their importance and universality. No explanation of these astounding phenomena is given in the *Bible*, as it is assumed that the *causes*, the *methods* and the *reasons* for them were well known and understood by all students of the Mysteries in those days. It is only in these later days of psychic research and scientific, laboratory investigations of super-normal phenomena that physical science and the public at large are beginning to understand the truth of such phenomena, although this knowledge was possessed by the initiated priests and by advanced students of the Mysteries in all ages.

The beautiful story of the Annunciation assumes the existence of hierarchies of spiritual Beings known as angels—the meaning of the word being "messengers"—who bring to mankind various directions from still higher Beings varying from the planetary and zodiacal Rulers to the many grades of Masters and other super-physical spiritual Teachers of mankind. It also assumes that under certain conditions—which are scientifically necessary—these various types of Beings *can and do appear* to and are heard by those mortals who have unfolded their inner faculties so as to respond to super-physical rates of vibration and who have been specially trained to receive, understand and record such messages. And the possibility of such communications has been amply scientifically confirmed by controlled experiments[7] in the laboratories of some of the great universities and elsewhere.

Any system of science or philosophy which treats the universe as a closed system of physical materials and

---

[7] For details see *Realms of the Living Dead*, Curtiss.

forces only, and interprets it only in materialistic terms, never rises above the rationalistic and personal plane. And since it ignores the super-physical planes of matter and consciousness, it thereby proves that it is unscientific. For just as the laws of radiant energy and thermodynamics permit the penetration of the atom and the transmutation of matter—both once thought by science to be wholly illusory—so do the laws of the super-physical worlds and consciousness prove that the universe is not a closed system but permits their penetration into the physical world by spiritual Beings as a divine intercession to produce physical manifestations.

This doctrine has been believed in, not merely by the ignorant masses of mankind, but has been confirmed and testified unto by the greatest minds of all races, the sages, philosophers and spiritual teachers in all ages. By this method many of the more important events of the *Bible* are represented as being especially announced either by angels, a voice, a burning bush or some other super physical and metaphysical manifestation.[8] And the truth of such manifestations is witnessed to, not merely by the sages and trained seers, but by every Soul who is sufficiently advanced in spiritual unfoldment to recognize an Inner Guidance of some kind, even if not an actual voice or vision.

We are all more or less impressed, warned and guided by our own divine Spiritual Self from within, even though we so often disregard it. For each step in our spiritual advance is announced by the angel of our Spiritual Self or by our Initiator, in a way which the world—the materially minded—cannot see, hear or understand, but which afterwards works out in our lives.

The beautiful doctrine of angelic beings and Divine Teachers (Initiators) in the invisible or heavenly worlds who have the power to communicate with humanity through chosen prophets and seers, is as old as recorded

---

[8] For examples see chapter *"The Cloud on the Mountain,"* in *Why Are We Here?*, Curtiss, 90.

history, and has been a source of comfort, inspiration and guidance to countless millions in all ages and in all religious beliefs. Altho invisible to physical sight, angelic beings are visible to the psychic sight, just as some things are visible in ultra-violet or infra-red light that are not visible in normal white light. And their reality was unquestioningly accepted by most of the ancient world, and by the early Christian church, as actual beings living in a fourth-dimensional or spiritual world. This almost universal acceptance is not because such a doctrine is a mere survival of folk-lore and tribal myths, but because *it is a fact in Nature*; a spiritual experience universally testified to by the spiritually advanced Souls throughout the ages. And it is *physically proved* by scientific psychic research through photographs, materialization, precipitated handwriting, recordings of phenomenal independent voices, and other physical proofs.

This universal method of angelic manifestation is emphasized in many places throughout the *Bible*,[8] but most conspicuously in *Acts, ii, 5*, where "devout men (Initiates) out of every nation under heaven" (under every sign of the zodiac) are represented as being gathered together "with one accord" or in perfect harmony, purpose and aspiration. It is stated (*i, 15*) that the number present was 120. This indicates that every sign of the zodiac was represented, hence all mankind. Twelve is the number of the zodiac and the extra 0 indicates a multiplication of that number, or many of each sign being present.

The point which most clearly confirms the character of the inspiration is that although they were of every language under heaven they all heard "in their own tongue wherein they were born." This testifies as to the true nature of the angelic and divine inspiration (from *inspiro*, "to breathe in") in which the idea is "breathed into" and recorded by the spiritual consciousness. Hence it is naturally expressed in the language of the one recording it.

The descent of the Holy Ghost, or the divine inspiration, was not an isolated occurrence which took place ages

ago only, for it comes to mankind continually today as in
the past. And it always will come to those who are "devout" or who are spiritually unfolded. For we are always
inspired when we touch the Cosmic Consciousness of God,
according to the degree that we respond. Thus will the
Holy Ghost ever bring to our remembrance or explain all
things whatsoever the Christ has revealed unto mankind.
(*St. John, xiv*, 26).

The word Gospel means, "good news" or the inner
guidance such as is given to all aspirants, often in symbol and allegory. In the *Gospel* story the four common
or fixed signs of the zodiac or the four ends of the fixed
cross—*Aquarius, Leo, Taurus, Scorpio*—are represented
by the four different versions of the story, those of Matthew
(*Aquarius*), Mark (*Leo*), Luke (*Taurus*) and John (*Scorpio*).
Each version is presented from the characteristic viewpoint
of the zodiacal sign which it represents, St. Luke representing the sign Taurus, the Bull, or Ox, the power to *do*, also
called the Physician.[9] The words *"according to St. Luke"*
indicate a mystical presentation of the story as viewed from
the great Healing Hierarchy which St. Luke, the Physician,
represents. An understanding of the words of the angel
from this standpoint will help us to gain the power to *do*
or to accomplish that for which we are striving, namely, to
bring to birth the Christ-consciousness in our lives.

St. Luke begins with a preface which must be very dis-
concerting to those who take the *Gospel* story literally, yet
which is very satisfactory to those who see in it a series
of mystical and spiritual events arranged in the form of
a legend which is handed down from mouth to mouth.
For *St. Luke* plainly states that he is merely setting forth
those things "which are most surely believed among us"
but which he had not personally witnessed, although he
had been taught them in the "Mysteries of the Kingdom
of God."

---

[9] See *The Key to the Universe*, Curtiss, 147.

This *Gospel* is addressed to one Theophilus, whose name means "the beloved of God." The use of this name indicates that the tradition is handed down not merely to one person, but to all who have awakened to a realization that they are "beloved of God." This preface also gives assurance to all who are seeking to understand and follow the *Pattern Life* that *all these events are essentially true and necessary* in their inner mystical meaning. It also indicates that the narrator perfectly understood the sense in which they were delivered to him by those who were "eye witnesses" or Initiates who had actually experienced these mystical events in themselves and who were therefore qualified to teach their true meaning or be true "ministers of the word." Such were the leaders of the many mystical Brotherhoods—Essenes, Nazarites, Gnostics, etc.—who had been trained to enter the Silence, commune with the Divine and receive inspiration and instruction from their Spiritual Teachers in the Higher Realms and from their own Spiritual Selves, or that which is immortal in man.

Since the *Gospel according to St. Luke* contains more incidents in the life story of Jesus than any of the others, let us follow this version in general in our interpretation, although the versions and incidents given in other *Gospels* will be drawn upon from time to time when found most appropriate. But in all our subsequent interpretations we wish our readers to bear in mind that our effort will be not to detract from their faith in and reliance upon the true meaning of the *Gospel* story, *but to add to it* by broadening and deepening their comprehension of this stupendous subject.

CHAPTER II

THE ANNUNCIATIONS

PART I. TO ZACHARIAS AND ELIZABETH

> "And there appeared unto him an angel of the Lord standing on the right side of the altar. . . . the angel said unto him, Fear not Zacharias; for thy prayer is heard; and thy wife Elizabeth shall bear thee a son, and thou shalt call his name John. . . . I am Gabriel, that stand in the presence of God, and I am sent to speak unto thee. . . . thou shalt be dumb until the day that these things shalt be performed, because thou believeth not my words." *St. Luke, i, 11, 13, 19, 20.*

> "In the zodiac the Annunciation indicates the time when the Sun enters the sign Virgo, August 22nd, where it foreshadows the 'birth' in *Capricorn*, the manger." *Appendix A.*

After the introductory verses of *St. Luke's* narrative the genealogy of Zacharias and his wife are given to show that both of them were descendents of a long line of initiates—the Priesthood, and the Daughters of Aaron—and that both were trained and devout occultists, "righteous before God, walking in all the commandments and ordinances of the Lord." In other words, they complied with all the rules of the Lord pertaining to inspiration and divine communion with the higher realms. Now Jehovah is the great angel and guide of the Hebrew people, hence was the one with whom Zacharias was accustomed to commune, so when the mighty Archangel Gabriel appeared to him as he "executed the priest's office before God" he hesitated to accept the message until he could be sure of its source.

Here Zacharias proved his training, for notwithstanding the overpowering glory of Archangel's presence, he obeyed the universal law as taught to the neophytes of all occult and mystic Brotherhoods, namely, that all who receive any form of communication from the invisible must see that the manifestation takes place on their right hand, and *must demand proof* of its truth or it cannot be trusted. For there are many earth-bound discarnate mortals in the astral world who try to impersonate angels or any other personage whose presence might be expected to flatter and impress the sensitive who receives such a manifestation or message.[1]

Zacharias was, therefore, not overawed even by so celestial a visitant, but boldly demanded: "Whereby shall I know these things?" St. Paul recognized the necessity of this rule to challenge all such communications when he warned his followers of the danger. "Beloved, believe not every spirit (*i.e.*, only those who pass the test) but *try the spirits* whether they be of God." (*I John, iv, 1*) We are also told to: "Prove all things; hold fast that which is good," (*I Thessalonians, v, 21*) even when received from tested spirits.

In response to his challenge Zacharias was then given a sign, as everyone has a right to demand. Moreover, his whole being was so illumined with the celestial radiance of Gabriel's aura that all, "perceived that he had seen a vision in the temple."

Since Zacharias was so unbelieving, the sign he was given was that he was to remain dumb until the event prophesied had transpired. This may seem to us to be a severe test, but it simply meant that because of his lack of understanding of the message he was not allowed to say anything more about it until the event proved the correctness of the prophecy. Thus are we often prevented from discussing intuitive messages from within which we doubt or do not understand.

---

[1] For details see *Realms of the Living Dead*, Curtiss 227. Also look up "Communications" in the other Curtiss Books.

It is in just these little technical details, seemingly so trivial that many wonder why the trouble was taken to record them, which prove to occult students not only the essential truth of the narrative, but also the importance of the little practical details that are taught them in connection with their psychic and spiritual training. This story of Zacharias is but another version of the fundamental truth that some day, as we reach up into the spiritual consciousness (the "temple of the Lord") and strive to bring down to our intellectual comprehension the realities of the spiritual world, we will receive the Annunciation of the coming birth of the Christ-consciousness within our hearts. But we must guard ourselves against self-deception and the many illusions of the astral world by following the age-old technical rules concerning such communications.

Zacharias and Elizabeth symbolize the advanced Soul whose masculine and feminine aspects (intellect and heart) are so balanced and so devout that the Soul is about ready to give birth to that intellectual comprehension (John) which must precede and become the forerunner and announcer of the coming Divine Birth, the Christ within. For only when the balanced intellect (Zacharias) and the intuition (Elizabeth) have matured or "grown old" "walking in all the commandments and ordinances of the Lord (Law) blameless," is their illumined child (John) ready to be born and receive and baptize the Christ-consciousness.

PART II. TO JOSEPH AND MARY

"And in the sixth month the angel Gabriel was sent forth from God unto a city of Galilee, named Nazareth, to a virgin espoused to a man whose name was Joseph, of the house of David; and the virgin's name was Mary. . . . And the angel said unto her. . . . Behold, thou shalt conceive in thy womb, and bring forth a son, and shall call his name Jesus." *St. Luke. i, 26-7, 30-1.*

"In the zodiac the Annunciation indicates the time
when the Sun enters the sign *Virgo*, August 22nd, where
it foreshadows the 'birth' in Capricorn, the manger."
Appendix A.

The second Annunciation came to Mary, whose name—
as we have explained in *Appendix A*—signified *mare*, the
sea, the Great Deep or the Divine Mother-force, through
which all things are brought forth. The sixth month is
specified as the time when the Annunciation is made to
the Virgin because *Virgo* (the Virgin) is the sixth sign of
the zodiac.

According to some numerologists number six is the number of the Christ-force,[2] the Universal Urge to Perfection
which pushes us on toward our ultimate destiny and perfection. Also, according to Eastern terminology, the Sixth
Principle in man is *Buddhi* or the Spiritual Consciousness.
Therefore it is quite correct for the *sixth* month to be specified, for the Annunciation cannot take place until the Soul
has reached a stage of unfoldment wherein it is possible
for the Spiritual Consciousness to become more than a
mere overshadowing; where its Buddic Ray begins to penetrate into the consciousness of the personality in which,
in the fulness of time, it will bring to birth the fully formed
Christ-consciousness.

It is only natural that the mighty Archangel Gabriel
should make the Annunciation to Mary as well as to
Zacharias, for Gabriel is the cosmic deity who presides as
the Regent of Mercury, commonly called "the messenger
of the Gods," which planet is closely connected with the
evolution of mankind.

While each planet has its own Regent, Gabriel is one
of the four Overlords[2] who embody both Divine Love
and Divine Wisdom, and is responsible for the part each
planet plays in man's unfoldment and perfection.[3] Under
the guidance of the Divine Mother, King Anael, the Ruler
of Venus—who manifests through two complementary

---

[2] *The Key to the Universe*, Curtiss, 195-6, 144.
[3] *The Message of Aquaria*, Curtiss, 380, 349.

subrulers, Lucifer and Uriel—gives to man the dual principle of mind and also Divine Love. Therefore it was necessary for Gabriel to be the one to make the Annunciation
of the coming of the fructifying Ray of the Christ-consciousness: that "true Light which lighteth every man that
cometh into the world."

The Annunciation is the first incident that is widely
found in the birth-story of many Lightbringers.[4] Since
this incident is found so universally in the birth-story it
must have some universal significance which can easily
be understood when spiritually interpreted. Applying the
symbology to the individual, the father (Joseph) represents the intellect, which is masculine in its nature, while
the mother (Mary) represents the intuition, the heart or
love-nature, which is feminine in essence. Since Mary
is represented as not yet married—only espoused—to
Joseph, this indicates that the intellect, no matter how
highly developed, is not "married" or completely joined
to the Spiritual Consciousness until toward the advanced
stages of Mastery, when union with the Divine, or spiritual
illumination, is attained.

While we are passing through the lower stages of unfoldment the Spiritual Consciousness is scarcely more than
a vague overshadowing, but after many incarnations we
reach a stage where our minds are willing to recognize and
admit that there is a Consciousness which transcends the ordinary human intellect. This is the Spiritual Consciousness
which, when contacted—through prayer, medi-

---

[4] The annunciation that the Hindu savior, *Krishna*, was to be an incarnation of
Vishnu was made to his mother, Devaki, by Vishnu himself. The coming birth of
Hercules was announced by Zeus to his mother, Alkmene, Queen of Thebes. The
birth of the Egyptian King, *Amenhotep III*, was announced to the maiden Queen,
Mautmes, by the messenger-god, Thoth. The birth of *Kung-foo-tz*se (Confucius)
was announced by a giant dragon called Ke-lin. An angel from Orion announced to
Sochiquetze, the mother of *Quetzalcoatle*, that she would bear a child who would
be the savior of his people. Even Plato's birth is said to have been announced by
Apollo, to his father Aris, to whom his mother was only espoused.

tation, aspiration etc.—fills us with light, life and love. We then realize that a closer union with Spiritual Consciousness is worth striving for. Only then does the mind become "espoused" to the heart. Still later a stage of development is reached when our heart realizes through intuition that a definite illumination is possible: the birth of a new consciousness, a new power, a new conception of Divine Love, the Christ-consciousness.

But ere this new birth can take place we must pass through the stages and experiences corresponding to the nine months necessary for physical gestation. Nine is the number of Initiation,[5] and it may require not merely nine months to prepare for this Initiation into the new life, but many years or even many incarnations—nine periods of unfoldment, according to our rate of growth to accomplish our spiritual gestation before the spiritual possibilities we have glimpsed at the time of the Annunciation can be brought down to earth and be born into the waking consciousness and we can bring them forth in the outer life.

The desire of Joseph to put Mary away privily when she was seemingly illegitimately "found with child. . . . before they came together" (*St. Matthew, i, 18*) was a perfectly natural reaction. Joseph knew that he was not the father of the child, so it is no wonder that he was so worried about it that he thought of jilting Mary. But this was prevented supernaturally by an angel's appearing to him and explaining the mystery. Likewise our finite intellect is suspicious of and often distrusts and seeks to put away privily that which comes to it from the heart through intuition, until it is enlightened by a ray (angel or messenger) from our Spiritual Consciousness. For "The natural man (intellect) receiveth not the things of the spirit of God: for they are foolishness (seemingly without logic or reason) unto him: neither can he know them (since they do not come through the head), because

---

[5] *The Key to the Universe*, Curtiss, 306-8.

they are spiritually discerned (through the heart)."[6] "A brut-
ish man knoweth not: neither doth a fool understand this."[7]

The message of the angel to Joseph was also meant
to assure all whose intellects at first refuse to believe the
revelations of the heart, that the inner divine life-story thus
symbolized was intended to be the story of God in human
form, no matter how historically inaccurate, illogical and
confusing the literal interpretation may seem to be. For
no truly enlightened mind will dare to put it away privily
as illegitimate.

Soon after the Annunciation, since all the birth stories
follow the cosmic events in the zodiac, the mothers are
always represented as being on a journey and having been
riding on an ass when the birth takes place.[8] Considered
as a physical journey, it is highly improbable that Joseph
would set out on a journey of some seventy miles in the
midst of winter with his wife near the term of her delivery
in her *enceinte* condition, knowing that the ass would have
to walk all the way to avoid jarring, and at the slow pace
of two or three miles per hour.

In the zodiac this period corresponds to the journey of

---

[6] *I Corinthians, II*, 14.

[7] *Psalms, XCII*, 6.

[8] *Isis* has to flee to the swamps of the Delta to bear *Horus*. *Devaki* was on a journey
to Kansa when *Krishna* was born. *Maha-Maya* was on a similar journey when
Buddha was born. *Myrrha* had to flee afar to bear *Adonis*. *Heré* went "far away"
to bear *Typhon* or *Dionysus*. *Rhea* went to Crete to bear *Zeus*. *Latona* wandered
far to bring forth *Apollo*. *Auga*, after her amour with Herakles, fled from home to
bear *Telephos*. *Cyrene* was carried to Libya to give birth to *Aristaeus*. The virgin
mother of *Lao-tsze* was away from home when he was born. *Mandane* went from
Persia to Media to give birth to *Cyrus*. *Evadne* goes away secretly to bear Apollo's
child, *Iamos*. *Rhoea* was cast on the island of Delos to bear Apollo's son, *Anios*.
Apollonius of Tyana was born after his mother had been warned in a dream to flee
to a meadow. The mother of *Confucius*, warned by a vision, went to a cave on
Mount Ne to give him birth. Zeus conveys the daughter of Opus to Locrus to bear
Iapetos. And so we find the same incident through the whole list of virgin mothers.
In all cases it is the Sun-child or Son of God who is to be born.

the Sun southward from the time of the Annunciation in *Virgo* (Aug. 22 to Sept. 23) until the Sun is "born" in *Capricorn*, the Manger (Dec. 25th). Also the great star Spica rises in the constellation *Virgo*—which rules Bethlehem—and with her companion, Joseppe, in the constellation *Boötes*, travels southward to a position corresponding to the journey from Nazareth to Bethlehem. Hence the birth of all the Lightbringers is announced by a great star.

Since the cyclic journey of the Sun has already begun before it is "born" in *Capricorn*, in the universal story it is only natural that the mother is represented as being on a journey, usually to pay taxes, and riding on an ass. This symbolizes that we must have consciously started out and been well along the Path of Attainment before the spiritual birth can take place. In this we must not shut ourselves off from the world and lead an ascetic life, but must be actively on our journey through earth conditions. We must be ready to meet and satisfy the natural demands of our position in the world, or pay the "taxes" the world demands, yet without letting them interfere with our spiritual ongoing. While we must "render unto Caesar the things that are Caesar's," we must not forget to "render unto God the things that are God's."

Since the ass is the symbol of our animal nature, its use by Mary indicates that through love (Mary) and consideration, assisted by the mind (Joseph), we must so subdue and train the animal nature that it will become a willing and obedient servant to carry us on to the attainment of our highest ideals.

From an historical standpoint many consider it most unfortunate that St. Luke should represent Joseph and Mary as making the journey front Galilee to Judea for the purpose of being taxed, altho the taxing incident is also connected with many other birth journeys.[8] The symbolic character of this journey is shown first, by the fact that such a trifling and historically unimportant incident is carefully recorded while many whole years of

Jesus' life-story are not even mentioned; and second, by the
fact that competent historical research by many authorities
has shown that there was no such custom as the census
actually in operation in the whole of Palestine until *ten
years after* the journey is said to have taken place! Rome
had but one census of Palestine taken. That was during
the reign of Quirinius in 6 A.D., some ten years after the
death of Herod, when the districts of Judea and Samaria
were thrown into one province. Hence the journey could
not have been made during that census. And even when it
was instituted the census applied only to Judea and Samaria
and not to Galilee. Hence Joseph's household would not
have been affected had there been a census at the time of
his journey. "Under the reign of Herod, nothing of the kind
(census) took place."[9]

Another historical discrepancy is the statement by St.
Luke (ii, 2) that the taxing was made "when Cyrenius was
governor of Syria." As a matter of history, Cyrenius was
not appointed governor of Syria until ten years after the
death of Herod! From the standpoint of the materialistic
critic these historical inaccuracies are serious enough to
discredit the whole story, but if we take them symbolically instead of literally the discrepancies vanish; for again
we find the incident universal, and historical names, dates
and places are used simply to give local color and veri-
similitude to the story, so it is not necessary that they be
historically accurate.

During our period of espousal, conditions on our spiritual journey through the outer life, put upon us a heavy
tax. Not only must we recognize our duty to our fellow
men and the world, as well as to our own personal development, and pay their tax, but we must go out from our
"cave" or spiritual retreat and our self-contemplation—
our mystical journey from Nazareth to Bethlehem—in
order that we may "render unto Caesar the things which

---

[9] *The Bible for Learners*, Hooykaas, III, 56.

be Caesar's" and thus do our full duty in the world while still maintaining our newly awakened spiritual life within.

For Joseph (intellect) the tax or testing is whether he should believe the miraculous story which Mary (intuition) has told him as to the visit of the angel and the wonderful Annunciation he had given her. How can he believe that such marvelous things can possibly come to such humble persons as they were? And if accepted, how will it affect his standing among his fellows? Just so does our intellect find it difficult to believe the revelations of our divine possibilities and spiritual destiny which come to us through the heart (intuition). Yet they come with such spiritual power, such conviction and such assurance, as of an angel, that we know they will come true in the course of our unfoldment, although we dare not proclaim them to the world.

For Mary the tax is the struggle between her knowledge that she is to bring forth a manifestation of the Christ and her love for Joseph. Hence her temptation is to subserviate her intuitive realization of Truth and her spiritual advance to the lesser spiritual comprehension of Joseph. Thus ever does intuition tend to be overpowered by the more positive assurance of the intellect. After the Annunciation this taxing involves a long journey which the enlightened Soul must take while in the throes of this momentous decision ere the Spiritual Consciousness can be born.

The birth can take place only after the great decision to follow the Divine Guidance has been made and our sincerity has been tested by great trials, only too often deciding between what seems to be expedient in the outer life and what the Inner Voice has announced. Yet, like Mary, we find that if we follow our Guidance in trust and confidence, the Great Law will work out the miraculous result, just as it does in Nature, to bring about the miracle of physical birth in due season. In Nature the taxing symbolizes the toll that is taken of what the season has brought forth, the grains that are reaped, the crops that are harvested, etc., as the Sun journeys toward its rebirth in December.

Among the four *Gospels*, which we have already shown represent the four Cardinal Signs of the zodiac,[10] *St. Matthew* represents the sign *Aquarius*, "the man from the East" or the power to know. *St. Matthew* is therefore represented as the Publican or the Tax-gatherer, and his *Gospel* expresses the events in the life of Jesus from the standpoint of the sign Aquarius. This *Gospel* begins with a long supposed genealogy of Jesus, which does not apply historically at all, because it relates to Joseph, and Joseph does not pretend to be the father of Jesus, hence Jesus could not inherit Joseph's genealogy or the "throne of David." This glaring and unexplained discrepancy is easily understood symbolically, because the Christ-consciousness, although not born of the intellect (Joseph), does inherit the throne of David, or rules through Divine Love.

The angel told both Mary and Joseph that the child's name should be Jesus, meaning the physician or healer, but in private they were told to call him Emmanuel or "God with us" or "God in human form." In other words, while the Christ-consciousness comes as the harmonizer and healer of conditions in the outer life, interiorly we know it to be far more. It is literally "God with us," giving us a spiritually illumined understanding of the great spiritual mystery which the story of Jesus' life was meant to teach all men.

Happy is he who receives the Annunciation.

---

[10] See *The Key to the Universe*, Curtiss, 146-7.

CHAPTER III

THE IMMACULATE CONCEPTION

> "Behold, a virgin shall be with child, and shall bring forth a son, and they shall call his name Emmanuel, which, being interpreted is, God with us." *St. Matthew*, *i*, 23.

> "In the Cycle of the Sun as a Lightbringer, the advent of its new cycle of light is announced in the sign *Capricorn*, without blemish, blot or stain. Hence its conception is immaculate that is, without blemish." *Appendix A*.

The paradoxes and flat contradictions of the *Bible* are often its salvation from the destructive criticism of the so-called "higher critics." For those very inconsistencies and contradictions only go to prove that the incidents so differently described in the different *Gospels* are not meant to be taken in the materialistic sense as being historically or literally true, as we have said before, yet they are spiritually absolutely true when interpreted symbolically and applied to the events in our spiritual lives.

The doctrine of the Immaculate Conception, as commonly understood, is a mere theological dogma, originating in the minds of speculative men in the early ages in an effort to give a physical explanation to a spiritual mystery. This is shown by the fact that the subject was not even brought up for discussion in the Church Councils for the first 400 years!

Soon after Nestorius was made Patriarch of Constantinople in 428 A.D. he caused a storm of controversy by his opposition to the custom of referring to Mary as "the Mother of God." Altho the Council of Ephesus was called in 431 A.D. to settle the controversy between the fol-

lowers of Nestorius and those of Cyril, Bishop of Alexandria, its decision did not become the official doctrine of
the Church. So the controversy still raged on more or less
actively and still unsettled for the next 1400 years! The fact
that it took the Church 1854 years to make up its mind as to
the actuality of the doctrine shows that there is still ample
room for sincere difference of opinion and interpretation
of the incident, for it is by no means universally accepted
by all the Christian churches today. It is rejected by the
independent Jansenist Church of Holland and by the Universalists[1] and the Unitarians in this country, also by the
Nestorians of the Near East.

There is perhaps no doctrine of the Christian religion
which so imperatively requires the spiritual and mystical
interpretation, instead of the literal and materialistic, as
that of the Immaculate Conception; for the actual dogma is
far from what it is popularly supposed to be. In fact, altho
discussed for centuries, the dogma is quite a modern one,
as it did not become an official *Article of Faith* until the
Papal bull, "Ineffebillis Deus," of Pope Pius IX was issued
on the comparatively recent date of December 8th, 1854.

Until that date our researches show that it was established only "by tradition, by the writings of the Fathers,
by feasts observed in honor of this prerogative, by the
general belief of the faithful."[2] But as far back as 1546 the
Council of Trent had exempted Mary's mother, Anna, by
"the foreseen merits of her future grandson, Jesus," from
the stain of "original sin."

While the Festival of the Conception, as distinguished
from that of the Nativity was celebrated by the Greek
Catholic Church as early as the seventh century, and was

---

[1] "Universalists are free to differ from one another about the natural birth, miracles
and all other questions raised by criticism." *The Universalist Church Commisson
on Literature*. See also *Unitarian Answers*, 8.
[2] *The New Catholic Dictionary* (1929), 470-1.

introduced into England in the twelfth century, becoming widely adopted by the Church in 1708 A.D., the doctrine itself remained the subject of bitter controversy for many centuries. For centuries it was espoused *as a belief* by the Franciscans and Carmelites, but was as vigorously denied by the Dominicans under St. Thomas Aquinas and St. Bonaventura.[3] It was largely to settle this bitter age-old controversy that Pope Pius IX in 1854 elevated the doctrine from a mere pious belief into a definite dogma or official *Article of Faith.*

The astonishing thing, however, is that the Pope's bull makes no mention of a miraculous generation of Jesus without a physical father as constituting the Immaculate Conception, which miracle most Christians think constitutes the doctrine! In fact, *the doctrine does not deal with Jesus or His birth at all!* It deals exclusively with Mary and her mother, Anna. The miracle was that Mary was absolved from the stain of "original sin." As stated in the papal bull, the doctrine of the Immaculate Conception is: "The doctrine which holds that the blessed Virgin Mary was preserved from the stain of original sin in the first instant of her conception in the womb of her mother (Anna). This was a singular privilege and grace of God, granted in view of the future merits of Jesus Christ. By her conception is meant not the act or part of her parents in it, nor the formation of her body, *nor the conception of Christ later in her womb. . . .* Her Soul was never stained by original sin, nor by the depraved emotions, passions and weaknesses consequent on that sin, but created in a state of original sanctity, innocence and justice."[2] In other words, the miraculous exemption *applied to Mary* and not to Jesus, except by inheritance.

---

[3] St. Thomas Aquinas, the greatest of the medieval scholastics, refused to admit the Immaculate Conception. . . . St. Bonaventura, second only to St. Thomas in his influence on the Christian schools of his day, hesitated to accept it." *Encyclopedia Britannica*, XIV, 334.

Here we have the Catholic Church officially stating that the doctrine does not apply to "the conception of Christ later in her (Mary's) womb."

From a strictly scientific and physiological standpoint, while there are many examples of reproduction without the aid of a male parent—called *parthenogenesis*—among the lower classes of animal life below the grade of vertebrates, once the class of vertebrates—to which class man belongs—is reached in evolution, no exception to the need of a male parent—called *gameogenesis* or sexual reproduction—is known in the annals of science.

The misunderstanding of this doctrine which is so common in the minds of most Christians has arisen largely through a misunderstanding of the meaning of the word immaculate. Immaculate comes from the root word *maculatus*, meaning spot or stain. Hence im-maculate simply means "not spotted" or without stain, hence pure, unblemished. Naturally this has nothing to do with *parthenogenesis* or conception without a father, as so many think.

As to the Soul being stained from birth with "original sin," since we have treated the so-called "fall of man" somewhat extensively elsewhere,[4] herein we can give only briefly our interpretation of the doctrine of "original sin."

The controversy as to whether or not all mankind was tainted with sin from birth because of Adams fall is not a peculiarly Christian one, for it has raged among theologians as far back as Mencius and Hsun Tzu in China in the third century B.C., *ages before the Christian era*. But it was brought into prominence again in the fifth century A.D. by the great controversy between Pelagius and St. Augustine, and again centuries later by Calvin.

As we have already pointed out: "This was *a mere theological speculation* which in time has become a dogma among many sects. But it is essentially ridiculous in view of modern scientific investigation, even if we take Adam

---

[4] See *The Truth About Evolution and the Bible*, Curtiss, 62.

to represent all humanity — or even the first physical race — and not one man. We are, indeed, all under the bondage of sin, but of our own making individually and collectively — in this life and in the past."[5]

"Through the Church's postulate of original sin the devil is given greater power than the Christ in that he is given power to blast every Soul born into physical life, while the Christ can redeem only those who seek salvation, and that with difficulty. Hence, from this postulate we might deduce that the devil was the original king of the world, instead of but the despoiler of Christ's kingdom. . . . Yet even today the devotee who fails to bow in abject submission to the belief in the devil's baleful rule or who dares to assert in Church circles that there is no devil outside man's perverted creations, is looked upon askance. Since all this is a vital belief, carrying life and energy and much creative thought-force, in fact, when we consider the voluminous treatises of the early Church on the devil, it is no wonder that we are suffering from its devitalizing effects in body, mind and estate."[6]

The original sin of man, now as in the earliest days, is the rebellion of the will of the personal self against the will of God, manifested through His laws and through the will of His incarnated Ray, the Spiritual Self. As we have explained elsewhere: "The exaltation of the intellect and *man's refusal to follow his Inner Guidance*, together with his effort to subserve the spiritual forces within to bring temporal domination, and the gratification of the lower senses, passions and desires, was the 'original sin' of the race symbolized by Adam, not the use of the creative powers themselves. This is clearly shown by the fact that the creative powers were built into mankind by his Creator, and he was told to use them: to 'Be fruitful and multiply and replenish the earth.'"[7]

Sin originates through a violation of Cosmic Law by

[5] *The Inner Radiance*, Curtiss, 142.
[6] *The Key of Destiny*, Curtiss, 177.
[7] *The Message of Aquaria*, Curtiss, 396.

the lower self. And as long as we refuse to follow the Inner Guidance of the Spiritual Self we naturally dwell in "original sin," or the sin which that refusal originates. Only when we surrender the personal self to the Spiritual Self and say: "Not my will but Thine be done on earth even as it is in heaven," can we be purged from our own sins and have the Christ born in us immaculately.

Returning to the fundamental Universal Solar Myth, we have seen that the physical Sun is annually born of a Virgin (*Virgo*) both without spot or blemish and also without a father. Hence, all representatives of the Spiritual Sun to mankind—all Lightbringers or Saviors—are universally born of a Virgin immaculately and without a father. This incident, therefore, like all the others in the *Gospel* story, is not peculiar to the Christian religion, but is found universally in the life-story of many other Lightbringers hundreds of years before the Christian era.[8]

---

[8] Our researches show that the Egyptian God, *Ra*, was conceived by his virgin mother, but was not engendered by a father. Also the Egyptian Savior *Horus* was conceived by the virgin *Isis*. The Persian savior, *Zoroaster*, is said to have been conceived immaculately by a Ray of Divine Reason. The Hindu savior, *Krishna*, was conceived by the virgin *Devaki*, and *Buddha* is said to have been conceived by a white elephant, symbol of divine Power, Wisdom and Love entering the side of the chaste virgin *Maya*. The Greek god *Perseus* was born immaculately from the virgin *Danae*. *Romulus*, the founder of Rome, was born from the virgin *Rhea-Sylvia*. The Greek *Apollo* was immaculately conceived by the virgin *Larota*, while *Mercury* was born of the virgin *Maia*. The virgin mother of the Siamese savior *Codom* was inspired from heaven to go apart into the forest where she was impregnated by the sunbeams.

Among the Chinese, *Fo-hi* was conceived by the coral seed of a lotus staining the garment of his virgin mother. The Chinese hero, *Hau-ki*, was born immaculately from a childless mother after she had become pregnant phenomenally by stepping on a toe-print made by a God. *Lao-tzse* is said to have been a Divine Emanation which incarnated in human form during the third year of the reign of Emperor Ting-Wang (604 B.C.). Two dragons are said to have hovered over the head of the virgin *Yen-she*, the mother of *Kung-foo-tzse* or Confucius, and impregnated her. And so we might go on through the whole list—Hercules, Bacchus, Bel, etc.,—and find the same incident, differing only in superficial details, according to race and language.

If so miraculous a phenomenon as the Immaculate Conception had been a physical event it certainly would have been known to the authors of the *Epistles* and have been mentioned by them. But since neither they nor St. Mark or St. John make the slightest reference to it, it is evident that they knew nothing about it. On the contrary, St. Paul states specifically: "Concerning his Son Jesus Christ our Lord, which was made of the seed of David *according to the flesh*." (*Romans, 1, 3*). Also "God sent forth his Son, made of a woman, *made under the law*." (*Galatians, iv, 4*).

If this is literally interpreted we must assume that St. Paul was right rather than St. Matthew. For certainly, in a small village like Nazareth, if Mary had become pregnant while only "espoused" to Joseph, it would have been well known to the gossips of the neighborhood. And if the conception was due to some miraculous spiritual phenomenon, it would soon have been noised abroad. Even though Mary "pondered these things in her heart," her cousin, Elizabeth, already knew it and quite likely many others. Yet the simple practical villagers would scarcely have believed Mary's tale, and she would undoubtedly have been stoned to death according to the Jewish law. And this law is still in effect today in the remote parts of the Near East.[9] So, in view of the flat contradiction between St. Matthew—the traditional—and St Paul—the literal—we must assume that our symbolic and spiritual interpretation of St. Matthew's account is the only correct one.

Since no two human personalities ever have identically the same incidents, and occurring *in the same order*, in their lives, how can the Immaculate Conception be found in the life-stories of some twenty or more previous Saviors of mankind unless it is a symbol of some *universal spiritual truth or law* connected with the *repeated* manifesta-

---

[9] The noted Assyrian author and authority on biblical customs, George Lamsa, told us that he had witnessed such a stoning when he was a boy in his remote native village.

tion of the Divine in human form? The conception of the
Divine Babe universally symbolizes the conception of an
inner spiritual consciousness, after the outer rational consciousness has received the Annunciation, and has been
appraised of the possibility of the coming Divine Manifestation. It must first be *perceived* through the head before
it can be brought to birth in the heart, altho it is already
conceived by the heart's response to an influx of Divine
Love. Only so can it gestate, grow and ultimately reach
its birth into the everyday consciousness of the outer life.

Following out the old medieval idea of there being
something impure in sex, most students have thought that
this passage indicated that there must be some mysterious
way whereby a physical child could be generated without
the use of the sex functions. But since we have seen that
this cannot be done without a physical father, it is evident
that this passage cannot refer to the generation of a physical body, but to the birth of the Christ-consciousness in
the heart of all who have reached the stage of spiritual
unfoldment where they can listen to the Annunciation of
the Inner Voice—Angel—and respond to the overshadowing of the Divine Mother.

God never made man a mere animal whose highest
end was animal gratification. Nor did God give man his
necessary animal functions and then prohibit their use.
We should realize that to use wisely all the powers and
functions given us by our Creator and to sanctify them to
the glory of God is the way by which we shall perfect our
incarnation. We must learn the great lesson that only true
love and the companionship of the ones whom God hath
joined "from the beginning of the creation" can lead them
into a full understanding of the mysterious path to that
wisdom which made them "as gods" referred to by Job.
For after Job had made this great discovery he took unto
himself a wife and enjoyed both happiness and marvellous
prosperity.

According to the *Bible* story the sex function cannot be

regarded as evil, for it was built into man's body *by the Creator Himself.* To think of the creative force as evil is to belittle the wisdom and goodness of God who gave it, and to attribute evil unto Him. Hence, God made no mistake in providing man with this function, as many theological "wise men" think He did. Not only did God not make any mistake in providing man with this function, but He picked out this function for particular commendation and *blessed it* and told men to use it normally for its proper purposes, as we have pointed out above.

Since the use of this function is the only method by which an immortal Soul or Spiritual Being can find incarnation on Earth, and since it is the only function man was *specifically told to use*, and whose use was *specifically blessed*, it certainly is not evil in itself, nor was its use prohibited. All such ideas have arisen from misconceptions of it due to a materialistic and unenlightened medieval interpretation of the allegory of the Garden of Eden.[10]

If we thus look into the spiritual meaning of this text we will see that only as the Holy Ghost—the Mother-force of Divine Love—comes upon or fills us, and "the power of the Highest"—the Father-force of Divine Will—overshadows us can we bring forth "that holy thing," the Christ-consciousness, whose manifestation within us shall truly make us sons and daughters of God.

The Immaculate Conception is, therefore, not a closed incident which happened ages ago to one pure woman, but takes place in all women who bear children in love and purity of mind, as well as all others who bring forth the Divine within them. Much less is it a mere decree declared by a certain group of fallible men in the Church Councils (no women being present) to absolve one woman from the stain of an imagined sin by giving birth to a God-given Soul. We repeat that since the physiological miracle of human gestation and birth is the *God-given and only known method* by which human Souls can in-

---

[10] For details see *The Truth About Evolution and the Bible*, Curtiss.

carnate on Earth, and by means of which man was told by God to "multiply and replenish the earth," we fail to see that it was a sin which needed a Pope's bull to set aside.[11]

No. The Immaculate Conception takes place in every human heart when it has reached the point of unfoldment wherein the Christ-consciousness is conceived of the Holy Ghost, preparatory to being brought forth to redeem the outer personality from the dominion of old ideas, thoughts, habits and atoms of the former and more material stages of unfoldment

This same law applies to us all, spiritually, mentally and physically, and also to the world at large. But our individualized Ray of the Cosmic Christ has to overshadow the personality, incarnation after incarnation, until it can spiritualize us sufficiently for our consciousness to respond to its illumination and give it recognition.

Until this spiritualization and expansion takes place our minds cannot conceive of such a divine consciousness—the Consciousness of the Spiritual Self—as being personally connected with us. But once this idea is conceived, then a ray of that Christ-consciousness definitely descends into our minds and incarnates in our flesh where it fructifies the germ of a new and finer body—the super mortal Spiritual Body—which then begins to grow within us. As this Spiritual Body begins to grow it will gradually drive out all inharmonious vibrations and impurities,

---

[11] "A compromise was attempted by putting forward the suggestion that the humanity of Jesus came from the flesh he absorbed from his mother, his divinity coming from the Holy Ghost, his father, and this became the accepted explanation by those who wanted their god to rank in every way as high as the gods of their Pagan neighbors.

For the next few centuries Christians occupied their time speculating as to how the virgin became impregnated, and various ideas were believed at one time or another. Tertullian thought it came about by means of a 'divine ray,' which was the explanation the Egyptians gave to account for the miraculous birth of Apis. Augustine, and other fathers of the Church, stated that the Holy Ghost entered through her ears, and ancient Christian art depicts this idea in various aspects." *The Psychic Stream*, Findlay, 698.

but not without a certain amount of suffering or "growing pains," however. Thus, the radio-activity of its out-shining will transmute and spiritualize our very flesh, although this process may be a long one if only begun in this incarnation. The result will be in proportion to the amount of the Christ-force with which we correlate and express.

As we have already pointed out above, *mentally*, we must *perceive* the possibility of a truth before we can *conceive* of it as a definite idea and bring it forth. If the new idea is a conception of a spiritual truth, then that idea forms the vehicle into and through which a new vibration, stream or current of spiritual force can flow into our minds to bring forth an entirely new state of consciousness, a new and Immaculate Conception of life and our place and mission in it. The radio-active force of such a new conception spiritualizes our minds, changes all our ideas, and purifies our thoughts and cleanses them from all stain or spot and hence brings them forth immaculate.

Just as this new and Immaculate Conception expands our consciousness and purifies our minds by compelling them to respond to a higher octave of vibration, so does it sound a newer and higher key-note for the physical body, so that the very cells of our flesh must respond to it or be eliminated. Reacting under the law of habit, the flesh naturally rebels at this higher vibration and claims its right to live its old life and follow its old habits. Recognizing this universal conflict at this stage of our spiritual unfoldment, St. Paul complains: "For I delight in the law of God after the inward (or spiritual) man: but I see another law (old habit reactions) in my members, warring against the law of my mind, and bringing me into captivity to the law of sin (impurity) which is in my members."[12]

This elimination of the old cells which were accustomed by long habit to respond to and express our former ideas may not be pleasant, for they are denied their former at-

---

[12] *Romans, VII*, 22-3.

tention and sustenance. Hence many of them fight to remain and express the same old sensations and desires. "He that is of the earth (the animal self) is earthly, and speaketh of the earth: he that cometh from heaven (the Spiritual Self) is above all."[13] "The first man is of the earth, earthy: the second man is the Lord from heaven."[14]

Physically, the reaction of our bodies to the character of the ideas we habitually hold is so definite that, as our minds become more spiritualized through the radiant energy of our new conceptions and these take the place of the lusts of the flesh which formerly occupied so much of our attention, our very flesh responds to the purifying and spiritualizing process.

But this is a phase of the transmutation process which must be passed through, even though it is often as distressing as the physical symptoms attendant upon human gestation. Indeed it may cause many obscure symptoms which physicians may class as "merely nervous" because they can find little physical cause. But in such cases it is well to be sure that there is no physical cause added to these symptoms of transmutation and regeneration. If such physical causes are found, use every means, physical as well as metaphysical, to eliminate them.

Aid this process consciously by recognizing that as the old and wornout cells of the past cycle are being eliminated, *new cells are constantly being born.* Therefore, concentrate upon the idea that *every new cell shall be of a finer type,* more sensitive and better able to respond readily to the manifestation of the higher octave of vibration which our new conceptions have set into operation. Thus will we prepare, not only our minds, but our very flesh, for the Immaculate Conception and the ultimate birth of the Christ-consciousness that is to follow in due season.

In the world at large, the Immaculate Conception should apply to every child that is born. That is, every child has a right to be born without the stain of a thought that

---

[13] *St. John, III,* 31.
[14] *1 Corinthians, XV,* 47.

there is something wrong or impure connected with its generation and birth, for such thoughts naturally overshadow the consciousness of the growing child and leave their impress upon it.

During the period of gestation the thoughts of the parents—the father as well as the mother—are especially potent in their effect. Hence thoughts of peace, love, harmony and purity should predominate rather than thoughts of mere animal gratification. Obviously the animal receives greater satisfaction if the thoughts are of a high character during the exercise of its various functions, for they thus bring to it the higher vibrations from the Real or Spiritual Self, the only source of true satisfaction.

A child conceived with the idea that there is something sinful and impure about its generation, is to that extent cursed for life or until that thought-force has been counteracted. This is one of the important lessons for humanity to learn in this connection. In fact, this is the vital truth back of the idea meant to be impressed by the sacrament of infant baptism.

Instead of this ceremony's being a cleansing from the supposed "original sin" assumed to be derived from the God-given process of birth and Soul incarnation, it should be a ceremony of rejoicing and joyful thanksgiving that a new life has been brought forth immaculately in love and purity; a new Soul descended from the bosom of the eternal Godhead to manifest Him on earth. It should, therefore, be a sacred dedication of the child to the manifestation of the Highest, and of the parents to bring up the child in the highest ideals they can conceive.

Marriage should be the union of the masculine and feminine aspects of the same divine or Spiritual Self,[15] and their union in the flesh is the most natural, normal, and should be the holiest and most sacred, of all functions. Consequently there should be no thought of impurity about

---

[15] See *The Key to the Universe*, Curtiss, 107-114.

the conception of a physical body in which a divine Soul can incarnate. And there is not, except to the extent that mistaken thoughts of its impurity make it so. "I know, and am persuaded by the Lord Jesus, that there is nothing unclean of itself: but to him that esteemeth anything to be unclean, to him it is unclean."[16]

Every function of the body necessarily has its physical organ of expression and therefore its animal aspect, but is not confined to that lowest animal aspect. One function of the brain is to transfer bodily sensations and physical stimuli from the outer world to the consciousness, and motor impulses from the consciousness to the body for expression in action. But the brain is not confined to those bodily functions. It is also the vehicle for the expression of the mind, which can soar up to the highest spiritual realms. The mind, therefore, far transcends the brain, the brain being but its physical instrument of expression,[17] not its cause.

So it is with the functions of conception and generation. They necessarily have their physical and animal aspect, but they are not confined to that aspect. For back of the bodily centers which seemingly govern the animal functions, there are higher and more spiritual centers which are intended to be the natural guides and helpers to raise those functions above the plane of mere animal consciousness and make them avenues for the manifestation of higher forces. These higher centers are developed and brought into play as we concentrate our attention immaculately above the mere physical aspect of their functions and aspire to higher ideals. All depends upon whether our attention is focused upon the bodily sensations or upon those spiritual ideals which it is desired to conceive and bring forth immaculately into our life.

There is no greater service that a couple can render to the Race and to the advanced Souls who are seeking the necessary conditions of peace, harmony and purity of

---

[16] *Romans, XIV*, 14.
[17] See *The Key to the Universe*, Curtiss, 260-6.

thought and of body in which they can incarnate, than to furnish pure and healthy bodies into which purity and love have been built. Such conditions will attract advanced Souls into incarnation because of such a high type of parents. The incarnation of such Souls brings joy, peace, harmony and love to the family and also to the world; for such Souls will be the ones to lead the world in all branches of discovery, art, science and religion. But they cannot incarnate except under conditions of an Immaculate Conception, for without these they can remain in incarnation but a few years. In other words, they must be immaculately conceived, not without a father, but without thoughts of impurity.

The growing spiritual body needs the Bread of Life for its nourishment and is poisoned by vibrations of inharmony, selfishness and impurity. Hence, it continually requires the forces generated by a continual Immaculate Conception. We repeat, only through purity of mind and life can this Conception take place and the spiritual birth follow.

Only as the expectant mother of a physical child aspires to the spiritual realms and makes possible such an over-shadowing of these two aspects of God—love and purity—can she attract the more spiritually evolved Souls who are waiting for just such conditions to be provided before they can incarnate. For if any thought of wrongdoing, sin or impurity is held, such a thought short-circuits the higher forces and prevents the incarnation of any Soul except those undeveloped Souls who are willing to incarnate under such lower mental and vibratory conditions.

Therefore, if the thoughts of the parents are immaculate or "without spot" or stain of impurity in the use of the function of creation, the incarnating Soul is born immaculate and without the sense or something impure concerning its generation and birth. Thus there can be brought into incarnation a beautiful "love-child" who will be a blessing and a joy through life. Such an immaculately born child does not need the ceremony of baptism with water to wash away the taint of something sinful or impure about its coming into the world in the only way God has provided for its incarnation.

As we have said elsewhere: "If the Race is to be propagated in vileness, every child that is born must bear the burden of a thought of something vile and impure in connection with its birth. . . . For this reason the salvation of the Race depends upon the pure in heart conceiving children in love and purity, for if the perpetuation of the Race is left to the impure and ignorant, conditions must grow worse."[18] This is one of the chief reasons for the incarnation of the large proportion of the unfit, from morons and the feeble-minded, to the insane.

By increasing the number of such immaculate conceptions we can help to shorten the days of tribulation and prepare the Earth as a purified and happy abiding place for the coming New Age.

Happy is he who experiences the Immaculate Conception.

---

[18] See *The Voice of Isis*, Curtiss, 225-6.

CHAPTER IV

THE BIRTH OF THE CHRIST

> "And the angel said unto her: The Holy Ghost shall
> come upon thee, and the power of the Highest shall
> overshadow thee: therefore also that holy thing that
> shall be born of thee shall be called the Son of God . . . .
> and the Lord God shall give unto him the throne of his
> father David: and he shall reign over the house of Jacob
> forever; and of his kingdom there shall be no end." *St.
> Luke, i,35,32.*

> "Astronomically, at the time of the birth of the Sun
> the sign *Virgo*, the Virgin, is rising on the eastern angle
> of the planisphere. Hence all Sun Gods or Lightbringers
> are represented as being born of a Virgin." *Appendix* A.

At the time of the winter solstice, after midnight on
December 21st, when the Sun has reached the lowest
point of its descent into the southern hemisphere and has
started on its upward journey, the whole world celebrates
the birth of a new era, the new year. In Christian countries this astronomical event is celebrated as Christmas
or the birthday of Jesus. But before the middle of the
fifth century there was no agreement as to an historical
date for His birth. Various churches and church authorities held as many as thirty-six conflicting dates, such
as January 6th, March 25th, Nov. 17th etc.[1] In fact the
early Armenian and Syrian Churches accused the Roman
Church of "Sun-worship" because it finally adopted the

---

[1] See *Appendix C*. "The first certain mention of Dec. 25th is made by a Latin chro-
nographer of A.D.354. It runs in English as follows: 'The Lord Jesus Christ was
born on Dec. 25th—a Friday—and the fifteenth day of the New Moon.'" *The Life
of Christ*, Cain, 263.

date of the solar event—which was also the birthdate of
the Sun-god *Mithras*, also of *Tammuz* and many others—
namely, December 25th, as the date of Jesus' birth.

The birth day of Jesus was first celebrated by Theodore
of Antioch nearly two hundred years after the event. And as
late as 245 A.D. the celebrated church Father and historian,
Frater Origen, understandingly and wisely repudiated as
infidel the celebrating of the literal and physical birth of
Jesus, "As if He were a King Pharaoh." Yet there was a
fundamental and scientific reason for the Church to adopt
December 25th as the date, for it is the date of the birth of
the physical Lightbringer in Nature, the Sun. And since
Jesus is the spiritual Lightbringer or the manifestation of
the Spiritual Sun to humanity, the day of His birth should
very properly be celebrated on the solar date of the Sun's
birth, as was the case with all previous Lightbringers.

At this season of rejoicing in the renewed advent of
the spiritual light, life and love, be our station in life, our
religion or our creed and belief what it may, we can all
greet it as one of the most sacred milestones that has ever
been set upon the pathway of life. For it commemorates an
event of world-wide significance; an event which, however
much critics may question its actual historical happening,
or cavil at its illogical seeming and its scientific and physical impossibility, is nevertheless recognized as the most
important event in the history of the Western world.

The doctrine of the Virgin Birth was not a part of the
original apostolic message. Nor was it among the original grounds on which belief in Jesus was demanded. The
Disciples never mention it, nor does Jesus ever refer to
it. And the greatest of the Apostles, St. Paul, apparently
never heard of it, for, as we have previously pointed out,
he says: "Concerning his Son, Jesus Christ our Lord,
which was made of the seed of David *according to the
flesh*." (*Romans, i, 3*). St. Paul also states specifically
that: "God sent forth his Son, born of a woman, *born*

under the law," (*Galatians, iv*, 4), presumably the law of human generation. And if Jesus had been born miraculously, such an event would have been well known in so small a village as Bethlehem or Nazareth, as we have already mentioned. Yet His fellow villagers know nothing about it, for they inquire: "Is this not the carpenter's son? is not his mother called Mary? and his brethren, James, and Joses, and Simon, and Judas? And his sisters, are they not all with us?" (*St. Matthew, xiii*, 55-6). Also, if Jesus was born immaculately and without taint of "original sin," why did He need to be circumcised when eight days old? and why did Mary have to remain in Bethlehem until her forty "days of purification" were over, like any other Jewish mother? (*St. Luke, ii*, 21-2).

This is the first of the many flat contradictions we shall find in the *Gospels*. Can both sides be true? If not, which side shall we take? In this case both sides are true. The one concerns the immaculate birth of the Christ-consciousness in the heart. The other concerns the body of Jesus. From the several lines of evidence at hand we must conclude with St. Paul that Joseph was the natural father of Jesus. In fact, His mother publicly proclaims Joseph as His father when she reproached Him for remaining behind in the temple after their party had left. "*Thy father* and I have sought thee sorrowing." (*St. Luke, ii*, 48).

On the other hand the whole story of the Immaculate Conception and the Virgin Birth is a part of the cosmic allegory that had to be added to make the life-story conform to the Universal Solar Myth so that it would carry the universal symbology of all Lightbringers and indicate that Jesus was a true Son of God or Sun-god.[2] St. Paul's testimony is so strong as to make it quite evident that the

---

[2] "As one old belief after another was draped round the name of Jesus over the first four centuries of our era, so the new religion grew up in the likeness of the old. The age-old beliefs were hung on a new peg, called by a different name, and the educated people were quite familiar with the sources whence they came." *The Psychic Stream*, Findlay, 308.

miracle was not to be taken literally and historically. This is a good example of the fact that the conflicting *Gospel* stories cannot be made consistent unless they are interpreted according to their universal spiritual symbology.

To reconcile these glaring discrepancies and make this beautiful story of vital importance to us, like all others in the *Gospels*, it must not only be spiritually interpreted, but its lesson must be applied to the life of each unfolding Soul. For each can find in it a pertinent truth, an individual lesson and a personal responsibility. In fact, this personal application is the chief reason for the story; for without this individual realization and application the astronomical, historical, intellectual or materialistic interpretations are but empty husks, without vital spiritual nourishment.

Therefore, let no heart turn away and refuse to recognize the birth, but let it respond to the joy of the season and the ecstasy of the realization, even though the materialistically trained intellect may say, as do some writers: "All this is but a part of the ancient Sun Myth, and belongs to the folk-lore and superstition of the early ages. It is but a medieval dogma outgrown and left behind long ago in these modern and enlightened days." For no matter how literally and materialistically it has been misunderstood or how dogmatically interpreted by the Church, *it is a great spiritual reality* that is enacted again and again perpetually, both annually in Nature and in the spiritual experience of every awakened Soul.

All birth is a mystery. How a pre-existing, super physical being with a definite personality and consciousness can appear from out the unseen into the seen, already fully organized and co-ordinated, is one of the miraculous mysteries of Nature. But it must follow certain definite laws, and take place at a certain point in a definite cycle. Yet because we are so familiar with its phenomena we overlook its mystery. The birth of the Christ is even a greater mystery, yet it follows the same laws, and passes through the same incidents, and *in the same order*, as does the birth of the Sun in the zodiac.

Astronomically the birth of the Sun takes place when it has reached its nadir or lowest point of southern declination. The sign *Capricorn*, in which the birth takes place, is symbolized by the goat, and astrologically is related to the manger and the stables. Hence, many Sun-gods, Lightbringers and Saviors are represented as being of lowly origin. Their birth is represented as taking place in *Capricorn*, not only because the Sun is "born" in that sign, but also because *Capricorn* expresses just those forces which will bring to humanity the experiences necessary for its ultimate spiritual birth. For the zodiac contains not only those newly discovered currents of force, called "cosmic rays," but other forces which profoundly influence the processes of Nature—such as growth, terrestrial magnetism, radio reception, etc.—and other physical events, but also forces which greatly influence the minds of men. And these forces are of vital importance in the development of the mystical centers and faculties in man at present little understood and yet which are necessary for man's ultimate perfect spiritual unfoldment.

There was evidently considerable uncertainty in the minds of the *Gospel* writers as to which was to be considered as Jesus' home village. *St. Matthew (ii, 20-3)* says that Joseph was warned to return from Egypt to Bethlehem, and was diverted from doing so only by fear of Herod's son, Archelaus, who then ruled Judea. Joseph therefore "turned aside into the parts of Galilee" only as a second choice or after-thought. But in *St. Luke (i, 26)* we are told that Jesus' parents had already made their home in Nazareth before the Annunciation was made to Mary.

The journey to Bethlehem was evidently made merely to comply with the tax decree. Jesus never referred to Bethlehem as His birthplace, and is not recorded as ever having visited it, altho it is only about six miles from

Jerusalem which He visited so often. If He was born in
Bethlehem and made it His home He would have been a
Judean, yet He is always referred to as a Galileean or a
Nazarean. No such village as Nazareth is mentioned in the
Old Testament or in the *Talmud*. And no such village can
be traced in history before the middle of the fourth century,
altho many other villages of similar size and of far less
importance are mentioned. This inaccuracy is but another
evidence of the allegorical nature of the entire birth story.[3]

As to the exact spot where Jesus' birth took place there
is also a similar conflict of testimony. *St. Luke (ii, 7)* implies that He was born in a stable, while *St. Matthew (ii, 11)*
tells us that the Wise Men found Him in a house. As one
writer summarizes it: "According to early Christian writers, such as Justin and Origen, Jesus came into the world in
a cave, and Jerome complains *(Epist. viii)* that in his time
the heathens celebrated the feast of the birth of *Tammuz*
at Bethlehem in the same cave in which Jesus was born."[4]

Tertullian also says He was born in a cave, while
Eusebius, the earliest Christian historian, says He was
born in the same cave over which Constantine built a
basilica in 330 A.D. which is now called the Grotto of
the Nativity. This is said to be the same cave over which
the learned and travelled Emperor Hadrian earlier built a
temple to Adonis when he rebuilt Jerusalem in 130 A.D.[5]

---

[3] The celebrated author, Hall Caine, was a very devout Christian, but after more than
forty years of scholarly research, and after many visits to Palestine, he wrote: "It is
impossible to regard the birth-stories in the Gospels as records of actual happenings.
They are obviously conceived in the spirit of legend and written in the language of
myth. Never have they any reality. . . . In every incident, except one, they contradict
and clash with each other." *The Life of Christ*, Caine, 1283. Also St. Augustine is
reported as saying: "Were it not for the authority of the Church, I should put no faith
in the Gospels."

[4] *The Christ Myth*, Drews, 101.

[5] *The Protevangelon* by James, the brother of Jesus, says that Jesus was born in a
cave. The Egyptian, *Horus*, was born in the stable of the "holy cow" or Temple of
Isis. The Cretan sun-god *Zeus* was born in a cavern, *Mithras, Dionysus* and *Hermes*
were all born in gloomy grottos or caves. *Krishna, Adonis, Apollo, Attis, Bacchus*
and many others were born in caves.

All Saviors are said to be born of a Virgin because as the birth takes place in the sign *Capricorn*, called "the stable," *Virgo* is the zodiacal sign which is rising on the eastern ascendant at the time the Sun is born in the southern hemisphere, which is so frequently called the "pit," "cave" or "stable." That this incident is *universal* and not exclusively connected with the story of Jesus is shown by the fact that more than twenty previous Saviors[6] of mankind, in other races and ages, are all represented as being born of a virgin in a stable, crypt or cave, and in the presence of the domestic animals, the bull, goat, sheep, ass, etc. This has been handed down from those ancient days (about 3000 B.C.) when the winter solstice began between the zodiacal signs of the Ox (*Taurus*) and the Great Bear, formerly called the Ass. For this reason we see those animals—especially the bull and the goat, both symbols of the procreative force in Nature—represented in nearly all pictures of the Nativity. Domestic animals in general symbolize both the material world and the animal world and their temptations.

This lowly place of birth indicates the universal Law of Birth into the physical world, for the generation and gestation of all forms of life take place in darkness and

---

[6] *Horus* was born of the virgin Isis; *Krishna* of the virgin Devaki; *Buddha* of the virgin Maya; *Romulus* of Rhea-Sylvia; *Bacchus* of Myrrha; *Hermes* of Mair; *Adonis* of Myrrha; *Agni* of Maya; *Mithras* of Marid; *Tammus* of Mylitta; *Attis* of Nara; *Apollo* of Leto; *Perseus* of Danae; *Dionysus* of Demeter; and the Persian *Mani* of the virgin Meis. Among the Chinese *Fo-hi, Lao-tzse, Confucius* and others are said to have been of virgin birth. *Cyrus the Great,* who was called "Chrestos, the Annointed One" and also "God's Messenger," was said to have been of virgin birth. Even the Greek philosopher, *Plato,* was believed to have been a Son of God by the virgin, Perictione, who had an immaculate conception by the god Apollo. Also *Rameses, Zoroaster* and *Quetzalcoatl* were said to have been born of virgins. The life stories of all these "sun gods" testify to the universality of the story and its symbology.

in lowly surroundings, and below the diaphragm and in the so-called "stable" with the animal functions. In the case of the Sun it takes place in the darkness of winter and in the "cave" of the southern hemisphere; in the case of seeds in the darkness of the earth and within the "cave" of the husk or shell; in the case of birds' eggs in the darkness made by the setting mother-bird and within the "cave" of the egg-shell; in all mammals, including man, in the darkness of the mother's body and within that particular portion (womb) which is in the nature of a cave.

A cave is said to have been the earliest form of temple or the first place of worship among primitive humanity. This was not only because it afforded privacy and protection, but also because it afforded secrecy, a feeling of awe, and the silence and darkness so necessary for the manifestation of primitive spiritual phenomena. As the rocks are the foundation which upholds the earth and focuses its magnetism, so our place of worship becomes the foundation of our spiritual life, and focuses its spiritual forces for us. The cave also symbolizes darkness and limitations, material conditions and materialistic thought, birth and death, the womb and the tomb.

Just so it is with the spiritual birth. It begins within the darkness of material conditions and within the "cave" of the heart, near which, and looking on as it were, are assembled those bodily centers which govern the "stable" containing the animal functions of the body, so aptly symbolized by the domestic animals.

The cave also refers to the crypt of the Chamber of Initiation in the Schools of the Mysteries where the Candidate receives his mystic "birth" or great spiritual illumination.

Not understanding the solar origin of these incidents, and hence not having the cosmic concept of them, the only way in which the pious Church Father, Justin Martyr, could account for the absolute uniformity of these events was to attribute them to the devil! He says: "It having reached the ears of the devil that the prophets had foretold the coming of Christ (the Son of God), he set the *Heathen Poets* (thousands of years B.C., Au.) to bring forward a great many who should be called *the sons of Jove*. The devil laying his scheme in this, to get men to imagine that the *true* history of Christ was of *the same character* as the prodigious fables related of the sons of Jove."[7] But we do not have to call upon the miraculous prognostication of the devil to account for the uniformity, once we have the cosmic concept and understand the personal application of the whole story.

What is the interpretation of this universal birth of all Lightbringers from a Virgin? Does it merely mean the annual birth of the Sun in Nature or merely the generation of a mortal without a father? Is it merely the repetition of an age-old myth? No, it means far more. It is a divine reality in the spiritual life of all mankind when its cyclic time is reached. In its physical sense it does, indeed, refer to the cyclic birth of the Sun in the cycle of the year, with the sign *Virgo* rising. And in the cosmic sense it refers to the cyclic manifestation (cycle of the Age) of the Celestial Being known as an Avatar, who comes as a Spiritual Lightbringer and hence periodically fulfills, in the spiritual unfoldment of humanity, an office similar to that which the Sun accomplishes periodically in Nature. But this universal symbology has a still more important and personal meaning.

As we have said elsewhere: "The story of the life of Jesus we regard not only as the spiritual history of one Great Teacher, but as an allegory of the life of perfected Man; the *Pattern Life* which all humanity must ultimately follow; the universal experience which each Soul passes through as the Christ-consciousness is born within and unfolds into perfect satisfaction and at-one-ment with the Father-in-heaven. Every incident symbolizes a step on the Path of Attainment of Christhood. . . . Therefore the story of Jesus is the story of the spiritual evolution,

---

[7] *Roman Antiquities*, 124.

unfoldment and manifestation of the Christ in the flesh."

In other words, the events in the life of Jesus dramatize not only the cosmic process by which the Divine manifests in the material universe—the Sun through the zodiac—but also the inner personal experience through which every Soul passes on its way to its ultimate union or at-one-ment with its Source.

Jesus, therefore like all Lightbringers, symbolizes the individualization and manifestation of the Christ-consciousness in man. This is not an intellectual process, but a spiritual one; the overshadowing, and finally the embodiment and birth, of the spiritual consciousness of our Real or Spiritual Self, or the Divine Man, in and through the human personality.

As we have already pointed out: "And because this Spiritual Self is the Ambassador of and of the same essence as the Cosmic Christ which vitalizes all divisions of the vast universe, through an acquaintance, realization and correlation with this Spiritual Self we can enter into an understanding of those cosmic centers of life, force and consciousness which have their miniature centers and points of contact within our bodies. The man who has thus found himself through realization and correlation with this Spiritual Self has found the Christ enthroned in the midst of his universe."[8]

St. Paul recognized that it was this mystical birth of the Christ-consciousness in the heart that the miraculous story symbolized when he said: "My little children, of whom I travail in birth again *until Christ be formed in you*." And again "when it pleased God. . . . to reveal his Son *in me*, that I might preach him among the heathen." (*Galatians, iv, 19* and *i,15*). "For God, who commanded the light to shine out of darkness, hath shined *in our hearts*, to give us the light of the glory of God in the face of Jesus Christ." (*II Corinthians, iv, 6*). And again, "Examine yourselves, whether ye be in the faith; prove

---

[8] *The Message of Aquaria*, Curtiss, 180.

your own selves (inner Spiritual Selves). Know ye not your own selves, how that Jesus Christ is *in you*, except ye be reprobates? (*II Corinthians, xiii, 5*). And it is evident that he refers to the Cosmic Christ when he says that the Spirit of Christ was in the ancient prophets. (*I Peter, i, 11*). It is evident that it is of the mystic Christ within to which St Paul refers in the above as in all his other references to the Christ, and not to the historical personality of Jesus, the Teacher.

It must be dearly understood that the spiritual birth is not due to a mere infusion into the rational mind of a new concept of God and His Son, but is the result of the inflow of new currents of spiritual life, light and love; the beginning of a new life-process. It involves breaking up of the old life and its reactions, and the building of a new life. It thus begins a never-ending reciprocity between God and man, between the Spiritual Self and the personal self. This results in a shifting of the field of consciousness from a lower to a higher level; from "conditioned reflexes" due to stimuli from the outer material world, to estatic response to stimuli from the inner spiritual world.

Returning to Joseph as a symbol of the intellect, naturally he is not represented as the actual father of Jesus, for, according to the story, Mary was only "espoused," not yet married to him at time. This indicates that no amount of intellectual activity can generate spiritual consciousness. That comes only from the spiritual world many octaves of vibration above the mental world. It comes from within, not from without, and is not generated by the mind. It first overshadows, and after proper recognition and response has been made, descends from the realms of spiritual consciousness into the "cave" of the heart —of which Mary is the symbol—where it must be nurtured in Divine Love, or by the Divine Mother-principle, ere it can be brought forth in the life and illumine the consciousness of the personality and seemingly become the son of Joseph.

"When the Christ-light is thus born in our hearts, our

consciousness is expanded and born into an entirely new world of spiritual light, joy and freedom. The change is even greater than that which the sprout must experience when it is born out of the darkness and limitation of the soil into the light and freedom of the sunlight. This new illumination is as much greater than the old ideas we formerly held as is the light of day to the newborn babe, as compared to the darkness of its mother's womb.

" 'If you would truly know how these things come to pass,' says St. Bonaventura, in a passage which all students of theology should ever keep in mind, 'ask it of Grace, not of doctrine; of desire, not of intellect: of the ardours of prayer, not of the teachings of the schools. . . . Not of illumination, but of the fire which enflames all and wraps us all in God with great sweetness and most ardent love.' "[9]

Electricity has been known to humanity for ages as a great cosmic power (lightning), but only when it was brought down to earth or was "born" on earth and utilized did it become effective in our lives. Likewise, the Cosmic Christ-force has been known to humanity for ages as a great cosmic power, but only as it is brought down from the heaven-world and "born" in our hearts can it become effective in our lives. To accomplish this we must say to ourselves: "Not only have I the Christ-force within me, but I must bring it forth to illumine my mind, warm my heart and radiate from me in streams of loving, transforming power." And we must repeat this again and again until we feel the birth take place.

As we have already said: "While the power of the Christ is within us, it is not ours consciously to use until we have *realized it* and endeavored to *give it expression* in guiding our daily life. For no matter how much we talk about it, nor how much we try to explain it, until through travail of Soul it is born in our consciousness and *begins to bring forth* in our life, it is not consciously ours.

---

[9] *Mysticism*, Underhill, 148.

But once the birth has taken place, once the realization has been attained, we have touched a live wire, we are standing on the third-rail tapping a power which, if we permit it to manifest, will bring to us whatsoever is needed—protection, peace, poise and plenty—plenty of mercies and joys."[10]

This new spiritual birth of the Christ-consciousness in its miraculous, immaculate birth in a virgin-heart, because its generation is not mortal, but Divine. According to the angel's promise: "The Holy Ghost shall come upon thee and the power of the Highest shall overshadow thee: therefore also that holy thing which shall be born of thee shall be called the Son of God." (*St. Luke, i, 35*). This evidently refers not to a physical child conceived without a father, but to the manifestation of the Spiritual Self, the Christ within us. The intellect appears to the outer world as the father, but is not so in reality, any more than Joseph is represented in the story as actually being the physical father of Jesus. This St. Luke frankly admits when he says: "Jesus himself. . . . being (*as was supposed*) the son of Joseph." (*St. Luke, iii, 23*). Yet, like Joseph, the intellect is needed to father the new-born babe, to guard, support, protect, and prepare conditions for the manifestation of the Christ-consciousness, hence must grasp and understand the miracle.

As we have said elsewhere: "Once the Spiritual birth has taken place in the heart, it must be recognized and fathered by the mind. Our consciousness must grasp a new idea of our Divine Source and the essential nature of our Real or Spiritual Self. Once this new idea is recognized by the mind, according to the laws of mind there is a modification of the mind in conformity with the idea. And if the idea is held continually or is recurred to frequently and positively, it grows and reacts upon the body with greater and greater power until finally the body is modified in conformity with the new idea, just as was

---

[10] *The Inner Radiance*, Curtiss, 156.

the mind. This is true of the birth of every new conception in proportion to the power we give it."[11]

This universal and spiritual interpretation of the story solves the whole problem of the conflicting genealogies[12] of Joseph which would seemingly deny the spiritual origin of Jesus in spite of Jesus' own words. "Ye are from beneath; I am from above: ye are of this world; I am not of this world." (*St. John, viii, 23*). Even if the genealogies were historically accurate, Jesus would still, according to the *Gospel* story, have no legal claim to the literal throne of David, for the story claims that He was conceived by the Holy Ghost and not by Joseph. So, if Joseph was not His physical father, He could not inherit Joseph's lineage. St. Paul even warns: "Neither give heed to fables and endless genealogies, which minister questionings, rather than godly edifying." (*I Timothy, i,4*).

Our spiritual interpretation also explains the seeming failure of the prophecy that Jesus would occupy the throne of His father David, and "reign over the house of Jacob forever; and of his kingdom there shall be no end." Literally Jesus never sat on any earthly throne, hence never reigned as king, and thus never fulfilled the prophecy. But spiritually interpreted He does not need the genealogy of Joseph; for once the Christ-consciousness is born in the heart it does sit upon the throne of David—Divine Love—and then: "Of His reign there shall be no end" through all our future incarnations.

All spiritual prophecies have two aspects: individual and collective. They are first fulfilled in the individual hearts

---

[11] *The Message of Aquaria*, Curtiss, 421.

[12] "The two genealogies given in *Matthew* and *Luke* differ from each other and their historical records. They may be said to exclude each other. Both cannot be true. . . . Joseph is said to have been only supposed to be the father of Jesus, having had no part in Him as a parent. Therefore the genealogies of Joseph are on different ground. It is of little consequence whether Joseph was or was not descended from David if he was not the natural father of Jesus." *The Life of Christ*, Caine, 264.

and lives of the few who can grasp their inner meaning, and then, as such individuals become more and more numerous, they make it possible for the prophecies to be fulfilled for a whole nation, a Race and finally for all mankind. Thus far only individually has this spiritual realization prophesied by the angelic host been fulfilled. For mankind has never yet collectively realized its common origin in the Divine, and hence its essential spiritual brotherhood.

Only the realization of this brotherhood can bring about the peace and good-will so long promised by the heavenly host. Every seeker for the Christ-consciousness therefore has an individual responsibility in helping to bring about this universal fulfillment of every prophecy concerning His coming, through exemplifying peace, good-will and brotherhood in his or her own life. And everyone who has passed through this stage of development and realization knows in his heart that, since the promised birth has been fulfilled in him individually, ultimately it must be fulfilled in all.

As the Earth, in its annual journey around the Sun, passes through the sign *Capricorn* during December, so is there a corresponding period in the spiritual zodiac of every Seeker for Truth which must be reached and passed ere the birth of the Christ-consciousness can take place. And only when this personal experience has been realized and exemplified in the lives of a majority of the worshipers of the Christ can the real Christ-mass be celebrated which, age after age, the angelic hosts have been waiting to sing, not for individuals alone, but for all mankind. This experience is realized at various times in various ways by different types of mind, but once experienced in the heart it can never be forgotten.

The birth of Jesus is represented as taking place in Bethlehem—the meaning of which is "the house of bread," or the sign *Virgo*, the sixth constellation, the harvest mansion, whose symbol is a woman with a spike of corn in her hand (*Ceres*)—because the spiritual birth must take place in the "house of bread" or center of spiritual nourishment, the heart.

An inn is not a home, only a place where many passing travellers meet and sojourn for a time, and perhaps discuss and argue over the topics of the day. It therefore fittingly symbolizes the head or the mind where many passing thoughts stop and sojourn for a time; where they reason and argue and then pass on.

Naturally, there is no room in the conflicting vibrations of such an intellectual maelstrom for the tender vibrations of Divine Love (Mary) to find a resting place and to bring forth the spiritual conception, the birth of the Christ-consciousness. For were the birth to take place in such company, the reasoning faculties would soon argue away the possibility of such a miraculous event's ever taking place and so convince the rational mind that we ourselves might doubt that the birth had ever taken place. Therefore there is no room in the mind for the Divine Mother and she is forced to go to a center lower down in the body, into the "cave" of the heart, where she is surrounded by the lower animal centers.

But the angels know that as the Christ grows up in the hearts of men and manifests in their lives, as He waxes strong in love, wisdom and power, all these crucifying conditions will be redeemed, and peace and good-will will reign upon Earth in reality as well as in name. For we can have true peace only as we feel good-will toward our fellow men. This means not only refraining from even thinking critically of our fellow travellers on the Path, but sending out the positive current of good-will to all while we mind our own affairs and do not interfere with other people's way of living and expressing, even to the extent of focusing our thought-force upon them. For we realize that each of us has to recognize the Christ within and work out our own problems, our own salvation, our own Karma, no matter what others may think or say about it. But while we thus guard our own flocks and keep hands off others, we can send to all those we contact our positive love and compassion.

Since the early Christian era the festival of the birth has been celebrated as an expression of good-will, happiness and unselfish helpfulness. But, alas, today it has become so commercialized that it is practically a social crucifixion to large classes of working people. Like all divine thoughts, concepts and symbols, the instant they are swallowed up in the world's misconception, they become a focus for greed, avarice, vanity and self-indulgence, and sink into the mire of callous selfishness. There are, however, many beautiful Souls who are sufficiently awakened and advanced to grasp the true Christ-spirit, and whose hearts do sing with the angels, "Peace on earth, good-will to men."

As the Christ is born a pean of praise, the great Christ-mass, "Glory to God in the highest" is sung by the angelic hosts. And this in spite of what must seem to them as the greatest crucifixion that the mind can picture, namely, the descent of the pure, spiritual Christ-light into matter and physical embodiment. The angels, in their enlightened consciousness, knew full well that ere peace on Earth could result, long cycles of war, slavery, toil and suffering must ensue. Yet, seeing the end from the beginning, with angelic confidence in the workings of the divine Law of Love, they celebrated the first Christ-mass, and have ever been singing it through the ages, while waiting for its sure fulfillment on Earth.

In its cosmic sense the birth is the descent of the Divine Light; the effort of Spirit to penetrate matter; that which is inner to express outwardly. In the personality it is the descent of the Soul into full embodiment. Mystically it is the descent of the Christ-child—the Son of God—into matter. The early church originally adopted this mystical concept, although through the ages of darkness and ignorance its mystical meaning has been lost to sight.

But the message of birth which our Cosmic Soul Science sends forth is not merely that of the Divine Birth in the heart of the individual, glorious as that is, but also of the Divine Birth for mankind as a whole, the advent of the Christ to humanity in the person of the coming Avatar.[13] The time of this Cosmic Birth is swiftly drawing near. In fact, The birth pangs of "wars and rumors of wars," of unbrotherliness, antagonism and conflict which are abroad in the land, and the cosmic disturbances which fulfill the prophecy, are already taking place. Hence, like a loving Father who sees His little children afrighted, He sends forth the call from the lips of His beloved Son, Jesus, the Christ, the comforting words: "Suffer the little children to come unto me, and forbid them not: for of such is the kingdom of heaven." And very soon, instead of the din of war and the cries of the desolate, "How long, O Lord, how long?" we shall hear the glad song of the Angels ring out: "Behold, I bring you good tidings of great joy, which shall be *to all people*. For unto you is born this day a Savior, which is Christ the Lord."

Happy is he who experiences the Birth of the Christ within.

---

[13] See "The Doctrine of Avatara," *The Voice of Isis*, Curtiss, Chapter X.

CHAPTER V

THE WISE MEN AND THE STAR

> "Behold, there came wise men from the east to Jerusalem, saying, where is he that is born King of the Jews? for we have seen his star in the east, and are come to worship him. . . . and lo! the star, which they saw in the east, went before them, till it came and stood over where the young child was." *St. Matthew, ii, 1,2,9.*

> "The three collinear stars of the second magnitude, known as the Three Kings or the Three Wise Men, rise from the East and travel West as Virgo rises in the East, until they come to the point where the star *Arcturus* rises over the manger of Io in the constellation Boötes. . . . By many the star *Sirius* is called the Star of Bethlehem." *Appendix A.*

One of the favorite passages which *Bible* critics delight to ridicule as superstitious is that which relates to the Three Wise Men and their Star. This Star is represented as going before them first to Jerusalem, then on to Bethlehem and finally we are told that it "stood over" a particular stable "where the young child was."

The critics claim that a star is a self-luminous body constituted like a sun and so nearly fixed that its displacement will be perceptible only after the lapse of several centuries. And even the moving planets have fixed orbits in which they can be located accurately at any desired time. And even the wandering comets have such nearly fixed orbits that their appearance can be calculated many years in advance. Yet ever since the early Christian era astronomers have eagerly searched the skies for some celestial body that would fulfill the requirements of the *Gospel* story, but without success.

The critics also say that altho new stars or *novae* do
suddenly blaze out in the sky, they do not travel for a time
and then stop, nor would they appear only to three persons
and not attract the attention of others. Much less could
such a star stand still over a certain country, far less single
out one little village and then a particular spot "where the
young child was" in that village.

They also claim that even if such a phenomenal star
could have stopped over a particular stable in Bethlehem,
such a marvelous phenomenon would have led Herod's
emissaries to the birthplace as easily as it is said to have
led the Wise Men. Therefore, the critics conclude that the
whole story is a fable conceived in the poetic imagination
of religious enthusiasts. But we hold that *it is far more*
than a myth or fable. In fact, the literal interpretation of
the incident is so physically impossible that it is evident
that the meaning must be symbolical.

In the life of the seeker after truth the mystical Star in
the East symbolizes that illumination which floods the Soul
whenever the heart turns in contemplation to the Christ.

The critics claim that the Three Wise Men were nothing more than wandering mendicants or story-tellers.
As a matter of fact the Magi were not mere "wandering
mendicants." Far from it.[1] They were extremely learned

---

[1] The celebrated Persian Magus, Gjamasp—called Hakim or "the Wise One"—was
the confidant and chief Minister to King Darius Hystapis, about 1000 B.C. He
wrote a book, *Judicia Gjamaspis*, in which he is said to have predicted the birth of
both Jesus and Mahommed, and that the Magian religion would be superseded by
their teachings. "Pliny mentions three schools of the Magi: one that he shows was
founded at an unknown antiquity: the other established by Osthenes and Zoroaster:
the third by Moses and Jambres." *Isis Unveiled*, Blavatsky, ii, 261. "The ancient
Magian astrologer, Aven Ezra, made the following prediction: 'In the sphere of
Persia there ariseth upon the face of the sign Virgo, a beautiful maiden. . . . She
bringeth up a child in Abrie (the Hebrew land), and the child's name is called Eisi
(or Jesus)!'" *American Journal of Astrology*, Winter Number, 1937, 59.

philosophers who were followers of the Persian prophet, Zoroaster, and had long anticipated the birth of another Messiah. In fact, they were such learned astronomers that, without the use of telescopes or other instruments, they were quite familiar with the zodiac, the planets and fixed stars, the precession of the equinoxes and the whole helio-centric system over a thousand years before the invention of the telescope! Astronomer Proctor has shown that the ancient Chaldean astronomers had developed a system of most accurate astronomy as far back as 2400 B.C., ages be-fore the invention of the telescope by Galileo in 1609 A.D.

In view of these unquestioned facts, it is scarcely logical for modern biblical critics, who know practically nothing about cosmic symbology, to belittle the learning of the Magi. We wonder how far they, or even modern astrono-mers, would get in organizing the heavens and developing such a complete astronomical and astrological science without their telescopes, spectroscopes, solar photography, etc., as did the Magi!

According to the Persian teaching there is one infal-lible, ineffable and truly Cosmic Soul Science which has always existed, but which is known only to the Elect. This science of the secrets of the heavens and their reflection in Nature, was revealed only at the time of Initiation. Since this science was cosmic in its nature it was far above the heads of the populace. Hence it had to be interpreted and adapted to the intelligence of the untutored multitudes of those early ages. And since the uninitiated were intellec-tually incapable of grasping the cosmic concept of those principles they were presented to the public in allegorical mystery-plays which the ignorant often took to be literal and historical.

But in these days of the almost universal spread of higher education, many of the public are now ready for at least an outline of these cosmic principles upon which all manifestation is based. Once these cosmic concepts are grasped they reconcile the seemingly opposed terms of science and religion, reason and faith, knowledge and belief, and authority and freedom.

As we point out in our *Appendix A*, astronomically the Three Wise Men represent the three bright collinear stars of the second magnitude—*Alnitake, Alnilam, Mintaka*—the sword-belt of the Mighty Hunter in the constellation of *Orion*. They travel from East to West, as the sign *Virgo* rises in the East, until the great star *Arcturus* rises over the manger of *Io* in the constellation Boõtes. Therefore it is only natural that the Persian Magi should be represented as travelling westward to the country in which they sought the birthplace of Mithras, the Savior-son of their Queen of Heaven, *Io*, or their rejuvenated or new-born Lightbringer.

But even when the Wise Men reached Jerusalem they found no physical star shining over a particular spot, but had to enquire locally about the actual place of birth. Only thus were they directed to Bethlehem, some five miles Southwest, altho the star is still said to go before them. Here we find the star radically changing its course. Whereas it formerly travelled from East to West it now turns at right angles and travels from Jerusalem in the North to Bethlehem in the South! Naturally this is another astronomical impossibility.

As one prominent writer attempts to account for such a physical star: "The famous star which appeared in Andromeda about the time of the Nativity, and which later was seen by Albumazar, the Arabian astronomer, in 945 A.D., again in 1264, and towards the end of the sixteenth century by Kepler, is one of those stars which have an orbit of great eccentricity with the major axis towards the solar system, so that they appear 'end on' when entering the field of vision, make a brief incursion, during which they appear to grow in luminosity, and then recede again and are lost to view for a period of many years. . . . Falling as it does in the sign *Capricorn*. . . . this star holds for us portents of singular interest. . . .

It may herald the birth of a new and great political leader or the rise of a new world power. . . . That it falls in the solar decan of the sign *Capricorn* is at least significant of such a possibility."[2]

Others have thought that such a star might have been an especially bright but temporary star or *nova*, such as the one seen by Tycho Brahe in November 1572, which outshone Venus in brilliancy and thus was visible in daylight. Or it may have been like the new star *Nova Aquillae* discovered in 1921 on the verge of the Milky Way in the sign *Capricorn* which rules Palestine. Or it may have been like the still more brilliant super-star, *Nova Puppis* (the stern of Argo, the ship), which suddenly blazed forth on November 4th, 1942, and within a week increased six million times in brilliancy to become the sixth brightest star in the heavens, only to fade rapidly away.

But unfortunately for the nova theory, since they do not lend themselves to mathematical calculation but suddenly appear and soon disappear, the uncertainty as to their nature and periodicity makes them of little prophetic value to the Magi. But if any such cosmic wonder had actually occurred, the writers and historians of the day would certainly have recorded it. But no one but St. Matthew mentions it.

On the other hand, the Cosmic Soul Science of the Magi taught that certain planetary conjunctions — especially of Jupiter and Saturn — [3] presaged great events on earth, such as catastrophies, the birth of great men, great religions and the like.[4] Similarly today modern material

---

[2] Sepharial in the *British Journal of Astrology*, July 1918.

[3] See *Appendix C*.

[4] The birth of *Rama* was foretold when Jupiter was in *Cancer*. Buddha's birth was predicted by the appearance of a "Messianic Star" when the constellation *Kwei* was in conjunction with the Sun. According to Jewish legends a brilliant star was seen by the Magi over the birthplace of *Moses*. Also *Abraham's* birth is said to have been heralded by the appearance of a brilliant star in the East which devoured the four stars which were with it. When *Krishna* was born his star—*Rohini* or *Aldebaran*—was seen by the prophet *Nared*. The Chinese say that a brilliant star heralded the birth of *Yu*, the founder of the First Dynasty, and also at the birth of *Lao-tsze*.

science tells us that the appearance and location of certain sun-spots definitely presages magnetic storms, radio interference, bad weather and the like.

Now, since every country is related to one particular sign of the zodiac, when the conjunction of Jupiter and Saturn occurred in *Pisces*, it is only natural that such a brilliant event would attract the attention of the Magi and indicate to them that the birth of their long-looked-for Messiah was about to take place in Palestine. Hence they would naturally be led to the capital of that country, Jerusalem. For according to the famous astronomer, Kepler, there actually was a conjunction of Jupiter and Saturn in the sign *Pisces*,[3] which rules Jerusalem, three years before the death of Herod!

Since the origin of the Star of Bethlehem has been the object of repeated research by both astronomers and astrologers for ages in an effort to account for some special star's appearing at or about the time stated, but without result, the astrological interpretation is the only tenable one, as *it covers all the facts* and *answers all scientific objections* as to the literal event. The learned Bishop Thorburn agrees with us in this statement when he says: "There can be little doubt, indeed, that the solution of this problem *must be sought in astrology* rather than in astronomy."[5]

The learned Magi well understood that an embodiment of the Light of the Spiritual Sun (Son of God) appears at the beginning of every Great Age that all mankind may have renewed spiritual life by absorbing and manifesting the new spiritual ideals thus revealed, and which that Age should naturally develop, just as the physical Sun shines forth at the beginning of every lesser cycle—the year—that all Nature may have renewed life by absorbing and manifesting the life-force which it pours forth. The light

---

[5] *Mythical Interpretation of the Gospels*, Thorburn, 50.

of this understanding should indicate to the spiritually wise men where the Manifestation or "birth" is to take place.

Such prognostication is neither psychic prevision nor prophecy, any more than the prediction that new chemical elements would be found at definite places in the periodic table of atomic weights, the reappearance of a comet, or that of a new planet, *Pluto*, would be discovered outside the orbit of his brothers Jupiter and Neptune. All are based on mathematically correct computations of phenomena regularly recurring in Nature, from the infinitesimal atoms to the stars in heaven.[6]

But it is not in the physical incident which we, as students of Cosmic Soul Science, are interested. The fact that such incidents have been recorded and handed down to us throughout the ages, long before the Christian era, suggests to an enquiring mind that they contain an inner meaning and lessons of importance. And to make those lessons useful we must seek to understand their symbology and apply it to our personal lives. For symbology, and even history, is of little value, except as a record of events, unless we gain a personal lesson and experience an expansion of consciousness from the story of the events. So is it with the life-story of Jesus. Unless we can make such a personal application, the story is little more than a beautiful biography filled with high ethical precepts. But spiritually interpreted, and with the spiritual forces symbolized actually contacted and applied, it becomes a definite and even scientific guide toward the unfolding of the Christ-consciousness within ourselves.

In the life of the seeker after Truth the mystical Star in the East symbolizes that illumination which floods the Soul whenever the heart turns in contemplation to the Christ within. The East is represented by the sign Aquarius the Man, or the wisdom that is able to sum up and correlate the forces of the entire zodiac. Hence it is

---

[6] For further details see "The Christ Star" in *The Inner Radiance*, Curtiss, 337.

said that all things pertaining to wisdom come from the East; not literally from the East, altho that too is a common source, but from that which the East symbolizes. For instance, it is commonly said that the Sun rises in the East, yet in reality the Sun is forever in the East and is forever sending its light and life giving rays to this planet of ours. It is the Earth that turns her face towards the East every morning and her back upon it every evening. So is it with every Soul who is striving for the light of the Christ within. That bright Christ-star, the Sun of Righteousness, remains forever in the mystical East. It is man who so often turns his back upon it.

From an occult standpoint the symbolic East is the most important point of the compass. It is the mystical point from which all spiritual life flows, from which all illumination comes. From the mystical South comes the warmth of love and the fructifying power to bring forth in our lives that which flows forth from the East. The West is the region of sunset and night, of compensation and fulfillment; the place where all that is conceived in the East, and brought forth in the South, is reaped and then takes its periodic rest. Then comes the storms from the North, whence Saturn sends forth his icy breath, the chill and death of his testing power. In the life of the Seeker these points of the compass are emblematic of the forces which perfect his spiritual growth and bring its spiritual fruition.

And just as the Earth periodically turns away from the Sun, so with humanity from the beginning of time. Altho again and again the light of the Christ-star has illumined humanity, through the teachings of those great Souls who periodically give humanity new conceptions of eternal Truth in each age, nevertheless, as soon as the icy wind from the North blows to test and prove him, man turns his back upon the Christ-star and sinks down into the darkness of materialism and apathetic slumber in the West. Yet at the beginning of each new cycle humanity again instinctively turns its face to the spiritual Light,

—the mystical Star in the East—for spiritual guidance and help.

As we have explained elsewhere, in the personality the Wise Men represent the three highest of our intellectual faculties, our three kings as it were. They symbolize those faculties which, through experience, reason and suffering, have evolved to the point where they have become like Sages or Wise Men to us, and hence are ready to recognize and follow the gleam of that Inner Light which shall ultimately lead them to the cradle of the Christ-consciousness.[6]

For when the intellect has evolved spirit-ward to the point where it is no longer dominated by the vibrations coming to it from the outer world, and is not only capable but is willing to recognize and respond to the higher vibrations coming from within, it recognizes that there is a power and an intelligence greater than the intellect; a power and intelligence which is back of all the manifold manifestations of life; a consciousness that is far beyond the mere human understanding gained through the reasoning faculties; the gleam of a Light that is high in the heavens, far beyond the human mind and the mental world. "Knowledge of the external world may come to man through other channels than the sense organs. . . . They express a rare and almost unknown aspect of ourselves."[7] This Light is the mystical Star in the East, the Star of Initiation, which, if faithfully followed, will lead our consciousness to the cradle of the Christ and then will become the Star of Bethlehem or the realization of the Christ within.

Since the East is the region in which the physical Sun arises to illumine and vivify the physical world, it naturally symbolizes the mystical East whence the Wise Men came, also the source from which the Spiritual Sun arises to illumine and vivify our spiritual lives. The mystical Star in the East therefore, in the universal sense, symbolizes

---

[7] *Man, The Unknown*, Carrel, 125-6.

the periodic rise of the Spiritual Sun and the revelation of the Cosmic Christ to humanity in each Great Age.

In the individual life this means that spiritual illumination and glory which elevate the human consciousness into a realization of the Light of the Christ within. For when we turn our backs on the lusts of the flesh and the allurements of the world and thereby no longer allow them to fill our sight and dominate our consciousness, but resolutely face the mystical East and deliberately open our hearts to the Christ Star of spiritual intuition, then the Christ Light will be revealed to us, and its slender gleam will guide us through the darkness of all outer conditions until we reach our Bethlehem and find that the Christ has already been born in us.

> "O star of wonder, star of might,
> Star of wondrous beauty bright,
> Godward leading, still preceding,
> Guide me with thy radiant light."

Also wherever we find the Hebrew word *beth*, or its combinations, its root meaning always refers to some kind of a "house or home," hence a birth-place. In us it symbolizes that center in us which corresponds to the mystical East; that center in which the Christ Light is born, namely, the heart center. Bethlehem therefore symbolizes that divine home, birth-place or spiritual womb—the home of Love— out of which the Divine Man or the Christ-consciousness must be born to govern our lives. For the prophecy is: "Out of thee (Bethlehem) shall come a Governor, that shall rule my people Israel." Out of the heart there shall come forth the Christ-force which shall govern our lives henceforth. For the Christ-consciousness is not born from the head or from the mind or the intellect, but from the love of the heart.

In our individual lives the Star of Bethlehem symbolizes that ray of spiritual consciousness which as Wise Men we have begun to recognize. As we have explained elsewhere: "As the gods said over the circle of unmani-

fested world-stuff in the beginning, so must we say: 'Let
there be light.' For we have recognized the radiant Star of
Initiation as the center of our circle of Life and it is now
our task to bring into manifestation that which we know is
within us.... the unveiling of the Christ Star which shines
in the center."[8]

"Just as in his earlier steps the Light shone above the
candidate as the Star of Initiation, which he had to follow. . . . even though at times the dark mists of earth
conditions hid it from view, so it is still the Light from the
one Master, his own Immortal Self, the Christ within."[8]

"The first creation is that of Light, symbolizing the
Light of the Christ-consciousness which breaks into the
darkness of man's ignorance and sin and turns his attention
toward the spiritual life. The light perceived in his heart is
called the Star of Initiation because the first glimpse of its
glory initiates him into a new world, and the memory of
that flash leaves him no peace until he seeks its source."[9]

"The light shines in the darkness of the unawakened
Soul and the darkness comprehendeth it not.... The darkness is pregnant with potencies of all things, both good and
evil, which at the breaking forth of the light become ener-
gized with new life and begin their slow evolution toward
perfection.... The instant the Star of Initiation sends down
its ray into the darkness of his earth life, every creeping
thing, not only in his heart, but also in his environment,
comes forth. . . . The loathsome creeping things of the
darkness were not created by the Light, but were all in the
darkness simply awaiting the energizing force of the light
to reveal them. The Light was sent into the darkness not to
stir up evil, but by the omniscient law, which recognizes
that only by fulfilling its destiny can evil be transmuted into
good.... This it does through the divine power of the Christ
Light when he says: 'Let there be light!'.... And the first

---

[8] *The Key to the Universe*, Curtiss, 364, 334.
[9] *The Voice of Isis*, Curtiss, 321-4-5-7.

beams of the Christ Star penetrate the darkness of his unawakened life."[9]

Applied to us personally therefore the Star of Bethlehem
symbolizes the Light of the Christ-consciousness (intuition) which arises in the mystic East (the heart), where
the Sun of Righteousness also rises later on. If this Star is
followed it will illumine our Path through life. It will also
illumine all our faculties and lead them to recognize, seek
and ultimately find the Christ-within. In occult terminology it also refers to the Star of Initiation, or the glorious
spiritual light which floods our whole being when the
Sahasrara center at the top of the head is opened and our
three dimensional, finite consciousness is so expanded as
to embrace something of the Cosmic Consciousness and
thus make us truly Wise Men.

The Christ Star is latent in every heart. It is not limited
to the Wise Men, for even the humblest shepherd can see
it. For when we deliberately turn and face the mystical
East, or even listen to the heavenly host, and open our
hearts to the Sun of Righteousness, the Light of the Christ
Star will gradually dawn for us. But it can shine forth and
illumine our lives only when we have become sufficiently
responsive or have become Wise Men enough to follow
the light of the Christ Star to its birthplace in Bethlehem.

As that treasury of spiritual philosophy, *The Voice of
the Silence*, tells us: "Fix thy Soul's gaze upon the star
whose ray thou art, the flaming Star that shines within the
lightless depths of ever-being, the boundless fields of the
unknown."[10]

Thus we must conclude that altho it was an astronomical and physical impossibility for a physical star to have
performed the actions attributed to it, the Star of Bethlehem
was a spiritual reality to the consciousness of the Wise
Men. And it still is a reality to all who are spiritually
awakened sufficiently to become Wise Men enough to

---

[10] *The Voice of the Silence*, Blavatsky, 32.

follow the Christ Star that shines within the heart until it leads them to the birth of the Christ within.[11]

Happy is he who has become one of the Wise Men.

---

[11] Those who wish to cultivate their response to the light of this mystic Star should repeat some such prayer as our *Prayer for Light*. "O Christ! Light Thou within my heart the Flame of Divine Love and Wisdom, that I may dwell forever in the radiance of Thy countenance and rest in the light of Thy smile." Visualize the Divine Light descending upon you like the beam of a giant searchlight above your head and flooding you with its radiance. See it awaken in your heart a tiny, bright Flame. See it illumine every fiber of your being with Divine Love and Compassion. Feel an actual glow of warmth spread throughout your body, purifying, spiritualizing and transmuting the very atoms of your flesh with its spiritual radioactivity. Then see it ascend and blend into the Divine Flame that is descending upon you. Then ascend in consciousness within the column of that Divine Light to the realms of Divine Consciousness where you lose yourself in oneness with the Divine. For further details see *Prayers of the O.C.M.*, Curtiss, 2.

CHAPTER VI

THE SHEPHERDS AND THE SHEEP

> "And there were in the same Country shepherds abiding in the field, keeping watch over their flock by night. And lo, the angel of the Lord came upon them, and the glory of the Lord shone round about them: and they were sore afraid." *St. Luke, ii, 8, 9.*

> "The sign *Capricorn* rules shepherds and the stables, hence the lowly origin of all Lightbringers, as they are represented as being born in a stable in the presence of an ox, ass, goat, etc., and laid in a manger and attended by shepherds." *Appendix A.*

The age-old picture of the humble shepherds quietly seated upon the hillside beneath the stars during the darkest nights of the year, surrounded by their sleeping sheep, is one of great pastoral charm for both young and old. Indeed, it has so often been reproduced in song, story and art that its beauty has touched the hearts of all. But why was so simple an incident recorded? And what does it mean to us today?

If we apply its logical symbology to our personal lives we will easily recognize not only its aptness, but also its importance. It not only reveals the law of communication from the spiritual world, but it also solves a problem which has puzzled so many generations of *Bible* students. The puzzle is why the birth of the Christ was announced to such humble and insignificant persons as the illiterate sheep-herders instead of the Priests of the Temple at Jerusalem or to the Wise Men, or at least to someone in authority in the spiritual affairs of the nation.

But before we take up the spiritual interpretation of this incident, our research shows that the story of the shepherds' being the first to find and watch over the Divine Babe is another well-nigh universal incident in the life-story of all celestial Lightbringers.[1]

Realistically examined, the incident of the shepherds watching their flocks by night out-of-doors on the hills in Palestine at the end of December is another one of those physical discrepancies which the higher critics delight to pounce upon. For in Palestine December is the height of the cold and rainy winter season. The nights are so cold that the sheep are usually kept in or are at least driven back to the sheep-fold at night, from the end of October until Spring. Hence the shepherds would not be literally out on the hills at night in the midst of winter.

So again the symbolic interpretation of the incident saves it from its material inaccuracy and inconsistency. The shepherds symbolize the simplicity, devotion, courage and steadfastness of our heart-qualities or love-nature, whose natural abiding place is upon the Mount of Attainment, the exact height on the Mount depending upon the stage of each Soul's spiritual unfoldment.

As we have already explained, it is not to the mind or the intellectual faculties—the Wise Men—to which the angels—the messengers of spiritual realization—come, no matter how highly developed those faculties may be, but to the simple, trusting love-nature. While the brain is the organ through which the intellectual consciousness manifests, it is the heart through which the spiritual consciousness manifests.

The reason why the Christ is first revealed to the shepherds is that the simple, trusting love-nature learns in a

---

[1] *Krishna* was first recognized as the promised Savior by the shepherd Nanda. The virgin-born *Aesculapius* was discovered and protected by shepherds. *Romulus* was found on the banks of the Tiber by shepherds. *Bacchus* was found and educated by shepherds, as was also *Paris*, son of Priam. Many other Greek and Roman heroes, demi-gods and Saviors were either attended or fostered by or first worshipped by shepherds.

burst of spiritual illumination, heavenly melody and joy where to find the Christ, while the intellectual faculties have to search far and wide, only at last to be forced to inquire of the heart.

Yet it is necessary for the Wise Men and the shepherds to worship together, for without love no amount of intellectual attainment or head-learning can ever find Christ. That contact and realization come only through the heart. On the other hand, love unbalanced by wisdom may be taken for mere mawkish sentimentality, or it may result in more trouble than comfort and inspiration to mankind.

Each Soul must therefore become a shepherd. And the sheep it must watch over, guide and protect are the flocks of appetites, passions and desires of the animal body, and the thoughts, ambitions and emotions of the human personality. Even though these flocks sometimes stampede like frightened sheep and carry us away with them into forbidden pastures, over precipitous cliffs or into noisome swamps of evil, they are not to be killed out or emasculated. They must be wisely led that we may utilize all their powers and products, each in its proper place, "to the glory of God." For all are given us by the great Shepherd of Souls to guide, develop, perfect and utilize, since all are necessary in their proper places for the perfect manifestation of the Spiritual Self through the body of flesh.

Our flocks must yield to the guidance of the true Shepherd, to the love, power and wisdom of the Christ within, that He may find expression through us. We should say to ourselves: "My sheep are all the thoughts, traits and circumstances that are given to me to guard and bring to perfection and utilize. Even if they are but passing fancies and conditions and have no permanent reality, nevertheless while I am here, living in this physical body and reacting to them, limited by my mental capacity, influenced by my karmic environment, all these things to which my consciousness reacts are real sheep to me and must be treated as such. Therefore there is nothing within or around me that I am not expected to train and direct and make the highest use of; nothing I am not to redeem, or from which I am not to absorb the forces and learn the lesson."

But like a good shepherd who calleth his sheep by name, we must face ourselves, recognize and call by name every hidden quality without deceiving ourselves. We must be ready to fight the wolves of selfishness and self-indulgence and not be deceived by wolves in sheep's clothing.

From another standpoint, as we have already pointed out, as a class: "The sheep are those gentle and docile Souls who follow unthinkingly in flocks wherever they are led; who must have a Shepherd and a sheep-fold wherein they are protected from the wolves; those who follow their shepherd lovingly, yet who will follow just as blindly one who would lead them to the verge of a precipice, or one who would flee and leave the sheep to their fate when the wolves appear."[2]

The shepherds as a class represent those who, although ardent and eager, are often without great learning, hence are unable to give their flocks deep intellectual analysis or profound metaphysical speculations. All they can give them for food is the green grass of simple truths of the plain, and afford them the clear outlook and wider view from the hillside heights. All they can give them to drink is the pure waters of inspiration or the intuitive knowledge of the reality of the spiritual life.

Thus it is that direct spiritual realization comes most often to the simple of heart, like the fishermen chosen as Disciples by Jesus, those whose minds are not over-burdened with elaborate intellectual conceptions nor crammed with the thoughts of others, even if such are supposed to be authorities.

The night in which the shepherds watched symbolizes the night of ignorance, materialism and spiritual blind-

---

[2] *The Message of Aquaria*, Curtiss, 277.

ness which marked the close of the Arian Age, for the
spiritual luminary or Christ-light of the then new Piscean
Age had not yet arisen. That was a period of overlapping
and transition similar to that in which we find ourselves
today as we are passing from the close of the Piscean Age
into the beginning of the new Aquarian Age.

The shepherds were awake, gazing in reverent awe and
wonder upon the beauty of the heaven world while their
sheep quietly slept. Thus even in the days of dense intellectual darkness, as well as in the present days of dense
materialism and inhuman warfare, do those of humble,
faithful heart find light and guidance even in the meager
rays of spiritual starlight that reach them from afar. On
these they meditate and feed until the time of their illumination comes and the heaven of spiritual consciousness
opens and its glorious light floods their Souls while their
ears are ravished by the angelic melodies.

When the time is ripe, the heavens of the spiritual consciousness always open at the call of spiritual aspiration
and love. But, alas, only too often the opening is delayed
or overshadowed by dark clouds of doubt and discouragement of the lower mind's formation. These are but the mists
of the valley which the rising Sun lifts only that it may
dissipate them. But if we ascend to the heights of aspiration we will find that there all is light, serene, comforting
and inspiring. For no matter how dark the night period of
the Soul, the light of the spiritual consciousness and the
warmth of divine love are always tenderly overshadowing
us. It is only through our simple, trusting and steadfast love
that we learn what the Christ-child has brought to us and
to all mankind; and when and where it manifests.

When the higher consciousness opens and the angels'
song is heard, the message seems to speak itself to the
inner consciousness, impressing the meaning upon our
minds and giving us a clear understanding of it. For the
true explanation of a thing we have prayed over and
meditated upon for a long time generally comes upon us

suddenly, just as described in the story of the shepherds. The heavens opened, "And, lo, the angel (or messenger) of the Lord came upon them, and the glory of the Lord shone round about them." And like many of those who suddenly receive an illuminating understanding and explanation of the problem of their prayers and meditations, at first the shepherds were "sore afraid."

But the messenger of the Divine Law (Lord) said unto them, "Fear not." In other words, recognition of the Law teaches us that all divinely given messages bring to the awakened Soul first a great joy and enthusiasm, and then a reaction of doubt and uncertainty as to the truth, not of the message or understanding received, but as to its source; the possibility of their having imagined what they so longed to hear. But an understanding of the Law brings the deep assurance that it was really an angel of the Lord, a messenger from the spiritual consciousness, who spoke and brought to them the glad tidings of great joy which they realize are not for themselves alone, but "to all people."

Once we have heard the angel's message we no longer sit in quiet meditation, watching our contented and sleeping sheep. Now there is a far higher duty, namely, to arise out of the daily round of our customary thoughts and activities and seek the new-born Christ-child. For the Christ must have willing and determined shepherds who will use wise and sensible means to awaken the world to a realization of His birth.

Alas, only too long has the message given to the shepherds lost its thrill of divine realization and its personal response. This is because it has been unwisely presented to the world, or given without taking into consideration the worldly duties we all must perform if we are to live in peace and harmony. For once the Christ is born in us its divine light, life and power bless all our worldly duties and all we contact.

After the angel's message is received, and the time for solitary meditation on the mountain-side is over, we must

arise and hasten to Bethlehem, the city of David, where
there is born a Savior who is Christ the Lord. Since "David" symbolizes love, the "city of David" is a term used to
symbolize the abode of Divine Love or the Spiritual Heart,
that center within us which is the focal point of the spiritual
consciousness of the "Heaven Born" or Spiritual Self.

Once the Christ-consciousness is born in our hearts it
literally becomes our Savior, our Savior from all evil, sin,
doubt or false teachings. For one who has passed through
the spiritual birth has but to ask and immediately he knows
what is true and what is false; all uncertainty, doubt and fear
are swallowed up in realization. Such a Christ-illumined
one is indeed a true shepherd. Such shepherds make no
claims as to their enlightenment, but prove it by their lives
and their works.

Only the outshining of the universal Christ-light can
illumine all minds and touch all hearts and unify all peoples. Yet to carry this message and cover this vast field,
it will require many illumined shepherds—many national
and racial expressions of Divine Truth—as each nation
will express it in the best way to carry conviction to its
people. Therefore the true shepherd must make faithful-
ness to the duty at hand his first consideration if he is to
prepare himself to realize the glory and understand the
angel's message; for to broadcast it to all who will listen
should be his deepest desire.

If we are true shepherds we will recognize that it is
our duty to our own sheep deliberately to select pastures
which are free from the poisonous weeds of atheism, also
bitter criticism of others, and from the wolves of sub-
versive doctrines. We must guide them into pastures of
intellectual and spiritual interest where they can profitably
feed in peace and harmony on the ideals which as good
shepherds our foresight and discrimination select for them.
For we must consciously lead them high up on the Mount
of Attainment, far above the dark canons of ignorance

and the dank, chilling fogs of doubt, cynicism and atheistic arguments.

This is important, for today, instead of the quiet pastures of normal life, under the stars of freedom and happy living, we have the turmoil and carnage of a world defending itself from atheism, aggression and enslavement. Hence our task as shepherds is more important because more difficult.

For during such periods especially, the old forces of habit, privilege and power put forth every vicious effort to kill out our new ideals and prolong the reign of the old. Hence the forces of the overlapping New Age are now calling to all the shepherds who are ready for the angel's message to put forth greater efforts to spread the glad tidings of the new day of spiritual enlightenment and upliftment.

As good shepherds we must not only guide our flocks, but also protect them from wild beasts and robbers. We must ever be alert to guard our thoughts against the ravenous beasts of lust and greed, which so often devour the tender lambs of our highest aspirations and whose indulgence consumes us and makes us one with the beasts.

Devotion to our ideals and to the guidance of the Christ must also protect us from those appeals to selfishness, self-indulgence and aggrandizement which rob us of our inner peace and serenity of mind so necessary for spiritual growth and the expression of the Christ-consciousness which has been born in our hearts.

Our flocks must also be trained to respond to the voice of our Spiritual Self as readily as the sheep do to the voice of their shepherd. For we cannot hear the voice of our Shepherd if we allow the turmoil and jangle of the outer world's activities to deafen us to His voice or so to enthrall our attention as to make us oblivious of His presence.

And our own voice must be gentle, firm and quieting, yet so positive and commanding as to secure instant

obedience. For it is a fundamental psychological principle
that through persistent, positive suggestions the subconscious mind of our animal nature can be trained to react
constructively as desired by force of habit before we have
time to think. Then if a wolf attempts to slip in he will
be instantly scented and immediately driven out by the
strong-horned rams—positive, protecting thoughts of our
flock. And just as a shepherd learns to recognize and love
his sheep, so will we learn to recognize and love, cherish
and take great comfort in shepherding our good thoughts
and desires and high ideals. If some thoughts are wayward
and wander far afield where they are subject to attack or
demoralization, like watchful shepherds we must go forth
to seek them and bring them back to the fold, not in anger,
but quietly and gently yet commandingly, lest they carry
us even farther afield.

But we must not make the mistake of thinking that we
can accomplish this in our own strength. For there is no
sadder sight than to see a personality rejecting the help of
the Christ within because of spiritual pride or intellectual
vanity. For back of every condition in life there stands an
angel who presides over it.

There is a heavenly host—divine emanations, angelic
messengers of God—surrounding, guarding and strengthening each one of us if we will only listen to their guidance.

There are angels even in department stores, shops and
factories, at the elbows of the weary ones, whispering into
their ears words of cheer and comfort, and strengthening
them with spiritual vitality. There are angels in our places
of business, in our homes, in all phases of our lives, helping us to turn everything into good and to the service of
the Christ within.

Then let us call the flocks of our thoughts and desires
together and drive out the wolves. Let us master the
pride and selfishness and self-sufficiency of the personality that the Christ may be born in us. Let us be humble
like the shepherds, and teachable. "I can of mine own
self do nothing. . . . but the father that dwelleth in me,

he doeth the works" (*St. John, v, 30; xiv, 10*), should be our watchword.

Let us cease our outer striving for a moment and sit down and fix our attention upon the heaven world and listen to the angels singing their heavenly anthems, telling us, in language unmistakable to those who have ears to hear, of the love and compassion and effort that is being put forth by the angelic hosts that we may enter into the Christ-consciousness and find safety and support and protection from storms and disasters on all planes. Then when the floods of changing conditions sweep over the world, since we have been faithful shepherds, our consciousness will be so uplifted that we can be guided and guarded and carried safely through them to the cradle of the Christ.

As we have already pointed out: "The divine Law of Love is indeed a Shepherd of Souls. And once a Soul has heard its voice and has followed. . . . he finds this loving guidance a deep and abiding reality. Hence that Soul wants nothing but to follow on wherever that voice leads. . . . We are contented to lie down at His command, no longer running to and fro bleating plaintively for food or for worldly things, but resting quietly on the Law. Then doth it lead us beside the waters of life that are no longer turbulent; that no longer gush forth from our eyes as tears, for the eyes now see clearly the glory of the Shepherd who leadeth us."[3] No matter how dark the night of the Soul, the love of God is watching tenderly over us all.

And to all faithful, humble hearts who, like the shepherds, have been guarding their flocks through the long dark night-period ere their spiritual unfoldment is attained, there will surely come a time—as surely as Christmas comes—perhaps in their darkest hour, when the heavens of their higher consciousness will open and in a glorious expansion of their consciousness "the angel of

---

[3] *The Message of Aquaria*, Curtiss, 216-7.

the Lord"—the messenger of the Law of Divine Love—
will proclaim the coming birth of the Christ-consciousness
in their hearts. Then will "the glory of the Lord" shine
round about them, and they will realize that there is with
them "a multitude of the heavenly host praising God and
saying, Glory to God in the highest, and on earth peace,
good will toward men."

But if we merely wonder at the glory and do not obey
the command to go to Bethlehem and seek until we find the
Christ, the glorious experience is wasted. If it is allowed to
remain merely as an ecstatic emotional episode, it is like
"good seed that fell on stony ground." It has no root and
therefore cannot bring forth its fruit.

There are certain fundamentals, however, without an
understanding of which we will lose the lesson. Firstly,
the shepherds—the loving hearts to whom the angels first
appear—were seated upon the ground watching their flocks
through the longest and darkest nights of the year. In eastern countries pupils of a teacher seat themselves upon the
ground at his feet, not only to listen to his words of wisdom, but as a symbol of their humility and teachableness,
and also to gather the earth-forces, so helpful in the development of their power to correlate their consciousness with
his and with the forces of Nature. The true significance of
this posture should be our conception of its symbology.
For now-a-days we can gain humility and teachableness
and can correlate with our teacher and the forces of Nature
without actually sitting upon the ground.

This is the attitude of mind which must be attained if we
are ever to hear the beautiful song of the angels. For if we
have truly seated ourselves at the feet of the Christ and are
singing our Christ-mass; if we are faithfully guarding the
flocks of our thoughts, tendencies and emotions, some day
the heavens of our inner consciousness will open and we
will hear the heavenly chorus, even though it seems but a
whisper that disturbs the stillness of the night.

This not a miracle, but is the natural flowering of our continued spiritual growth. It is not a unique or isolated phenomenon which occurred only once nearly two thousand years ago, nor is it a mere symbol or figure of speech. It is a Soul reality experienced more or less consciously by every Soul as it nears the time for its spiritual birth.

Happy is he who is a good Shepherd to his flocks.

Chapter VII

THE MANGER AND THE SWADDLING CLOTHES

"And she brought forth her firstborn son, and wrapped him in swaddling clothes, and laid him in a manger." *St. Luke, ii, 7.*

"The star *Arcturus* rises over the manger of *Io* in the constellation Boötes. . . . The sign *Capricorn* rules the stables, hence the lowly origin of all Lightbringers, as they are represented as being born in a stable, in the presence of an ox, ass, goat, etc., and laid in a manger." *Appendix A.*

Careful research shows that the placing of the Savior-babe in a manger or basket—some form of basket being the usual form of food-box in the stables in Eastern countries where wood is scarce—and connecting him with shepherds, is another one of those universal incidents in the lives of nearly all Lightbringers.[1]

There is an important distinction that should be made between the symbology of the stable and that of the

---

[1] *Krishna* was placed in a basket and entrusted to the Gopis or shepherds. The infant *Dionysus* was wrapped in swaddling clothes and placed in a golden *likon*,—basket or manger—on what is now called Christmas day. At the birth of *Ion* he was carried by *Hermes* with "cradle, swaddling clothes and all," to the temple of his father, Apollo. *Sargon* was placed in a golden basket at birth. At the birth of *Mithra* at the winter solstice, be was enveloped in a golden nimbus, and surrounded by shepherds. The infant *Horus* was cradled in a lotus leaf at the winter solstice. That Egyptian savior-babe was also worshipped in a manger or crib. *Hercules, Jupiter,* and a number of other savior-babes, were similarly wrapped in swaddling clothes and placed in a manger, crib or basket, usually with the domestic animals looking on. All these testify to the universality of the symbol.

manger. Since the stable is where the domestic animals live, as applied to the personality it refers to that region of the body below the diaphragm—the abdomen—where the vegetative organs which nourish the body are located. These organs may be called domesticated because they are quietly carrying on the animal functions of the body under the control of the subconscious or animal mind. But since the subconscious mind is extremely sensitive and responsive to suggestion it is quite willing to respond to and obey the influx of the higher self-conscious mind without argument, especially when guided by love.

The manger is a feed-box to hold the grain and hay for horses and cattle. It is elevated above the floor of the stable and hence symbolizes that part of the body above the diaphragm, namely the chest, where the heart—the organ of spiritual nourishment—is located. Therefore in all the nativity stories the Divine Babe is placed in a manger or golden basket, as in Botticelli's celebrated picture of the nativity.

This indicates that while the Christ-consciousness must be born in and make use of the "stable" of the animal body, it is "laid in the manger" or functions through a higher organ (heart) than those which minister to the animal functions, instincts and desires.

For while the intellectual consciousness (Joseph) functions through the head, the spiritual consciousness (Jesus) functions through the heart (Mary). Since the spiritual nature requires a finer kind of nourishment than does the animal nature, those experiences which are as grain to nourish the animal nature must be ground to flour so that their essence may be made into nourishing bread to promote our Soul growth. Then the animal nature will no longer find its former food in the manger, but must now partake somewhat of the spiritualizing Christ-force.

And just as it requires the heat of the flame to transmute the food of the beasts (grain) into food for man (bread), just so does it require the flame of Divine Love to transmute the sensations of the body and the ex-

periences of our outer daily lives into spiritual realization
or the Bread of Life for our spiritual growth, that we may
truly manifest those high ideals which establish our character. And it is our rough, hard experiences in the world
which become the two millstones—the positive and negative aspects of the Rock of Truth—that grind the grain that
we may learn the lessons from it or mould it into loaves
which will become as spiritual bread when transmuted by
the fire of love.

The fact that the spiritual Babe is laid in the manger
of the animal body should teach us that the animal instrument, through which we must contact earth conditions and
express our Spiritual Self, must not be despised. It is a
necessary part of God's creation and more useful and essential to man than the horse or the ox. Its needs must be
recognized and supplied and its legitimate wants satisfied
on its own plane. And since it is blessed by the presence of
the Christ within, it is His will that must be done "on earth,
even as it is done in heaven," and not the uncontrolled will
of the animal self.

When this new conception has finally been brought
forth we realize that it is too sacred and holy to be exposed
to the incredulity, the arguments and the scoffings of our
worldly friends; for until they, too, have passed through the
same experience they cannot understand or comprehend it.
Therefore, we must not publish abroad to our friends of the
outer life our sacred spiritual experiences, especially the
news of this spiritual birth. It must be wrapped in swaddling clothes of silence, meditation and cherishing love,
both to protect it and support it until it has grown strong
enough to stand alone.

The swaddling clothes also symbolize the mystical language of parable and allegory which surround the sacred
mysteries of the inner life, and hide them from the curious gaze of the worldly-minded casual observer until he
is willing to follow the light of the Star of Intuition and is
willing to ask of the humble shepherds where to find the
inner truth about the Christ within.

As we have explained in previous chapters, the birth of the Christ-consciousness in us is a great spiritual event. But to ensure this birth we must prepare the manger of our hearts. The love-nature is ever ready to promote the gestation and birth, but we must prepare ourselves to receive it.

When the Christ-babe is laid in the manger where our animal nature has been wont to feed, we will find that henceforth all our functions and faculties must partake of His divine nature and be under His control. Each one of us has all these animal traits within him. Formerly they all strove for their own expression and satisfaction, and often led the whole personality astray through self-indulgence. But now that they find the Christ-child in the manger, they must learn to "feed on Him with joy and thanksgiving." Then they will use all their forces for "the glory of God" so as to manifest Him in the flesh.

If you cannot understand this mystery then the babe is still concealed from you by the swaddling clothes of ignorance or lack of understanding. If you hold back from seeking to find Him, you are wrapping the swaddling clothes the tighter, almost smothering Him. If He cannot manifest through you, at least to some extent, then you have not unwrapped Him and brought Him forth to be seen of the shepherds and the Wise Men.

From another aspect the swaddling clothes symbolize rigid censorship imposed by the intellect, the sophistries of the mind and the misunderstandings and misconceptions under which the Light of the Christ has been obscured, but which in this new Aquarian Age must be removed, through enlightened understanding and realization, so that the Christ-light may shine forth to illumine all mankind.

The awakening of those who are perfectly satisfied with the outer life, who sleep while the shepherds watch, and who have little conception of that which lies wrapped up and swaddled within them, must await a later stage of their spiritual growth. For only when they are ready to become shepherds can they hear the angels' song and be willing to set out to find the Christ.

But to all these there ultimately comes a time when they must learn to unwrap the swaddling bands of ignorance and indifference and listen to and obey the inner "voice from heaven" that speaks from the manger of the heart within. Such an awakening often requires a period of dire distress, because they have allowed the Babe to lie dormant so long. But once the heart has had its first illumination it must follow it as the day-star of its life until it leads to the cradle of the Christ and the realization that He is born within.

Then we must unwrap the swaddling clothes and bring Him forth into manifestation. For if the Christ-consciousness cannot manifest in our lives He is still wrapped in swaddling clothes, incapable of expression and without wisdom as far as our conscious outer life is concerned. Only as we bring Him forth before the world can that living principle of Divinity be free to use its spiritual Light to illumine our Path through life, and its wisdom to guide our actions. Therefore we must remove the swaddling clothes and let every mystical power of the Divine Babe show forth in our lives.

As we have previously pointed out: "After the Christ has been born in the heart of man, has been laid among the animals in the stable of his physical existence; wrapped in swaddling bands of mind-stuff, subconsciously manifesting in the astral world, awakened and manifesting in his spiritual nature, then may the Jesus-man, the Divine Physician, the Healer, be said to have come to Earth in our lives. For only as the personal man is taught to follow the Jesus-life can the Christ manifest consciously in him."[2]

Happy is he who has removed the Swaddling Clothes.

---

[2] *The Message of Aquaria*, Curtiss, 180.

CHAPTER VIII

GIFTS OF THE WISE MEN

"Behold, there came wise men from the East. . . . And when they were come into the house, they saw the young child. . . . and fell down and worshipped him: And when they had opened their treasures, they presented unto him gifts: gold, and frankincense and myrrh." *St. Matthew, ii 1, 11.*

"The three Wise Men are the three bright collinear stars of the second magnitude—Alnitake, Alnilam, Mintaka—in the belt of the mighty hunter, Orion." *Appendix A.*

In the ancient days the Wise Men were those who had spent their lives in the study of higher thought, of deep philosophy, prophecy, esoteric truth, symbolism and the like, and had been initiated into some one of the several Mystery Schools.[1] They all sought to follow the Light as revealed to them until they found the Christ within. They were, therefore, much wiser in many things than the shepherds; for as representatives of the mighty hunter, Orion, they had spent their lives hunting for Light instead of tending sheep.

They had crossed the deserts of the outer material conditions, had passed through the psychic swamps and morasses of the lower astral planes through psychic research, without finding the Christ. They had climbed the dry, rocky mountains of intellectual attainments without their hearts being touched with the fire of Divine Love. And at last they were forced to come to the humble shepherds to ascertain where they could find the Christ that they might lay their gifts at His feet.

---

[1] Schools such as those of Zoroaster, Dionysus, Cybele, Attis, Eleusis, Orpheus, Isis, etc.

In general the three Wise Men symbolize the three great classes of thinkers—not the unthinking masses—who are supposed to be wise, or at least are seeking to follow the Light of Truth as far as it has been revealed to them.

First there is the *philosophical type* of mind which loves to delve into the records of the past. They study the ancient philosophies and find that there must be some degree of truth in any system of thought which persists throughout the ages, or it could not survive. They study comparative religion and find that all religions have certain basic truths in common. And those who are sincere set out to follow the Light of Truth revealed by both philosophy and religion, and so are finally led to find the Light of the Christ within.

As the celebrated scientist, Dr. Alexis Carrel, has pointed out: "Men of genius, in addition to their powers of observance and comprehension, possess other qualities, such as intuition. . . . Through intuition they learn things ignored by other men. . . . All great men are endowed with intuition. . . . This phenomenon, in former times was called inspiration."[2]

The second class of Wise Men is the *scientific type*. They know that everything in the universe, from the various components of the atom to the components of a solar system or a universe, manifests according to cosmic laws which underlie them all. They therefore recognize that there must be a mighty Source whence all substance, life and intelligence emanates. Hence all this orderly manifestation must be the result of the plan, purpose and design of a mighty Cosmic-consciousness so all embracing that the tiniest crystal or infusoria or a blade of grass—even the structure of the atom—are built on the same engineering principles as are the planets that circle around our Sun. And since man is the most highly evolved form of life on Earth these Wise Men know that he too must

---

[2] *Man the Unknown*, Carrel, 122-3.

embody some ray of that divine life and Cosmic-consciousness, and they therefore seek its realization and ultimately find it in the Christ within.

The third class of Wise Men are the *sincere skeptics*. They have been trained in the materialistic school of hard facts. But they have so often been astounded by the physical facts which their investigations have revealed, that they realize that almost anything may be possible. Hence they are too intelligent to ridicule and scoff at anything which they have not investigated thoroughly. And to the degree that they are honest and sincere, to that degree their investigation of the Source of all life and consciousness leads them to the manger of the Christ within. But the great mass of mankind are still living the vegetative life, merely reacting to the stimuli of the material world through their "conditioned reflexes." Hence they are not yet spiritually awakened or wise enough to see their cause.

In addition to the general classes which the Wise Men symbolize, what do they signify in our own personality, and what qualities do their gifts indicate? What is it that could make us Wise Men? We know that knowledge comes from without, but wisdom comes from within. That which enables us to become wise from within is our mind. Therefore our teaching is that the three Wise Men symbolize the three chief faculties of our minds.

The first Wise Man, *Melchoir*,—supposed to be a sage of 60 years—symbolizes the intellect. His gift is gold, formerly regarded as the most precious of metals and therefore a suitable gift for a king. This indicates that intellect is the most valuable possession of the human side of the personality. For without it we would have to be classed with merely intelligent brutes. But if we are truly Wise Men we must use our wealth of intellect to lift us above the domination of the brute instincts of the animal nature, even as it is so often allowed to enslave us to the animal plane.

One basic characteristic of gold is that it is incorruptible. Also no disease germs develop upon it. It therefore symbolizes that precious possession, that purity of heart, mind and life, which all truly Wise Men present to the Christ.

The ancients teach that the more intellectual and scientifically minded a race becomes, the more it is ruled by mundane things, the more it loses its spiritual vision. It becomes self-sufficient, loses touch with the higher worlds and the divine overshadowing which can inspire and guide it only when recognized and responded to. Hence the more materially civilized we become, the more selfish, materialistic and unspiritual we tend to be.

As gold must be refined by being purified of its dross of baser elements before it can be used for its highest purposes, even so must we purify the intellect of its pride of learning, from its greed for power, and from its materialism, before it is fit to lay the wealth of its powers—its gold—at the feet of the Christ and prove it to be the gift of a Wise Man.

For it is often a great sacrifice for the intellect to become as a little child and bow to and obey the Voice of Intuition. But ultimately it finds that neither learning nor physical gold can satisfy the inner craving of the heart for spiritual food. But once the surrender has been made, it will intelligently follow the light of the Star. And ultimately the intellect will become the high priest who uses all his powers to serve at the altar of the Christ.

Since the intellect can devise ways and means to attain the gold of this world, it has not become truly wise until it has devised ways and means to conquer and control the "money power," as it is called, so that the gold of the world is used primarily for the good of humanity, instead of being manipulated to amass a few great private fortunes. Its powers should be used to establish the reign of the Christ— through love, brotherhood and co-operation—instead of perpetuating the reign of the Beast.

Only when the intellect puts all its treasures at the

service of the heart can either one fully express the Christ-consciousness and make us truly Wise Men. Some of those who have given of their physical gold to the Christ and His work, often feel that because they have given of the world's precious metal they are entitled to greater importance, power and prestige in the eyes of the Christ. But as long as they hold such an idea they have not become Wise Men. For the Christ notices and rewards only the gifts that are given in love and humility, and without the secret desire for personal aggrandizement.

As we have said elsewhere about the first Wise Man as a class: "He represents those whose intellect has made them financially successful in obtaining the gold of the world, yet whose success does not satisfy their heart-hunger, and who are seeking how best to utilize their wealth in His service, yet who must seek unsuccessfully the world over ere they are willing to ask of the humble shepherds for final guidance. . . . The testing of the first Wise Man will be whether, having obtained much gold, he will use it for the Christ's work as he. . . . at first vowed he intended to do. Has he recognized that he should use his gold to help support and spread the teachings of the Christ."[3]

When the intellect is truly sanctified to the service of the Christ we will find a way to place all our gold and worldly possessions at His feet without anticipation of reward. Then it can no longer be said of us: "The children of this world are in their generation wiser than the children of light."[4] Only when the intellect puts its treasures at the service of love can either one fully express the Christ-consciousness and make us truly Wise Men.

The gift of the second Wise Man, *Balthazar*,—aged 40—is frankincense. This symbolizes *thought* which, when turned to the Christ, should rise like incense before His throne. Thought seeks to dominate all the channels

---

[3] *The Inner Radiance*, Curtiss, 349, 350.
[4] *St. Luke, xvi, 8*

of expression. But before it can become one of the Wise
Men it must learn to listen to "the still small voice" of the
Christ within, and follow it.

Balthazar represents those intellectuals who think it is
necessary to spend years delving into the musty records of
the past, through comparative religion, anthropology, etc.;
to cling to old rites and perpetuate ancient ceremonies to
find the truth (Christ), while all the time the living inspiration of the Christ within can reveal the truth to them here
and now. His test will be whether he is willing to be guided
by intuition as to the proper interpretation and application
of new revelations of the truth as well as the old. He must
be taught to wander no longer, but to be guided by the Light
of the Christ-consciousness within.

As we have already pointed out: "The second Wise
Man brought frankincense. This symbolizes that praise
and worship whose ingredients must be gathered, laboriously and with great learning, from the study of ancient
manuscripts and philosophies—hermetic, theosophical,
rosicrucian, etc.—and the comparative study of religions.
This group includes even some of the liberals in the orthodox churches. And there are many teachers, schools and
centers who feel that this resurrection of the best of the
ancient teachings is their contribution to His worship. This
gift is indeed a valuable one to lay at His feet, for through
it the proof of His periodic manifestation in each Great
Age is made known and the reality of His second coming
in this Age is assured."[5]

"The chief test of the second Wise Man will be, is he
wise enough to give a proper interpretation of the ancient
mysteries? Is he able to separate the dust of the ages and the
chaff of decayed ideas and outgrown conceptions—suitable perhaps for bygone ages and conditions, but outgrown
today—from the everlasting and living truths which underlie former Manifestations."[5]

If your gift is the frankincense of a well-ordered and

---

[5] *The Inner Radiance*, Curtiss, 350.

Illumined mind, one that can delve into the mysteries and not be mystified by them, then it should cull from their subtleties the wisdom that understanding the grand truths of life should bring. Then you will forget the vanity of your mental powers, for you have become wise enough to lay them all at the feet of the Christ.

Balthazar also symbolizes those whose worship of the outer personality obscures the realization of the inner Presence; who worship the person but do not live the life; who profess allegiance but fail to follow the lead; those who sing and pray about their Savior but will have none of His salvation. Only as these not merely talk about but really follow the Star, will they ever find the Christ

The third Wise Man, *Gaspar* or Casper—a youth of 20—represents the *awakened will* which provides all the youthful energy and determination necessary to follow the Star until it finds the Christ. This is no longer the selfish will whose goal of attainment is worldly possessions, position and power. It has learned that none of these outer things can bring true, inner satisfaction and happiness. It has seen the spiritual light of the Star and has determined to give up all else and follow it over all obstacles until the Christ is found. And then the mighty power of the will must become a servant of the Christ and lay all its might at His feet.

Incense containing myrrh was offered to those who were about to die, or was and still is burned in memory of those who have died, for it induces melancholy, sadness and depression.

The gift of *Gaspar* is said to be myrrh whose volatile, acrid odor symbolizes the bitter experiences and suffering we often have to undergo before we are willing to give up our personal will to the divine will and say: "Father. . . . not my will, but thine, be done." Then the bitter suffering of uncertainty and repeated disappointment is turned to the sweet joy of realization. The will alone may express as courage, devotion, determination and sincerity, but may reap much bitterness unless tempered with the spiritual qualities of tolerance, tenderness and love.

If we feel that we have no gifts to bring but disappointment, unhappiness, sorrow and tears, then we must be wise enough to bring even those to the Christ, lay them at His feet and be released from them. Kneel before Him and say: "Here, Lord! This is all I have to give! This is all the world has left me in life! But now I know that they can be redeemed. Now I know that my Redeemer liveth, for I have followed His Star and it has led me to His feet. Take all these negative conditions of poverty, misery and unwillingness to submit to Thee, and transmute them through the fire of Thy divine love into incense that shall ascend unto heaven and rain down upon me as the blessings of love unspeakable, of comfort beyond words, of peace of mind, and rest from the tensions and inharmonies of the body."

But if your gifts are once given they cannot be taken back. For you cannot let the peace and love of God enter your heart and dwell there tonight, and then tomorrow take up the old burdens and carry them around with you again. If you do this you have not really laid them at the feet of the Christ, or given up your will to His and been released from them.

We therefore repeat that: "The third Wise Man represents those who bring myrrh for their offering, the symbol of sorrow, anguish, crucifixion and death. There are many of this class today who are giving forth the doctrine—and trying to exemplify it in their lives—that if the kingdom of heaven is to manifest on Earth we must give up all joy of life, must frown upon all innocent recreations, gaiety and happiness, must sell all we have and give to the poor or to their society, and live a life of poverty, austerity and self-abnegation. Their sincerity, their courage and their devotion to what they believe to be the Truth would do much to help spread the Light of the Star, if they were willing to lay their limited ideas at His feet. But they must be tested as to the sincerity and the correct-

ness of their conceptions, also as to what extent their teachings are tempered with loving tolerance for the views of
others, rather than condemnation and self-righteousness"[6]

The ages commonly assigned to the Wise Men represent
three different periods in the life of all who are wise enough
to follow the light of the Christ Star. In any period we can
find the Christ within if we are willing to be guided by
this light. We do not have to wait for old age, although in
youth the will is the hardest and last to surrender. Yet it is
never too late to begin.

"We are told that there was still another or fourth Wise
Man, although he is not mentioned in the *Gospel* story.
Four being the number of the earth-plane, the story would
not be complete unless representatives of all four corners of
the Earth, and the four great types of seekers for Light, recognize, worship and lay their gifts at His feet. The fourth
Wise Man represents a large class of seekers who start out
well and with the full intention of following the Light of
the Star, and whose gift is *service*. Therefore, the fourth
Wise Man is represented in the legend as being so intent
upon rendering *service* and giving so much of his time
and substance to those in distress whom he met upon the
way, that he failed to keep up with the other three Wise
Men and so was not present when they reached their goal.
Indeed, when Herod. . . . sought to destroy the new born
babe—the Christ consciousness—this fourth Wise Man is
said to have told an apparent untruth in order to save the
Christ-child and His mother, whom he had hidden in his
house. Even though he denied that he had seen the Child
and His mother pass by—for they had not passed by, but
had stopped and stayed with him—nevertheless the Child
and His mother—Divine Love—were safely hidden in his
heart."

"The class represented by the fourth Wise Man are
more numerous in the world today; for never has the
world known such stupendous exhibitions of philanthropy

---

[6] *The Inner Radiance*, Curtiss, 351-2-3.

and service for the welfare of humanity; such wealth and huge Foundations established for the education of the people, for the eradication of disease, for social welfare and for the promotion of the finer arts of life and the moral uplift of humanity. Since their form of worship is service, this class of seekers have little time for, and see little need of meditation or the special study of spiritual philosophy. Hence they are often considered or even condemned as irreligious. Yet they ultimately do recognize the Truth and find the Christ hidden away in the love of their hearts.

"The test of the fourth Wise Man will be as to how wisely he has rendered *service*; whether from mere sentimental reasons, or from real compassion and a sincere desire to help suffering humanity; whether personally, for the sake of shining in the world as a philanthropist, or impersonally for the sake of the resulting good to his fellow men."[7]

As we have previously explained: "But the Wise Men of this Age must be scientifically sure; must. . . . explore many deceptive, misleading trails, ere they can find the Christ. For today, although the Christ is lying in the manger of the heart of everyone born into the world, for many it is still wrapped in the swaddling clothes of misunderstanding and misconception.

"Today, also, the so-called Wise Men are searching the heavens, are exploring the atom and studying the relativity of matter, space and time in their search for Truth. Yet ultimately. . . . the truly Wise Men will find the Christ-child and truly worship at His feet. For they will find Him manifesting where'er they sincerely seek: in the mystery-cradle of the atom, in relativity and in the marvels of inter-planetary space."

"It must be these Wise Men who will help to teach humanity to stop their childish quibbling over the literal meaning of the words of the allegorical stories. . . . Spiritual stories to be spiritually discerned."[7]

---

[7] *The Inner Radiance*, Curtiss, 351-2, 218, 353.

In this sense, "Remember that these Wise Men are not certain personalities or even groups or centers, but certain classes of seekers. And the gold that one class has gathered is greatly needed in publishing the Announcement of the Shepherds and in advertising and spreading broadcast the 'glad tidings' unto all people. The ancient wisdom gathered by another class is also needed, but clarified and made so simple that the multitude may see it rising like frankincense before the throne."

"Even Myrrh—symbol of misunderstanding, bitter persecution, sorrow and suffering—has been needed that the Shepherds might more fully understand the suffering of others. . . . And above all, there is needed among all advanced seekers and followers of the Star, consecrated service and co-operation which shall be so practical, yet so sincere, unselfish and pure, that the world will gladly accept it and be led to the feet of the Christ."[7]

Happy is he who lays his gifts at the feet of the Christ

CHAPTER IX

HEROD AND THE WISE MEN

> "In the days of Herod the king, behold, there came wise men. . . . saying, where is he that is born king of the Jews? for we have seen his star in the east, and are come to worship him. When Herod heard these things, he was troubled, and all Jerusalem with him. . . . And he sent them to Bethlehem, and said. . . . when ye have found him, bring me word again, that I may come and worship him." *St. Matthew, ii, 1-8.*

> "As the constellation *Draco*. . . . or Herodes—rises in the East, the constellation Aries—the Ram or Lamb—flees before it in the West." *Appendix A.*

The meeting between Herod and the Wise Men may be but a minor incident in the *Gospel* story, but when symbolically interpreted it gives us the key to many otherwise unexplained experiences in our own personal lives.

The Wise Men asked Herod: "Where is he that is born king of the Jews?" Upon careful consideration it is evident that this sentence, like so much of the birth-story, must not be taken literally, but must be interpreted according to its spiritual symbology. Literally and historically Jesus was not "born king of the Jews," nor did He ever attain that position, nor "sit on the throne of his Father David." Far from it. As already explained, He could not have inherited whatever claim He may have had to the throne as the son of Joseph, for, *according to the Gospel story*, He was not conceived through Joseph, but through "the power of the Highest" which overshadowed Mary. Jesus' genealogy must therefore depend upon that

of Mary alone. Both Mary and her cousin Elizabeth were
of the house of Aaron of the tribe of Levi. Hence Mary's
son could not be of the house of David, who was of the
tribe of Judah.

Therefore Jesus could not literally have inherited the
throne of David nor become king of the Jews. He could
never have been more than a pretender to that throne,
even if there had been such an office, which there was
not. Furthermore, since the story says that Joseph and Mary
were not even married, only "espoused" at the time of
Jesus' birth, the very wording of the story seems put in
such a way as to point out to the thoughtful reader the impossibility of taking the story literally. For no one would
want to think of Jesus as a fatherless pretender to a throne
that did not exist. Thus the spiritual and symbolical is the
only possible interpretation for those who have become
Wise Men or who have advanced beyond the unthinking
stage where the unexplained dead-letter of the text satisfies.

When the Jews are spoken of as the "chosen people,"
it does not refer to the small Hebrew tribe of Judah. For
surely that relatively small tribe would not alone be "chosen of the Lord" above all the other tribes — who were not
"Jews" but Hebrews or Semites — nor above all the other
countless millions of other races and peoples who are also
God's children, and just as dear to His heart as the little
nomadic tribe of Judah, even though they never heard of
the Hebrews and their God, Jehovah.

The "chosen of the Lord" are those who have chosen
to follow the Lord God or the Law of God, symbolized by
Moses the Law-giver. Therefore all of us are "the chosen
people" in this symbolic sense, if we have had the divine
law revealed to us by some Law-giver and are being prepared to recognize the Christ as the King and Governor
of our lives. They are all who recognize and worship the
power of the Christ manifesting within them and in their
fellowmen, and are Wise Men enough to lay their gifts at
His feet.

In our personal lives Herod symbolizes our lower personality and all the selfish powers which predominate in the outer world. He is selfish King Desire, the ruler, not of the temple of our inner life, but of the outer life; those outer and material desires which so dominate our lives in the earlier stages of our spiritual unfoldment, ere we become Wise Men, that we give little attention to anything else.

Altho the birth has been recognized by both the Shepherds and the Wise Men, it must still be concealed from Herod or King Desire, who has for so long ruled our lives and will brook no interference, and will stop at nothing to continue his reign. Thus do the selfish desires of the personality and the animal man war against and seek to slay the spiritual conceptions which have finally been born in our hearts. But if we keep them wrapped in the swaddling clothes of reticence for a time, they are never captured or slain.

Following the gleam of their inner Star of Intuition, the Wise Men set out to reach and pass through Jerusalem, the Holy City, where all the great spiritual powers are focused. There the Temple of the Living God is erected. This symbolizes the advanced state of spiritual consciousness in which we recognize just what it is that has heretofore been ruling our outer lives (our Herod), and what it really is that our Souls have hungered for and have been seeking. But on their arrival the Wise Men find the city ruled by the ruthless Herod.

The inquiries of the Wise Men greatly disturbed Herod, "and all Jerusalem with him"; for he was familiar with the prophecy: "And the Lord God shall give him the throne of his father David: and he shall reign over the house of Jacob forever." (*St. Luke, i, 32-3*). It is prophesied of nearly all Sun-gods that they will ultimately supplant the reigning monarch.[1] For this reason the monarchs first try to prevent their birth. But always failing in this, they try to destroy the Babe after his birth. They

---

[1] For examples see page 18.

also seek the help of the Wise Men to this end, but the Wise Men are too wise to fall into the trap.

And we find this same situation in our own lives. When we first realize that there is a higher life than merely our physical life and a higher power than that of our intellect, we begin to be troubled. For we do not see how we can, or why we should desire to change our habits and readjust our whole life to this new set of ideas that the Wise Men have brought to our attention. All our habits of thought and desire (Herod) rise up against such a radical change in the rulership of our lives. And naturally we are greatly troubled, and "all Jerusalem"—all our friends and acquaintances—with us. For the consciousness of our human personality instinctively believes what the Wise Men have revealed to it, and recognizes that should this new authority be set up within its kingdom: should the Christ be found and set up as King and Governor of our lives, the rule of animal desire and selfish personality will come to an end.

Through the power of the Christ ruling our lives, personal desire for self-indulgence will soon be turned into unselfish desire to do His will. That is, our lower desires will be so transmuted as to become harmonious expressions of Divine Will, so that we will do the Will of the Father here on earth, even as it is done in heaven. Naturally then, these lower desires of the personality strive to prevent the change and do their best to kill out the new ideas which we have elevated into *ideals*, which already threaten to usurp the rule of the old *ideas*. They are so clever about it that they present to our minds all kinds of sophistries to deceive us, and even pretend to be interested in and desire to worship the new-born King.

Not only Herod, but "all Jerusalem with him" are troubled. The news that those who are wisest in spiritual things were seeking their King greatly troubled both Herod and his advisers, just as the news that we are earnestly seeking a personal realization of the Christ within that we may lay our gifts at His feet and make Him henceforth the ruler of our life greatly troubles all our worldly minded relatives and friends. They are upset when they see us determined faithfully to follow a Light which they cannot see. They instinctively realize that with our new ideals as the ruler of our life and its activities, their influence over us, their advice and their desires as to how we should live—which may formerly have had great weight with us—will no longer be paramount. They realize that now we mean to follow this new Christ-light without regard to the desires of Herod, or those former standards or persons, to which or to whom we formerly looked for advice and guidance. Hence they try in every way to discourage us in our search. Like Herod, they also try to deceive us with pretended interest. But the only gifts that the Herod-power ever gave the Christ and His followers are misunderstanding, antagonism, persecution, martyrdom and the sword.

We can trace this result all down through the history of the ages. For the Herod-power represents all those forces in the world, all those rational, literal and materialistic ideas and teachings, which refuse to recognize anything that does not pay tribute to them; those powers which refuse to bow to any ruler or authority other than their own desires or to which they have not given birth or sanction. Hence they naturally seek to slay the new-born King of Love.

And we see this same Herod-power abroad in the world today in war, in a lack of tolerance, a lack of brotherhood, love and compassion: all that seeks to belittle and ridicule and kill out the higher, advanced spiritual teachings which are being given out through so many avenues of illumination today. The Herod-power includes all that seeks to control and limit all independent expressions of Truth; which seeks to deceive even those who should be the modern Wise Men, and lead them astray. But "being warned of God in a dream" the Wise Men ever refuse to betray the Christ. Hence in none of the many versions of this divine birth-story throughout the ages is the Divine Babe ever found by His adversaries or slain.

When the forces of Herod are rampant, those who have been Unwise Men enough to call attention to what they believe to be the birth of the Christ within themselves are the first to attract the attention of the critics and scoffers. But when the Christ-child is really born He is so humble and lowly that He does not make claims for Himself, hence does not attract attention, and so escapes into the protecting obscurity of "Egypt."

The truly Wise Men teach that: "It is only to those who know how to retain a secret that the secrets of Nature are given; not to the babbler who is constantly calling attention to his spiritual, mental and psychic power.[2]

Those things which the Unwise Men proclaim to be manifestations of the Christ within are but the offspring of vanity and self-righteousness. They cannot stand the inspection of Herod's soldiers, yet they cannot be hidden, for they have already attracted attention. Hence they get their just deserts. And so a great cry of lamentation goes up. Some little dagger-point of worldly criticism has killed their cherished babe. But if the Christ-child has really been born within us it has no desire for worldly recognition and honors, but nestles quietly in our bosom so that the soldiers of Herod pass it by, saying: "Surely this humble manifestation cannot be the Christ-child, so we will let it live."

This explains the suffering of many who have boasted of their spiritual progress and attainments, for they have been wounded to death by the first spear thrusts of the world's scoffing.

Although the real Christ-child may be driven into the sheltering obscurity of silence for a time, some day the babe we have brought forth through pain, anguish and travail of spirit will come forth to comfort and illumine our lives and confound "the doctors in the temple" with His wisdom.

"And being warned of God in a dream that they should

---

[2] *The Dawn of Truth*, Barkel, *161*.

not return to Herod, they departed into their own country another way." So often we waste our higher intellectual powers wandering about, following the attractive lights of the world which seem to rule, and even the outer, intellectual teachings of philosophy and occultism. Thus we vainly strive to find that inner peace, satisfaction and happiness which comes only when we correlate with something that is of divine origin. Only when we become Wise Men enough to notice and follow the inner light of the Star of Intuition, no matter how faintly it may be gleaming in the dark night of our outer conditions, are we ready to be led to the cradle of the Christ. But once we have found Him we will be wise enough never to allow our faculties to return to the rule of Herod. But they must return to their own "country" or function "another way." Each faculty must return to its own place and still perform its own function, but now under the enlightening rule of the Christ-consciousness and not under the desires of Herod.

Each one of us may have had some realization of the birth of the Christ-light in our hearts. But perhaps some may not have been Wise Men enough to recognize it or may not have had the courage to follow it. Some may have wrapped the Child in many, many swaddling bands of old ideas and conceptions which have hidden Him from view lest the world think they are peculiar or "queer."

Perhaps some have felt that the world's opinion (Herod) demands so much of time and attention and so much tribute from our lives that have no time to pay attention to this inner birth. Or perhaps we have thought that to acknowledge this precious Child would upset the current of our lives, might disturb our business and make our lives more difficult than they were before. Or we may not be quite sure that which we thought was our Wise Men would quite approve of so great a change in the allegiance of our lives as from the outer to the inner guidance. And so we may have failed to acknowledge the spiritual birth and hence have neglected the Divine Child within.

CHAPTER X

THE FLIGHT AND MASSACRE

> "The angel of the Lord appeareth to Joseph in a dream, saying, Arise, and take the young child and his mother, and flee into Egypt, and be thou there until I bring thee word: for Herod will seek the young child to destroy him. . . . . And (he) was there until the death of Herod; that it might be fulfilled which was spoken of the Lord by the prophet, saying, Out of Egypt have I called my son. Then Herod, when he saw that he was mocked of the wise men, was exceeding wroth, and sent forth, and slew all the children that were in Bethlehem, and in all the coasts thereof, from two years old and under." *St. Matthew, ii, 13-16.*

> "As the constellation *Draco* or *Ophincus*—the Dragon, Hydra or Herodes—armed with a cudgel, naturally rises up over Libra in the East, the constellation *Aries*—the Ram or Lamb—flees before it in the West and disappears below the horizon towards Egypt or the Land of Darkness, so that the Dragon of Night (Herodes) seems to devour all the stars in his path. All infant Lightbringers are therefore represented as being pursued by some vindictive ruler and fleeing to some far-off place of safety. But in none of the stories is the child ever caught, so the pursuer orders a slaughter of the innocents as the stars pale and disappear at dawn." *Appendix A.*

Herod's "massacre of the innocents" is another of those incidents which delight the historical critics and are the despair of the literalists. For although we find the incident given only in *St. Matthew*, the whole setting is flatly denied by the account of the birth given in *St. Luke*. It is not a question of *St. Luke's* merely failing to record the incident, but of his recording events which *directly contradict* the whole story of the flight into Egypt.

According to *St. Matthew*, "And when they (the Wise
Men) were departed, behold, the angel of the Lord appeared to Joseph in a dream, saying, Arise and take the
young child and his mother and flee into Egypt. . . . When
he arose he took the young child and his mother by night,
and departed into Egypt (presumably the same night after
the Wise Men had left). And was there (in Egypt) until the
death of Herod. . . . Then Herod was exceeding wroth. . . .
and slew all the children that were in Bethlehem, and all
the coasts thereof, from two years old and under." (*St.
Matthew, ii, 13-16*). And yet neither St. Peter nor St. Paul
knew anything about this tragedy.

On the contrary, *St. Luke (in ii, 21-2)* states definitely
that instead of fleeing to Egypt that same night, the parents
remained eight days in Bethlehem, had the child circumcised and then *remained there for over a month longer*
until the 40 days of the mother's purification were over.
Even then, according to *St. Luke*, there was no flight into
Egypt, for then, "they brought him to Jerusalem, to present
him to the Lord." They had no fear of Herod or of a massacre "of all the children that were in Bethlehem, and in
all the coasts thereof, from two years old and under." For
"when they had performed all things according to the law
of the Lord, *they returned into Galilee*, (not into Egypt)
to their own city Nazareth." Instead of being in Egypt for
some years, "his parents went to Jerusalem *every year* at
the feast of the passover." (*ii, 39, 41*). In this account there
is no mention of Herod, or a tragedy at Bethlehem, or of a
flight into Egypt. There is no mention of a massacre or of
"lamentation, and weeping, and great mourning," for the
children slain is so great a holocaust.

There is the flat contradiction between the two accounts.
Which shall we accept? If we are literalists we are face
to face with an unsolvable problem. But if we are universal symbologists, we naturally accept the account that
appears in the life-story of all the other Savior-babes as

an essential part of the Universal Solar Myth, namely, the flight and massacre. But we accept it only in its symbolic meaning, not as an historical fact *for which there is no corroboration*, either religious or secular.

The great problem for the literalists to explain is that if such a wholesale massacre of children actually took place,—which would have aroused the indignation of the entire race—there certainly should be some record of it, especially in Jewish if not in Roman history. Yet no such record is to be found in either! It was supposed to have taken place at the close of the reign of Herod the Great. But as he died in the year 4 B.C. it is generally supposed that, since there is no record of the year, much less the month and day, in which Jesus was born, He must have been born before 4 B.C. Astrological authorities say it was 7 B.C.

The great Jewish historian, Josephus, who gives a minute account of all the atrocities of Herod up to the day of his death, would surely have recorded such an unheard-of crime had such a massacre occurred, for it would have been even more notorious than Herod's other crimes. Yet not even a passing reference to such a thing is made by him.[1] Roman history also records Herod's crimes in detail. On his accession to the throne he ordered the massacre of all of the forty-five members of the Jewish Sanhedrin, and confiscated their estates. He executed all the members of the family of the best beloved of his ten wives—*Miramne*—one the daughter of his brother, another the daughter of his sister. He slew his grandfather, *Hircon*; his own father, *Alexander*; his own mother, *Alexandra*; his uncle, *Antigones;* his brother, *Aristobulus;* had another brother, *Pheroras*, and a sister, *Salome*, strangled at Sebaste, and finally killed his own beloved wife, *Miramne*. These atrocities gave rise to the saying: "It is better to be Herod's swine than his son."

With all these *personal* crimes recorded in such detail, it is hardly possible that such an atrocious *public* crime as

---

[1] *Antiquity of the Jews*, Josephus, Book XVIII, Chapter III.

the so-called "massacre of the innocents" could have gone
unrecorded if it ever took place. Not only Josephus, but the
great Roman historian, Tacitus, who so minutely recorded
the crimes of other despots, also does not record any such
country-wide massacre.

The number of children slain is variously estimated. The
Coptic *Acts of St. Matthew* in Kahamot gives the number
as 14,000, and Canon Farrar as not exceeding 20,000. The
date is supposed to have been about two and a half years
after the birth of Jesus. Tradition says that the interval
was occupied by Herod's journey to Rome to secure from
Caesar permission for the slaughter.

No one who is familiar with Roman history, customs
and the exactness of its laws—upon which our present
common law is based—could believe that such a public
holocaust could have taken place throughout a whole province without its perpetrator's being deposed and punished.

This completes the list of miraculous events connected with the birth and childhood of Jesus. Since St.
Paul was so anxious to prove that Jesus was the Christ
and the expected Messiah, that had he ever heard of the
angelic Annunciation, the Immaculate Conception, the
Virgin Birth, the Adoration of the Wise Men, the Star of
Bethlehem and the Flight and Massacre, he certainly would
have made the best use possible of them to substantiate his
claim. And since the first *Gospel* to be written (*St. Mark*)
was recorded some fifteen or more years after St. Paul's
first Epistles (*Thessalonians*), it would seem that St. Mark
knew nothing of any of these events either.

As the *Gospels* which do mention these events were
written many years after that of St. Mark, it is evident
that this whole series of events was added after the time
of St. Mark and St. Paul by someone who was familiar
with the Universal Solar Myth.[2] If we ask why they were

---

[2] "Contemporary with Augustine lived Jerome, who translated the Hebrew scriptures into Latin. . . . The Pope then commissioned him to translate the Gospels
and epistles from Greek into Latin. To this request Jerome replied that it would be
difficult to know where to start, as there were as many different versions of these
in existence as there were copies in circulation. However, he undertook the task,
trusting in God to direct him as to which were the right ones to use." *The Psychic*

thus inserted into the story, the answer is twofold. The only rational explanation of the use of these highly improbable and historically unrecorded events, and the flat contradictions in the different *Gospels'* accounts of them is, firstly, they were necessary "that it might be fulfilled which was spoken by the prophets," (*St. Matthew, ii, 23; xxvi, 56*), to show that Jesus was the expected Messiah, for He never referred to any of these events.

In the second place, these events were a part of the universal cosmic allegory, all the events of which all of the previous Sun-gods of history are said to have fulfilled. They were therefore appropriated and applied to the life story of Jesus by the writers of St. Matthew and St. Luke to help prove that Jesus was a divine, individualized manifestation of the Spiritual Sun and the spiritual Lightbringer or vehicle of the Cosmic Christ-force to humanity in the cycle of the Piscean Age. This is evidenced by the fact that He fulfills all the incidents, in their proper order, in the Universal Solar Myth, just as does the physical Lightbringer, the Sun, to the physical world in a shorter cycle, the year

That this is another universal incident, and does not apply to Jesus alone, is shown by the fact that all Lightbringers have been considered as dangerous children because of the universal prophecies that their growth and destiny threatened the rule of the then reigning monarch.[3]

Stream, Findlay, 1116-17.

[3] "A heavenly voice whispered to the foster father of *Krishna* and told him to fly with the young child across the river Jumna, which was immediately done. This was owing to the fact that the reigning monarch, King Kansa, sought the life of the infant Savior and sent messengers *'to kill all the infants in the neighboring places.'*" *Life and Religion of the Hindus*, Gangooly, 134. The Egyptian Lightbringer, *Horus*, was obliged to flee to the Isle of Buto from his uncle Seth, or Typhon. Frescoes on the walls of ancient Pompeii represent this incident, feature for feature, with the biblical story. *Hadad*, another name for the Syrian Sun-god *Adonis*, escaped into Egypt when David's general, Joab, is said to have slaughtered every male in Edom, Astyages, king of Media, warned in a dream that his daughter, Mondane, would give birth to a son who would reign in his stead, sought to have the babe, *Cyrus*, destroyed, but never succeeded. Soothsayers informed *Nimrod*, king of Babylon, that a child—*Abraham*—soon to be born would become a great prince. Nimrod then issued orders that all women with child should be guarded, and all children born of them should be put to death. Also *Zoroaster* was considered a "dangerous child." He was obliged to flee into Persia, pursued by

Hence, they are all pursued, and as they are never captured, in most cases a general massacre of all the young children in the region follows.

Since it is evident that this is not and has never been a literal, historical incident in the life of any *one* person, what is the spiritual interpretation of this incident of the massacre, flight and concealment of the babe until he grew up into a child?

From the astronomical standpoint, the Sun, after its birth in the sign *Capricorn*, the sign of the manger, flees or hides below the equator in the darkness of the southern hemisphere — symbolized by Egypt — until it has so grown in strength that it is ready to appear in the northern hemisphere and begin its mission of bringing light and giving renewed life to all Nature in the spring. The astronomical basis of this incident is that as the constellation Draco — the Dragon, also Hydra or Herodes — rises in the East, the Dragon of night (Herod) seems to devour or slay all the stars in his path as their light disappears below the horizon.

Egypt is allegorically a symbol of darkness and obscurity, but the obscurity in which something fructifies. It is the region that is self-impregnated by the inundation of the Nile when the Sun touches the zodiacal sign *Virgo*, the Virgin.

---

the King, who sought to destroy him. *Buddha* as a babe was persecuted by King Bambasara. He was placed in a copper chest and set afloat in the river Ganges. The same incident is found carved on the rock walls of the cave-temple in the island of Elephanta in India. *Hadad*, the child King of Edom, fled to Egypt to escape the terrible massacre when Solomon ordered Joab to slay every male in Edom. (*1 Kings, xi, 16, 17*). And the same incident is found in the life-stories of Perseus, Aedipus, Paris, Jason, Bacchus, Han-ki, Salivahana, Aesculapius, etc.

The flight into the land of darkness sets forth the truth that the light first manifests in the darkness, but the darkness comprehendeth it not.

The great lesson is that allegorically Jesus was not only taken into Egypt, but that He *came out of it*, thus fulfilling the prophecy, "Out of Egypt have I called my son." Thus we have the assurance that no matter how obscure and dark conditions may be, if we realize that we have the Christ with us we will come out safe into the Promised Land of spiritual light and realization.

After the birth there is a reaction in which our realization is swallowed up by the darkness of Earth conditions. The first reaction of the outer personality and the world (Herod) to any manifestation of spiritual forces is to "massacre" or destroy them. And the Herod forces are still with us today, and will be until the millennium. For the advent of the spiritual forces in our lives so stirs up the forces of Herod in us that they are stricken with terror lest their rule be soon at an end. This is not a terror of physical conditions, but of the unknown, something intangible; an unknown fate that is impending, such as often breaks down the strongest minds. As long as the Herod of pride and selfish desire rules in us it ever seeks to slay the innocent ideals our heart conceives. The more we are governed by selfish and worldly conditions, the more we become hardened against spiritual forces, and so become our own Herods.

The first-born in every heart is a desire to express its joy at the birth, an overflowing enthusiasm to do great things for the Christ, for this mighty love melts our hearts. But soon Herod—the desires of "the world, the flesh and the devil"—strives to find and kill the child, but never succeeds. For although many of our mind-born ideals are killed by a scoffing world, the Christ-consciousness flees into the darkness of protective silence for a time, and escapes, only to return in due season.

There are many persons of the Herod type still with us today; the intellectually vain, the agnostics, the sophists, the wiselings of scholastic reasoning, and those whose highest ideals are to follow after Mammon and the lusts of the flesh. Such will go to any atrocious length to prolong the rule of their self-indulgence. The slaughter of the innocents is a continuous process until stopped by the death of the Herod forces.

It was not without reason that Jesus was called the "Lion of the tribe of Judah," for it required the courage of the lion to face misunderstanding, skepticism, ridicule, contempt, sneers, hyprocrisy, betrayal and final crucifixion. And His followers today have need of the same courage in these days of materialism and atheism.

We have already pointed out[4] that in the life-history of each Soul Joseph symbolizes the intellect, which is not the real father of the new-born Christ-consciousness, but is only its supporter and protector. The "angel" or messenger that appears to him in a dream is a message from the Spiritual Self warning him that both the new-born spiritual consciousness and the Divine Love (the mother) which brought it forth must be hidden for a time from the forces which have been ruling the outer life or they will kill the child. He must therefore take the new-born conception of the Christ within and the Mother-love to which he is now wedded and flee into Egypt, or conceal them by silence "until the death of Herod" or until the outer opposition is over or the rule of the desires of the flesh is ended and his realization of the Christ-consciousness has grown clear and strong enough to resist attack and come forth and bless mankind.

Such Inner Guidance at first is often considered "only a dream," yet if followed good always results. Subsequent events always prove that to ignore it is a mistake for which we have to pay, often in sorrow and suffering. This does not mean that we should blindly follow every impulse, prompting or "hunch" that comes to us, but must ask for guidance, and challenge "in the name of the

---

[4] *Chapter III.*

Christ" everything that comes, and demand that its truth be confirmed to us.

This journey into the land of darkness is a universal fact and a vital necessity; for only so can the newly-born spiritual child and its mother (Divine Love) escape being overwhelmed by the forces of the outer world which relentlessly seek to stamp out all that seems likely to interfere with the indulgence of the lower self in the pleasures of the senses.

Not only must there be a voluntary veiling of the inner illumination in silence, but from another aspect, after one has had the transcendant experience of a realization of the Christ within, there comes a reaction in which all memory of the experience seems swallowed up in the darkness of uncertainty, and we wonder if we have not been subjected to some form of mental illusion or psychic delusion.

The rational mind cannot reason out or comprehend such an experience, for *it transcends reason* and enters upon the realm of intuition and direct realization. Therefore it must be put aside until the rational mind has had time to adjust itself to the new current of force from the higher or Spiritual Mind,[5] the mind of the Spiritual Self. Every Soul in which the conception of Divine Truth has taken place must, therefore, keep this new realization of the Christ within sacredly hidden in his or her own heart, for if it were proclaimed abroad or told even to friends, it would either be laughed at or mocked or in some way be belittled, and killed out and forgotten.

The new current of spiritual consciousness from the Spiritual Self now begins the establishment of a new highway of communication with the personality. This is a bridge of understanding (*Sattva*) called *Antaskarana* which must ultimately span the gulf which separates the rational or so-called mortal mind from the Spiritual Mind of the Real Self. This bridge is a literal thing composed

---

[5] For the divisions of the mind see *The Voice of Isis*, Curtiss, 167-9 or *The Key to the Universe*, Curtiss, 260-2.

of radiant light from the Spiritual Self although it is impenetrable darkness to the outer world. Every step we take toward spiritual enlightenment not only strengthens this bridge, but also shortens our journey across it and gives the Spiritual Mind greater influence over the human personality. This is sometimes called the "bridge of swords" over which we must pass with naked feet; for once we start to cross it we can never again go back or accept conditions in life as we did before our awakening. And our understanding (feet) may receive many sharp cuts and bleed as we progress until our lower conceptions and understanding of life can no longer be wounded by or suffer from the higher ideals revealed to us by the Divine Light.

Just as in Nature the seed of the future plant or tree lies buried in the darkness of the soil until it sprouts and grows strong enough to push up through the soil into the light of day, so does the seed of the Christ-consciousness lie buried in the darkness of the physical body until it has germinated and put up its mystical sprout of divine understanding into the light of our outer consciousness. But until that time the tender sprout must be concealed by the darkness of its Egypt

If we dig a seed up to show to some horticulturist, or to see if it is growing, or that we may find out what kind of plant or tree it will be, we simply delay or even prevent its growth. Just so does a babbler kill out the sacred inner realization if he tries to display it before the world that he may be admired for his advanced development. The law of the outer Nature applies as well to our inner nature or Soul-experiences. If we dig them up to show our friends or expose them to the light of reason and ridicule we prevent their growth and manifestation. The world will become aware of them in due season if we let them "sojourn in Egypt" until the time has come when we are ready to manifest our new understanding and realization. For it is in darkness, where God works silently His wonders to perform, that all things germinate and are brought forth.

Egypt is commonly used as a symbol of spiritual darkness, sorrow and lack of understanding, where we are
under the bondage of ignorance and are slaves to King
Desire. It also refers to the physical body in which the
incarnating Soul is in bondage to the senses. But to those
who bravely "flee into Egypt" at the command of the Inner
Voice, it has quite a different meaning. It now symbolizes
that inner sanctuary of the heart or the Temple of Silence
in which the newly-awakened Christ-consciousness is hidden until we fully understand the Inner Radiance which
can and will shine forth clear and steady if we will but fix
our gaze upon it instead of upon the tiny candle of self-
admiration. Then will the Inner Radiance, and the sacred
joy which we have found, yet dared not to speak of until
it grew strong enough, come forth and dispute with the
doctors in the temple.

When we pass through the thrilling Soul-experience
in which we awaken to a new realization of the Divine
Presence within, we feel that something so wonderful has
come into our lives that we must change our entire mode of
life if we are to live up to it. Because of previous erroneous
teaching, some feel that they must give up all expressions
of joy and gladness and go about their work in the world
with a long face and a solemn manner. Such a conception
of the flight into Egypt would indeed be a punishment
instead of a joy. But if we realize that for us now Egypt is
not a place of utter darkness and sorrow, but is the silence
of a sacred shrine into which we can retire and worship
the Christ, realize His mighty love, and truly "feed on Him
in our hearts by faith and thanksgiving," then the experience fills us with such happiness and joyous ecstasy that
we cannot help unconsciously radiating it in our lives to
all we contact.

In the personal application of this incident, after our
realization of the Christ-consciousness and the reaction
which plunges us into the darkness of Egypt, where our
conscious touch with the Divine seems swallowed up and
lost, both the desires of the flesh, old habits of life and

doubts of the reality of our recent experience, arise in our minds and seek to reason us out of our belief, seek to slay or darken our memory of this beautiful experience. Thus do our new ideals and resolutions, in fact, all the offspring of our experience of spiritual realization, seem to flee from our consciousness and memory.

But altho that realization has left us for a time it cannot be killed, but will return again in due season and rule our lives, even though, as we said before, it may be a great sorrow that brings it back. In the meantime, like Joseph, we must care for and guard our first-born; for it needs both the intellect (Joseph) and the Mother-love (Mary) to nourish it until it can take care of itself when recognized and perhaps be laughed at and ridiculed by the world.

It is significant that after their adoration of the Babe the Wise Men "being warned of God in a dream. . . . departed into their own country another way." Thus it is that after having been brought face to face with the Christ within, even though its manifestation is but as that of a babe, we can never go back the way we came. We can never submit our tender realization of the Christ to the hatred of Herod. Neither can we any longer recognize him as king and ruler of our lives. Being warned of God we must go back to the daily routine of our lives another way.

As this child of the Christ-consciousness grows within us it absorbs all that is good, constructive and helpful from both mind (Joseph) and heart (Mary). But it must be fed by our constant recognition of the God-power within us and the possibility of our manifesting it, which by this time we should have proved to ourselves. It is this idea which we must nourish by *constantly contemplating it*, until we grow to love it as our great source of love, comfort and help, both in our periods of silence and devotion and as often as we can turn our minds toward it during the day. For our great lesson to learn is that God is love, and we must learn to know this in spirit and in truth.

CHAPTER XI

TWELVE YEARS OF AGE

"And the child grew, and waxed strong in spirit
filled with wisdom: and the grace of God was upon
him. . . . When he was twelve years old, they went up
to Jerusalem. . . . The child Jesus tarried behind. . . .
after three days they found him in the temple sitting in
the midst of the doctors, both hearing them, and asking
questions. . . . And he said unto them, How is it that ye
sought me? wist ye not that I must be about my Father's
business?" *St. Luke, ii, 40-50.*

"When the Sun has completed its circuit through the
12 signs of the zodiac it is said to be 12 years (or cycles)
old, and is ready to be about its Father's business or
ready to start out on a new cyclic round," *Appendix A.*

Between the record of the flight of Jesus into Egypt[1] as
a babe and the next mention of Him at the age of twelve
there is a long period concerning which there is no record, although there have been many speculations as to
how those years were spent. Some authorities claim to
account for those years either from ancient records which
they claim were found in a Buddhist lamasary in Thibet,[2]
or to have read the story psychically direct from the im-
perishable Akashic Records[3] in the unseen worlds, while

---

[1] The Coptic Christian Church of Egypt claims to have actual physical documents,
rescued from the great library at Alexandria when it was pillaged and burned by
Bishop Theopholis in 389 A.D., which give details of *three* sojourns of Jesus in
Egypt. During our visit to Egypt in 1938 we were present at an elaborate baptismal
ceremony in the very cave or grotto in which is claimed the Holy Family lived
when they fled from Herod with the infant Jesus. The Copts claim that Jesus was
trained in the school of the Essenes by whom he was called "St Issa."

[2] *The Unknown Life of Jesus*, Notovitch.

[3] *The Aquarian Gospel of Jesus Christ*, Levi,

others have made up a more or less plausible record of what they imagined might have taken place. But the historical inaccuracies and anachronisms inherent in such stories show that they are only human speculations. Even though some claim to have received the details from teachers in the astral world, yet such teachings are still only the human speculations of discarnate mortals alter all, and are without proof either in history or in symbolism, myth or allegory.

The fact that the *Gospel* record is absolutely silent on the details of that long period is in itself very significant. But once we understand the allegorical and symbolical nature of the story, *i.e.*, as an outpicturing of the events in the unfolding of the Christ-consciousness in each heart when a certain stage of spiritual unfoldment is reached, we will see the reason for the lack of details prior to that time.

Twelve is a most important and mystical number. It is called "The Manifested Universe,"[4] because the universe requires twelve zodiacal signs to complete the circle of its manifestation. Likewise man must incarnate in and master the forces of all the twelve signs before he can complete his own "manifested universe," or the manifestation of his Spiritual Self which he came to earth to express. Hence we are born again and again under each of the twelve signs until we have learned and built into our consciousness all the lessons of the zodiac.

Usually when one is born with the gifts of a Prophet or Seer they begin to manifest by the time he is twelve years of age. Samuel and Daniel both prophesied at twelve and Solomon's "wise judgements" began at twelve. At twelve Jesus seems to have been aware of His divine mission and had already begun to be "about his Father's business." This His mother did not seem to understand. She seems to have forgotten the prophecies made about Him by the angel before His birth, also those of Simeon and Anna (*St. Luke, ii, 32-6*), the message of the shep-

---

[4] *See The Key to the Universe*, Curtiss, 29.

herds and the reason for the massacre and flight into Egypt.

In the individual, the age of twelve is an important milestone in the manifestation of the Soul. In Oriental countries that is the average age when puberty occurs. The fact that the power to procreate is present at that time is evidence that the several stages by which the incarnating Soul takes possession of the body have been completed. The incarnation is then attained and the Soul is ready to "be about my Father's business" or accomplish the object for which it incarnated.[5]

As we have explained elsewhere: "The age of the boy Jesus when found by His mother in the temple expounding the law to the elders also has reference to the relation of the evolution of the Soul to the forces of the zodiac. That this incident is but another step in the manifestation of the Spiritual Sun is evidenced by the corresponding accounts found elsewhere. . . . For according to the Sun Myth, at the age of 12 the incarnated Sun God or Savior has passed around and completed the circle of the zodiac, and altho but a child, has attained the Light of Wisdom which enables him to consort with the Masters in the temple, for he has demonstrated his ability to rule all 12 influences of the zodiac.

"Another significance of the Lightbringer's prophesying and teaching at the age of 12 is that when the Soul—the individualized Sun-god of its cycle—has really correlated with the influences exerted through the 12 signs, he is mystically 12 years old; that is, at the age of 12 the Soul is fully incarnated. In Oriental countries a boy has reached his majority at 12 and is initiated into his cast, religion or tribe, according to the practice in the various countries. . . ."[6]

---

[5] See *Why Are We Here?*, Curtiss.

[6] *See The Key of Destiny*, Curtiss, 54-37. "Strauss points out the extra-Scriptural stories of Moses leaving his father's house at twelve to play the part of an inspired teacher, and Samuel beginning to prophesy at that age. . . . In Strabo's account of Judea. . . . the parents went to Delphi. . . . while the child itself had gone to the temple of Apollo. . . . in one part of the Egyptian ritual Isis is figured as wailing for the loss of her child, the boy Horus, who was afterwards found in the Temple of the Sun teaching the priests." *Christianity and Mythology*, Robertson, 310-11

"When the evolving child has reached this period, the Soul has taken possession of the body. . . . The child must therefore take upon itself new duties and responsibilities or 'be about its Father's business.' The Soul must now take its place in the Temple of the personality as a Lightbringer, for it has now reached a point where it has realized the character of the lessons and recognized the forces of each of the 12 signs and has begun consciously to control and utilize and impress them upon the personality. . . .

"It is at the age of 12 physically that the child must begin to assume personal responsibility, for it is only then that the Soul has fully incarnated in the body. The incarnation may be said to begin at the time of conception. . . . Another stage is reached at the time of 'quickening' and a third stage with the drawing of the first breath. . . . The possession of the body by the incarnating Soul steadily progresses as center after center in the bodies of the child is developed and made available for the Soul to function through, until the age of 12 (approximately) or when puberty is reached. The actual age of puberty varies somewhat according to race, climate, etc., but theoretically it should occur at 12. . . . The power to create, which appears at that time *and not before*, is evidence that the Soul is *only then* in full possession." [6]

At this period the child usually has dreams, visions or memories of the last incarnation, and sometimes there is a morbid depression as though from a Soul-memory of some great mistake or failure in the past. Usually, however, there is a great self-confidence and a realization of an inexhaustible power to accomplish, as though from a memory of what the Soul has already accomplished and the great lessons learned, together with a more or less conscious impression of its mission in this incarnation.

This might be called a Soul-memory of its "manifested universe," or that which the Soul has manifested in the past and a prophetic vision of that which it hopes to manifest in this life.

At this time children frequently make decided changes in their disposition and character, and often make a definite choice of their life work. They realize, even if but vaguely, that they must be about their Father's (the Soul's) business. This is a period of inspiring idealism. The child is full of zeal and takes pleasure in studying the highest ideals he hears or reads about. If this idealism is encouraged and wisely guided at this time, a strong character, based upon spiritual principles and realization, can be formed which will withstand the shock of disillusion which comes later in life as the selfishness and sordid materialism of the average unenlightened person becomes evident.

Plutarch tells us that the Egyptians understood this vital period in the child's life, for at the age of 12 those who were qualified were admitted to the temple to prophesy.[7] The parents paid serious attention to the remarks, dreams, visions and desires of children during puberty, and tried to guide them accordingly. But, alas, few parents or teachers today understand the laws back of these things, so the child's Soul-memories and ideals are laughed at and pushed aside as mere imagination, when they should be carefully, sympathetically and understandingly considered, and the germ of his Inner Guidance sifted out from what is truly only childish imagination or suggestion from outside sources. Failure to do this often forces children into careers for which they are totally unfitted and which either prevent or at least retard the unfoldment and mission they incarnated to attain.

In view of the above it is only natural that after the

---

[7] "Thus, then, although the gospel story of the abnormal wisdom of the child Jesus represents a development alike on Pagan and Jewish lines, the story of the finding him in the temple is a specifically Pagan Myth." *Christianity and Mythology*, Robertson, 311.

incidents of the birth and the flight the life-story of Jesus is not resumed until the mystical age of 12 is reached. And there would have been no need to specify the age unless it was mystically important. For there is no need for a record of the incidents of the childish growth-period. Those who attempt to supply or fill them in thereby exhibit their lack of understanding both of the law of incarnation and the meaning of the allegory as a whole.

While the Christ-consciousness is growing within us the little incidents of its unfoldment are only of minor importance. But when in our spiritual development we have reached the stage mystically symbolized by 12 we should emerge from the obscurity of our spiritual childhood and take our proper place in the world and become responsible for accomplishing our part of the Father's business. In other words, we should begin to express our 12 or "manifested universe."

The mystical age of 12 does not mean that it requires only 12 years to unfold the Christ-consciousness to the point where we consciously realize its presence and allow it to rule our life. If the process has been almost completed in past lives it may take but a short time in this life, but for most persons it may require many years or even many incarnations. For to reach this stage we must pass at least 12 times through all the signs of the zodiac and learn the characteristic lesson of each sign so perfectly that we have not merely understood it intellectually, but have built its force into our lives. Only then can we so embody the forces of the zodiac and its Planetary Rulers that we truly express the mystical meaning of 12 and become an expression of our "manifested universe" which is now reflected in us for us to express to the world with as much or as little fruitage as we have been able to bring forth. For only then are the centers in us which connect our consciousness with the forces of the zodiac sufficiently developed to enable us to consciously correlate with them and truly begin to "rule our stars." Only then can the Christ-consciousness take complete control

Jesus is represented as being found in the temple sitting in the midst of the doctors. The temple symbolizes the human personality, while the "doctors" or learned ones, represent our intellectual and other faculties which have learned many valuable lessons and gained many powers through experience in the outer world. Hence, like Jesus, we must ask them questions and thus avail ourselves of their worldly wisdom. As St. Paul reminds us: "Know ye not that ye are the temple of God, and that the spirit of God dwelleth in you?. . . . for the temple of God is holy, which temple ye are."[8]

"And all that heard him were astonished at his understanding and answers." Once the center of the Christ-consciousness unfolds and comes to the attention of our outer faculties (the doctors) we are astonished at the understanding of the problems of daily life that it gives us. When our intuition asserts itself the intellect recognizes its wisdom and marvels. When the Christ-consciousness expounds the law, the wisdom of its guidance in answer to our questions fully satisfies us. But this newly recognized Inner Guidance has only begun its influence at this period and must still grow and develop and prove its wisdom to the outer faculties before they can completely trust it.

We are all children of the one divine Father and must learn the Father's business by performing the daily tasks brought to us by the law of life, and learn the lessons from them. Previous to the age of 12 or puberty, the life of the child has been acquisitive; everything is absorbed and utilized for growth. But after puberty is attained there is present the power to give out or create and procreate.

Similarly, until the mystical age of 12 is attained all our efforts have been for self, for our own aggrandizement. But after we reach 12 we begin to be about our Father's business; we begin to work for the Father unselfishly. Previously we may have worked for the Father a little at times but then we turned away to play. But

---

[8] *I Corinthians, iii*, 16-17.

now we realize the seriousness of the Father's business and put it first in our lives. We each begin to expound the law and the teachings through love and realization to the best of our ability as the Father gives us understanding and power. Even though we may be but children spiritually we must now begin to take our evolution in our own hands and be responsible for it.

In our solar system the zodiac represents the temple, the Planetary Rulers represent the "doctors" and the Sun in the center is the Lightbringer to the system. Similarly, when the Christ-consciousness occupies the central place in our lives, around which all our activities circle, and is recognized as our source of light and life, it is able to expound to our faculties (the "doctors") all the forces of the zodiac so that we are able to grasp and correlate with them almost unconsciously. This is accomplished both through the inner illumination of the Christ-light and the deep intuitions of our hearts, and through the way we are guided to react to the experiences of daily life and to the karmic conditions we have brought over from past lives, but which we now gladly assume and work out.

The Lords of Karma[9] apportion to the Soul, in exact justice, as much of the fruits of the causes we have set up in the past as each Soul is strong enough to conquer and work out. It is the Inner Guidance of the Christ-consciousness, sitting in the midst of our faculties, who gives us the light to recognize these conditions and the power to work out and conquer them. Thus, out of bitterness shall come sweetness, out of seeming evil shall come good, and out of experience shall come wisdom. Thus does the Christ within drink of the Cup of life with all mankind in loving sympathy and compassion as we pass through the adjustment of the inevitable results of our thoughts, words and deeds.

This incident again connects the *Gospel* story of Jesus' life with the incidents of the Universal Solar Myth, rep-

---

[9] See chapter on '"The Lords of Karma" in *The Inner Radiance*, Curtiss, 129.

resenting Him as the Lightbringer and Savior to mankind as a whole, as the Sun is to the zodiac and as the Christ within is the personal Lightbringer and Savior to each personality. But when we refer to this mighty story as the Christian version of the Universal Solar Myth, many find it difficult to make a reality of the personal application. And often a feeling of sadness comes over them until they realize that the very fact that the life story of Jesus embodies and follows *exactly and successively* every incident of the Solar Myth, plainly shows Jesus to have been a Divine Being, and that the story of His life expresses the mightiest truth given to man. It illustrates the steps in the unfoldment of the Christ-consciousness within for the guidance of our lives.

As the Sun is the light, life and glory of the zodiac and of all Nature, it should remind us as we see it each day that the Spiritual Sun or the Christ within should be made the light, life and glory of our lives and our natures. Then we will see the doors of our temple of the higher spiritual consciousness swing open and will feel a mighty love fill us. Then we will hear the Still Small Voice, like the soft sighing of a summer breeze, whisper: "I am the herald of the dawn of a new day, a new spiritual springtime in your life. I bring you the Christ's message of light, love and peace, and call upon you to awaken to your opportunities and to the reality of your inner spiritual life."

"You are no longer a spiritual child hidden in the darkness and doubts of Egypt, but must now take your rightful place in the world and be about your Father's business. Shake off the lethargy of Egypt which has for so long benumbed your heart and darkened your understanding. You are no longer left to fight your way up the Mount of Attainment alone, for the ever-living, indwelling Christ is always with you and waiting to bless you and guide you and endow you with His power. When misunderstanding, trial, fear or sorrow seem to overwhelm you, call upon Him in your heart and He will answer and say:

'Peace, be still. Fear Not. Put your feet (your understanding) in the footprints that I leave and follow me. Forget the darkness of outer conditions, tread the Path of the Christ and follow on'"

Happy is he who is about his Father's business.

CHAPTER XII

THE BAPTISM

PART I. JOHN THE BAPTIST

"In those days came John the Baptist, preaching in the wilderness of Judea, and saying. Repent ye: for the kingdom of heaven is at hand." *St. Matthew, iii, 1-2.*

"When the Sun enters the Milky Way—the river Jordan—that celestial river spreads apart or the 'heavens opened' and the constellation Cygnus, the Swan, or the heavenly dove, 'descends' or becomes visible directly overhead. At the same time the Water Bearer of *Aquarius* pours out the water from his urn in baptism into the mouth of the Southern Fish in the third decanate of *Capricorn*, and thus causes the Baptism. *Pisces* occupies 30° of the zodiac, all Sun Gods receive their baptism of water at the mystical age of 30." *Appendix A.*

The sacred sacraments of all religions both symbolize and embody certain cosmic forces which produce corresponding effects in the spiritual lives of those who participate in them. These effects have been known and their meaning recorded in many myths and fables, while their forces have been invoked and correlated with, through suitable ceremonies, by the Initiates of all ages, races and religions. For it should be remembered that the Christian religion has added no new sacraments to the list. All are found in more or less the same form in the so-called pagan religions ages before the Christian era.

Among ancient peoples there were many forms of baptism used for many reasons, yet all for purposes of purification, varying from sprinkling to submersion. Since water is the universal solvent and cleansing agent, all baptisms by water symbolize the washing away of the magnetism and influence of old mistakes, habits and former conditions of life. The use of water also symbolizes the downpouring of the mystical Waters of Life which promote the opening of the spiritual faculties, just as physical water promotes the opening of the buds and blossoms in Nature. It also symbolizes the state of purification through which the candidate is supposed to have passed ere he becomes a member of the sect conducting the ceremony.

By many the purification from sin by the use of water is supposed to be an exclusive Christian ceremony and indispensable to salvation. But that is not the case, for it was a common rite used for the remission of sin in many lands long before Christianity was founded. In spite of the injunction of Jesus (*Matthew, xxviii, 19*), and although it was advocated by Tertullian, Bishop of Carthage (155-222 A.D.) in *De Baptismo*, it was not regularly instituted until the rule of Stephen, Bishop of Rome, about 250 A.D. Previous to that time candidates were admitted to the Church by prayer and laying on of hands.

The Hebrews "were all baptized unto Moses in the cloud and in the sea."[1] In Mongolia and Tibet the child is dipped three times into the water. Among the followers of Zoroaster the children were brought to the temple to be baptized. The rite was also celebrated by the ancient Egyptians, Etruscans, Mexicans, Greeks, Romans and others. Both Tertullian and Justyn Martyr claimed that those earlier rites were invented by demons to discredit the later true Christian Baptism.[2]

---

[1] *I Corinthians, X, 2.*

[2] Tertullian tells us that: "The nations who are strangers to all spiritual powers (the heathen), ascribe to their idols (gods) the power of impregnating the waters with the same efficacy as in Christian Baptism. . . . The devil signed his soldiers in the forehead, in imitation of the Christians. . . . He baptizes his followers. . . . he promises the remission of sins. . . . and thus initiates them into the religion of Mithra." *De Praescriptione Haereticorum*, chapter XI.

Among the Brahmins several forms of baptism are used, from sprinkling in certain ceremonies to being plunged three times in the waters of a sacred river during other ceremonies. Initiation into the Mithraic and Bacchic Mysteries was marked by the baptism of the candidate, after which his forehead was marked with the sign of the cross. Among the Egyptians candidates for initiation into the Mysteries of Isis were also baptized. Since baptism was the first sacrament of initiation into the Mysteries of practically all ancient religions ages before the founding of Christianity it is only natural that it should also mark the first step of initiation into the Mysteries of Jesus.

Why has baptism thus held its place through the ages as the first and universal sacrament? Because mankind has universally recognized that man is prevented from contacting and correlating his consciousness with the Divine both by the limitations of his unillumined mind and by the vibrations of mistakes due to ignorance and to the domination of his sins and his animal desires. While such desires serve a useful purpose when normal, they must not be allowed to go to excess or to dominate, but in the spiritual life they must be purified and controlled through transmutation and made to subserve their normal functions. For mastery is attained not by killing out, but by the perfect control of all normal functions.

The word baptism comes from the Greek word "photisma" which means illumination, that inner illumination which comes only through the descent of the Spirit. Complete baptism, therefore, consists of three stages, each often requiring many years for its completion, namely, (a) the purification of the body and the desires from the lusts of the flesh; (b) the purification of the mind from self-indulgence, misunderstandings and false conceptions, the resulting illumination of which reveals the Path and all that it involves, and (c) the birth of the Christ-consciousness within which makes us truly Sons of God.

True baptism is both a mystical and a magical ceremony.

Through the use of an appropriate formula—such as, "Sanctify this water to the mystical washing away of sin. . . . in the name of the Father, and of the Son, and of the Holy Ghost. Amen,"—the true priest has gained the ability to speak the Word of Power and makes the Sign of the Cross over the water. He thus invokes the superphysical forces which give the water a property it did not have before. This added spiritual energy reinforces the spiritual forces of the candidate and helps to protect him from any evil forces from the unseen.

True baptism is therefore not a mere mechanical ceremony, but marks a definite preparation which must be made by the candidate when he reaches that cycle of unfoldment wherein he recognizes that he must put away the childish pleasures of the self-indulgent life and prepare to enter a new and higher life.

Just as the Earth is prepared for a new Age by a great baptism due to extensive continental submersions or other cleansing cataclysms of water, so must there be a definite cleansing of the body, mind and life of man often through cataclysms of illness, sorrow and misfortune that certain obstructions may be removed ere it is possible for him to respond to the higher octaves of spiritual force which wash away the desire for the old life and prepare him for a new life. In other words, baptism marks the first *consciously recognized* and *voluntarily sought* stage of that purification and regeneration so necessary ere we can be "born again"; for, "Except a man be born of water and of the Spirit, he cannot enter the kingdom of heaven."[3]

In all ancient Mysteries, as well as in the early Christian Church, there were three definite baptisms which marked the three major stages of bodily and spiritual regeneration and symbolized the manifestations of the three aspects of the Trinity, i.e., the baptism by *water*, the baptism by *fire*, and the baptism by the *Spirit* or the Holy Ghost. The baptism by fire is the invocation of the Light of the

---

[3] St. John, III, 5.

Shekina upon the candidate; that spiritual fire which enters into the finer bodies of the candidate through the seven sacred centers when the proper preparation and purification has been completed and which results in spiritual illumination. The baptism by the Spirit or the Holy Ghost refers to the descent of the Divine Self into the human personality or that at-one-ment with the Divine which is the object of all religious endeavors and for which all previous steps and ceremonies are but preparatory. Although the Christian Church no longer celebrates the baptism by fire, nevertheless, it is still celebrated in India by having the candidate jump three times through the flames of a sacred fire.

The Baptism of children is a Christian rite which arose from the false and misleading medieval doctrine of a supposed "original sin" of Adam and Eve,[4] but which occultly is unnecessary and mystically of little value. In the early centuries the catechuman could not be baptized until he was familiar with the requirements of the faith he was embracing, and was willing to accept its obligations. But with the growth of the idea that every child was born in sin and cursed with original sin, it was thought essential that the babe be cleansed from that stain lest it die in sin.[5] Later on, this ceremony became conventionalized into celebrating the obligation of the parents to bring the child up with the knowledge of the tenets of their particular church.

The three stages of baptism are all combined and marvellously illustrated in the story of the baptism of Jesus. He is represented as first (a) being baptized with the water of Jordan. After that (b) the heavens opened and the Light or the Spiritual Fire of the Shekina descended upon Him with cloven tongues of flame resembling the wings of a dove. Then (c) the Voice spake and gave recognition to the fact of His spiritual Sonship. "This is

---

[4] For explanation see *The Truth about Evolution and the Bible*, Curtiss, 62-3.

[5] For the purity of birth see Chapter III, 3.

my beloved son in whom I am well pleased." These three phenomena—the opening of the heavens, the descent not of an actual dove, but of a blazing ray of spiritual Light "like a dove," and the Voice—are recognized only by the illuminated consciousness. They represent the three aspects of the Trinity which must descend upon and manifest in man ere he can attain the full status of Christhood.

We see three similar stages of manifestation in Nature. The seed must have the forces of the water, the earth and the Sun in order to put forth its sprout into the new world of light, air and freedom. Similarly, the Christ seed needs the water of Divine Love to soften the protecting shell of the intellect; it needs to assimilate the strength gained from the lessons of earth conditions; and finally it needs the fire of the Spiritual Sun to illumine its manifestation.

Since baptism is a universal symbol, its three stages must apply to a sequence of changes which take place within us, once we have reached the point in our spiritual unfoldment where we recognize the necessity of acknowledging our failures and mistakes and of cleansing ourselves of all impurities, that our bodies and minds may no longer be clogged by accumulated impurities but be free to vibrate to the forces of the indwelling Spirit or Higher Self.

In the *Bible* story John the Baptist symbolizes the human intellect which has begun to respond to the inner urge to turn away from the old life of materialism and follow the life of inner Divine Guidance. He also represents the all-compelling call of the conscience summoning the personality to repentance, purification and renunciation of the world's dominance, which are indispensable to the success of the quest for spirituality and Christhood.

As the intellect follows this higher guidance it begins to serve us as prophet and priest. But first it must be ready to recognize that there is a power within—the Christ-consciousness—far greater than itself and to say with John: "There cometh one after me, the latchet of whose shoes I am unworthy to stoop down and unloose. . . . but he shall baptize you with the Holy Ghost."[6]

John is represented as being clothed in skins and crying in the wilderness: "Repent ye: for the kingdom of heaven is at hand. . . . Prepare ye the way of the Lord, make His paths straight." For the intellect is clothed in its animal body (skin) and wanders in the wilderness of the outer life until it is awakened to the possibility of something far greater coming to it. Then it realizes that it must make straight the crooked paths of error and sin ere the Christ-consciousness can flow in. Hence it cries out: "Repent ye" until its Path through the outer life is changed and made straight so that the influx of Divine Love can bring forth the Christ-consciousness.

In other words, when once recognized, the intellect readily admits the superiority of the Christ-consciousness, and feels that it is unworthy even to unloose the coverings (shoes) of the understanding (feet) which shall bring about the baptism of the Holy Ghost. For when the heart hungers for spiritual food, for the warmth of Divine Love and the light of illumination, the giant intellect (John) realizes its helplessness to satisfy that Soul-hunger. It can give a cold analysis of conditions and a mental explanation of the process and the results that should follow, but *it cannot confer the power.* Only the Holy Ghost can accomplish the miracle of awakening the Christ-consciousness, and reveal its glory.

The meaning of the word John is "the Lord graciously gave." In other words, no matter how wise, learned and capable the human personality may be, it can never attain Christhood through its own unaided powers. That is attained only by baptism in its three-fold aspect which "the Lord graciously bestows from above" when the personality prepares for it both through repentance and by making all its powers and faculties subservient to the Divine. Only thus can man attain that Christhood symbolized by the three-fold baptism.

[6] *St. Mark, I, 7, 8.*

The first impulse of the newly awakened Soul is an ardent desire to get away from the old life and environment: to give up the comforts and pleasures of the world and dwell apart as in a wilderness, that he may thereby find the Christ. This stage requires courage and the power to dare; for like all who are truly awakened spiritually, he dares all conventions and the criticism of his family and friends, as well as the limitations and privations of the wilderness. In the next stage he has an overpowering realization of the new life and of his duty to make it known to others; his responsibility to help save the world. To express this desire to accomplish or do something for humanity he is eager to take the responsibility for humanity on his own shoulders. He, therefore, cries out: "Repent ye: the kingdom of heaven is at hand." Thus he goes about his chosen work determinedly and courageously, even if not always wisely or lovingly, and may bring many to a realization of their need for repentance and to desire the baptism of the higher illumination.

Applying this symbology to the changes which take place within the consciousness of the awakened personality, John the Baptist represents the intellect which has awakened to the fact that without the higher spiritual consciousness life is but a wilderness in which it finds itself clothed in a garment of camel's hair. This was a cheap, coarse outer garment commonly worn by the poor in Palestine and symbolizes the animal body with which the intellect finds itself clothed, and whose instincts it must learn to dominate and make subservient to the higher ideals it has just realized.

The girdle symbolizes the orbit of the Sun and identifies the wearer as a priest of the Sun[7] such as "the curious girdle of the ephod. . . . of fine twined linen, and blue and purple and scarlet,"[8] which identified Aaron and his sons as priests of the Lord. Physiologically it refers to the current of vital force which encircles the body just

---

[7] For details see *The Key to the Universe*, Curtiss, 36, 322.

[8] Exodus, XXIX, 5, XXXIX, 29.

below the breasts which is especially strong in those whose centers are highly unfolded. As the Feast of St. John is held on June 24th, as the Sun reaches the highest point of the summer solstice in the sign *Cancer*—symbol of the breasts—geographically the girdle symbolizes the Tropic of Cancer which girdles the globe just below its "breast."

A wilderness is not a desert but a confusion of overgrown bushes, brambles and vines, a region uncultivated and without roads, only the meandering and aimless paths made by wandering animals seeking food and drink. Yet a wilderness is full of possibilities for primitive human habitation, happiness and comfort once it is cleared of its underbrush, properly organized and cultivated.

Until the Christ-consciousness comes to it for recognition, the awakened intellect finds life just such a wilderness. It strives to satisfy its hunger for spiritual food with outer conceptions comparable to the most primitive food, locusts and wild honey. Locusts are pestiferous insects which completely ruin the beauty and devastate the landscape over which they swarm. But they are made to serve a useful purpose by many primitive people who dry, roast and grind them into flour so that they are made, temporarily, a chief article of diet for about four months. Wild honey, while having a certain sweetness, is often made bitter and acrid by the blossom nectar of certain weeds, and in some cases it contains narcotic and even poisonous substances. It symbolizes the sweetness of the world's enjoyments which, although the result of the greatest bee-like planning and industry, so often leave a bitter taste or even unsatisfied cravings. We recognize that this is as far as the intellect can satisfy us, so we must feed on what food the wilderness supplies until the Christ comes with "the bread which cometh down from heaven."[9]

How true a picture of the condition in which the awakened Soul finds itself when forced to subsist on the

---

[9] St. Luke, VI, 50.

temporary, primitive and unspiritualized food of the outer life! Its former intellectual activities, once so satisfying, no longer appease the Soul-hunger. The intellect now realizes that the paths by which the vibrations of the higher consciousness can reach it, must be made straight, that all the old mental twists, misconceptions and habits of life which prevented the inflow of the Christ-consciousness must be straightened out.

In technical training the Hindus claim that this also refers to that stage of unfoldment wherein the positive and negative currents of force—*Ida and Pingala*—are no longer allowed to twine and twist around the spinal cord, but must be blended into one and be made to pass straight up the *Sushumna* canal in the center of the cord ere the complete Illumination of the Christ-consciousness can be attained.

The intellect now realizes that "the kingdom of heaven is at hand" or within, but that it cannot be attained except through repentance. The personality must realize, face and acknowledge the conditions it has set up through its mistakes of ignorance and through its sins of omission and commission, and be sincerely sorry for them and positively determined that they shall not continue. It, therefore, calls upon all its faculties, habits, thoughts and desires which have not been constructive—especially those which have been most influential and which offer the greatest resistance, like the Pharisees and Sadducees—to repent or "turn back" from the old life and begin to follow the new; to prove their sincerity by bringing forth "fruits meet for repentance."

We must realize that the old life was not the Way; that it did not reveal to us the Truth nor did it lead us into the true spiritual Life. The repentance must, therefore, be more than a mere intellectual recognition of our sins and mistakes, for it must be followed by the baptism or a *definite cleansing* of both body and mind. This is accomplished only by deliberately Immersing oneself in and correlating with the waters of Divine Love.

In the condensed *Bible* story the heavens seem to open immediately after the baptism, but in actual life it may require a long period in which to change the habits of life and purify the mind and body so that the Inner Light is revealed. And it may be still longer ere the inner Voice speaks with authority and the at-one-ment is attained. But "the way, the truth and the life"[10] has now been recognized and actually entered upon, and it requires only faith, courage and repeated and persistent efforts for the goal to be attained. And every conscious effort we make toward that end is a step up this Mount of Attainment.

Owing to ancient misconceptions the word repent carries a fearsome meaning to certain sensitive Souls. In medieval times to express true repentance it was thought necessary to don sackcloth and ashes, retire into seclusion for a time, abuse and mortify the flesh and bemoan one's past mistakes like a worm of the dust. Hence to many earnest and loving Souls who have searched diligently to attain a definite realization of the Christ, such a conception of the word repent is like a stone of stumbling in their path; for they have not been vicious or evil and their mistakes have been only the unwitting ones due to ignorance. But when we understand that to repent simply means to recognize and turn away from wrong thoughts, acts and habits that we may follow the guidance of the Inner Man instead of the outer, we see that the word repent is really but the call of the loving Christ who said: "Suffer the little children (*i.e.*, the well meaning but ignorant ones) to come unto me and forbid them not." The intellect cries, "Repent," but the Christ cries, "Come unto me."

From another standpoint John the Baptist represents that class of newly awakened ones who ardently seek to bring the worldly ones to the loving Christ by denouncing them and picturing the disasters that will follow a continuation of the old life. Such exhorters seek to *force* repentance through *fear* instead of *inspiring* it through

---

[10] See lesson *The Way, the Truth and the Life*, Curtiss.

a *realization* of mistakes and the cleansing power of love. Instead of teaching their followers to purify their lives and perfect their conditions of life, such teachers often mistakenly seek to lead their students away from their positions and duties in the world and to live apart in retreats and colonies, forgetting that mere change of location is not sufficient to produce the cleansing baptism. We do not have to change our abode or move to another city or live an ascetic life apart from our fellowmen to repent and be baptized. We have only to recognize the futility and the sorrow-producing habits of the old life and seek to correct them through the love-power of the Christ within, no matter where we may be.

But even such teachers, when sincere and true, are recognized by the Christ, for only He can fully understand what they call their mission. There are many John the Baptists wandering in the wilderness of earth conditions and preaching repentance today, yet their zeal is clothed only in the most primitive ideas, almost naked or clothed only with camel's hair and a leather girdle or only the crudest understanding of how to save the world. Yet they often have a true divine eagerness to "make straight the paths" of the Christ, and there are always those to whom such teachers and such methods appeal.

Jesus plainly recognizes both the value and the ability of such teachers. "What went ye out for to see? A reed shaken by the wind?—A prophet? Yea, I say unto you, and much more than a prophet."[11] This recognition of the good that such John the Baptists accomplish is most comforting and encouraging. No matter how imperfect the understanding and how crude the methods of such workers for the Christ, *if they be sincere and earnest* and willing to learn, the Christ will surely come to them and recognize them and accept their efforts to make straight the paths by which His children may come unto Him and be purified and baptized with the fire of the Spirit.

(To Be Continued)

---

[11] *St. Luke, vii,* 26.

Chapter XIII

THE BAPTISM

Part II. The Christ

"Then cometh Jesus from Galilee unto Jorden unto John, to be baptized of him. But John forbade him, saying, I have need to be baptized of thee, and comest thou to me? And Jesus answering said unto him, Suffer it to be so now: for thus it becometh us to fulfil all righteousness." St. Matthew, iii, 13-14.

"Ye yourselves bear me witness, that I said, I am not the Christ, but that I am sent before him. . . . He must increase, but I must decrease." St. John, iii, 28, 30.

If John the Baptist is regarded merely as an historical personage sent forth by God as a messenger and forerunner to prepare followers for the forth coming of Jesus, then his mission was almost a complete failure so far as turning over to Jesus a following of several thousand already baptized and organized disciples was concerned. For we are told: "Then there went out to him *Jerusalem and all Judea,* and all the region round about Jordan, and were baptized of him' (*St. Matthew, iii,5,6*). Therefore Jesus should have had thousands of John's converts who were ready to follow Him whom John had announced as the Messiah, and ready to acclaim Him as soon as He appeared. But we know that was far from being the case, for at first Jesus is represented as laboriously trying to gather even twelve followers. It is therefore well that we consider John the Baptist not from the historical, but from the allegorical standpoint. Then, as usual with all

the other incidents in the life of Jesus, we will find the key
in the Universal Solar Myth.[1]

The Feast of St. John the Baptist is held on the day of
the summer solstice (June 22-24) in commemoration of
his birth. At that time the Sun reaches its highest point in
the heavens as it enters the watery sign *Cancer*—the sign
of the breasts—called the Nourisher. Since *Cancer* is a
watery sign it is only natural that John's baptism should
be of water. Also John is but a variant spelling of the name
of the Babylonian Water-god *Oannes* or Joannes. At this
time the constellation of the Southern Fish rises as the Sun
sets and disappears as the Sun rises. Here John represents
both the physical Sun and the physical man ruled by his
intellect, while Jesus represents the Spiritual Sun and the
Spiritual Man, ruled by the Spirit.

The birth of the Spiritual Man is placed at the time of
the winter solstice (Dec. 22-25) when the Sun is born in
Capricorn. After that the days begin to lengthen until the
time of the Ascension. This increase is especially notice-
able from the time of the Resurrection (March 21st) when
the Sun crosses the equator and is thus resurrected from
the Southern hemisphere, until it reaches its zenith at the
Ascension on June 24th. Thus the Spiritual Man continually grows in strength until the time of Baptism, after which
he takes control of the personality, instead of allowing the
physical man to dominate.

Since John is six months older than Jesus, as the days
shorten after the Baptism, naturally John is made to say:
"He must increase, but I must decrease," as the two phases
of the Sun necessarily follow each other. Thus is it said:
"He that descended (on Dec. 22nd) is the same also that
ascended up (on June 21-24) far above all heavens, that
he might fill all things," (*St. Matthew, iii*, 5, 6), just as the
Sun as it ascends fills all things in Nature and thus enables
them to reach their zenith or their fruition.

---

[1] See *Appendix A*.

Jesus is represented as being 30 years of age at this time, since the Baptism takes place when the Sun has entered 30° into the sign *Cancer*. Jesus is said to have ended His work after only three cycles or years, for the Sun shines undimmed in the mid heaven only three days (June 21-24) before the days begin to shorten and its power declines.

As explained in the previous chapter, in the personal application of the story of the Baptism, John symbolizes the intellect after it has awakened to the realization that there is a greater consciousness than the intellectual, to be attained, the Christ-consciousness, represented by Jesus. John's message was an expression of that all-compelling yearning of the awakened conscience which is so necessary as a preparation for the coming of the Christ-consciousness. This call of the conscience must be recognized and responded to ere the Voice of the Christ can be heard or understood. And the baptism by water must be accomplished ere the baptism by fire is possible.

Up until the Baptism we are told only of the babe, the young boy, and the carpenter's son, Jesus the man. Only after the Baptism do we learn of the christened or Christed One, Jesus the Christ. The Baptism by water marks the entry of the Christ-consciousness into the personality, the initiation of the personality into the Christ-life. For only when we have courageously looked within and repented and purified ourselves are we able to look up and see the Christ approaching. John, therefore, represents the awakened personality with all its powers purified and at the service of the Christ, while Jesus represents the regenerate or Spiritual Man. Not only was John's coming foretold by the prophets (*Malachi, iv, 5*) and heralded by the angels (*St. Luke, i,13*) as a forerunner, but his mission was and is, and always will be, an absolutely necessary preparation for the mission of the Christ, both in the individual and in the world as a whole.

Next there is recorded a most curious incident. Jesus comes to John to be baptized by him. Quite naturally

John demurs, saying: "I have need to be baptized of thee, and comest thou to me?" But Jesus replies, "Suffer it to be so now; for thus it becometh us to fulfill all righteousness." There is no explanation given anywhere in the *Gospels* as to why Jesus needed to be baptized by anyone. Certainly He did not need to be purified, nor can we suppose that John had any powers to confer on Jesus which He did not already possess. Why then the need of baptism by John? Also, John baptized sinners only, and only after they had confessed their sins and repented. Since Jesus had not sinned He had no sins to confess and no need of repentance, yet He came to John for baptism. Why? If we follow the symbolic interpretation it is so simple that we can easily understand the law.

The law is that that which is Immortal cannot manifest on earth except through that which is mortal. There must be a physical vehicle. Just as the Soul cannot manifest on earth without using the physical body as its instrument of expression, and is limited in that expression by the stage of development and character of the body, so must the Christ-consciousness use the human intellect as an avenue of expression. Yet its expression is limited by the capacity of the intellect to recognize and understand what is wanted and what is taking place. For the intellect is generally both unresponsive to the higher octaves of force and is also easily influenced and even warped by its preconceived opinions and habits of thought.

Altho the River of Life (Jordan) is always flowing through man and trying to wash away the impurities of the lower animal instincts, nevertheless it is hidden from his recognition until the Christ comes to be baptized by its waters. The Christ recognizes the mission and importance of the intellect and insists on being baptized with all its powers. Only when the Christ-consciousness is consciously recognized within and is baptized with all the powers of the newly awakened intellect can "the fullness of righteousness," which is man's heritage and which gives him dominion over the beasts of the field, be manifested. If man denies the Christ-consciousness and refuses to respond to it and follows only his intellectual guidance, he is wilfully denying the Christ as did Peter. The Christ never forces us, yet knows His lack of power to manifest except as we recognize and give Him the use of all our faculties.

As we have repeatedly pointed out, altho the Christ-consciousness is born in our heart—not in our head—in a moment of ecstasy, it must dwell for a long time obscured in the Galilee of outer conditions, working through three cycles of completion (3 x 10=30 years of age) as a carpenter until it has prepared the "house" or the character of the personality to receive both its outer recognition by John and its illumination through the Baptism. Thus it grows so strong that the intellect must bow before it and give it recognition.

Many, many times does the Christ come to us for recognition but we refuse to admit that there is a faculty or power superior to our intellect or reason. Yet as we emerge from the obscurity of the wilderness of the outer life, ultimately the time comes when we recognize that life without spiritual realization is indeed but a wilderness and that something must be done about it. When we are ready to repent or change our former mode of life and recognize the redemptive power of the Spirit, then the Christ comes to us for baptism. With the Baptism the Presence is revealed. For John the baptism of Jesus was the end of his career, for he is soon beheaded—the intellect is soon removed from dominating our life—but for Jesus it is the beginning of His manifestation.

Like John, the intellect at first refuses, realizing that it is unworthy to unloose the latchets of His shoes, i.e., release the coverings (shoes) which have hitherto confined the understanding (feet) of the Christ in its contact with the outer life (earth). But the Christ points out that to enable Him "to fulfil all righteousness" the intellect must both recognize and confer all its powers on Him that He may use them for His manifestation in the mental and physical worlds.

While the intellect which has heretofore dominated our lives must willingly give up its rule, or be "beheaded," and obediently follow the guidance of the Christ within, yet it must not be utterly despised and cast aside. For the intellect is no longer merely the expression of a current of force flowing through the mental world, but is now illuminated and becomes a spring of living water filled with everlasting life, bubbling up from the Christ within. We are not told to do this and not to do that like babies, but must now seek deep within and ask of the Christ which course of action will most please and serve Him.

Later on, as our illumined intellect points out to King Desire (Herod) his illegitimate use of the creative force (*Matthew, xiv, 3-12*), it is temporarily overwhelmed or put in prison at the demand of lust (Salome) and ultimately is "beheaded" or recognizes that it cannot overcome all the former conditions in its own strength and so gives itself up completely that the Christ alone may manifest. For John can impart to his disciples no greater wisdom than the outer Mysteries connected with the plane of matter, of which Water is the symbol. His Gnosis is that of the exoteric and ritualistic dogma, of dead letter orthodoxy; while the wisdom which Jesus would reveal is higher spiritual wisdom, the Fire Wisdom of the true Gnosis or *real* Spiritual Enlightenment.[2]

Instead of condemning the shortcomings He may find in us, the Christ temporarily says: "Suffer it to be so now," but shows us how they can be corrected and redeemed. From this time on the disciple begins to point out and draw others into the Path of Attainment through love and the example of his life instead of intellectually trying to compel them through fear that, "He will thoroughly purge his floor and gather his wheat into his

---

[2] *The Secret Doctrine*, Blavatsky, II, 598.

garner; but he will burn up the chaff with unquenchable fire." (*St. Matthew, iii, 12*).

To cry, "Repent ye" is a form of condemnation. To cry, "Suffer it to be so now," is to draw to us through compassion the hearts of mankind. Nor should we let the intellect think it can help others by telling them of the wonderful experiences it has passed through and the marvelous visions given it, lest we be like the hypocrites publishing their attainments and making great claims as to their powers, on the street corners, that they may have glory of men. Only as our Soul communes with God in secret will He reward us openly.

Happy is he who has been baptized by the Spirit.

(To Be Concluded)

CHAPTER XIV

THE BAPTISM

PART III. THE JORDAN

"The Baptism in the Jordan is the Rite of Initiation, the
final purification, whether in sacred pagoda, tank river
or temple lake in Egypt or Mexico. The perfect Christos
and Sophia—divine Wisdom and Intelligence—enter
the Initiate at the moment of the mystic rite." *The Secret
Doctrine*, Blavatsky, iii, 159.

"The Jordan symbolizes the celestial river Eridanus,
the Milky Way." *Appendix A.*

Although the river Jordan is used primarily as a mighty
symbol of the mystical inner cleansing which is essential
for crossing into the "promised land" and for the reception
of the Christ-consciousness, that is not its only meaning.
Physically the Jordan is a swift, muddy stream, falling 610
feet during its course of sixty miles, as it passes through
the Sea of Galilee and falls into the Dead Sea. "It has never
been navigable, no important town has ever been built
upon its banks, and it runs into an inland sea which has no
seaport and is destitute of aquatic life. . . . on the whole, it
is an unpleasant, foul stream, running between poisonous
banks, and as such it seems to have been regarded by the
Jews and other Syrians."[1]

Ancient Hebrew authorities on the Talmud say that its
waters are so impure, because so mixed and muddy, that

---

[1] *Encyclopedia Britannica*, XV, 509.

it should never be used for baptism, not even for sprinkling. And yet it is this same dirty and unclean water, which was never used by the Jews for baptism, in which Jesus is represented as being baptized. It is, therefore, evident that its use was symbolic, for all the people of Palestine knew that it was never used for actual baptismal purposes.

When John's mission has progressed to the proper stage: that is, when in every sincere Soul the intellect has reached the point where it recognizes the Christ, not as a mere expectation or a logical belief which it is willing to accept and prepare for, but as a real, vitally living force, consciousness and power which comes into the life of every true seeker after righteousness just where he is and as he is, then he becomes what *The Voice of the Silence* calls, "He who has entered the stream." From this standpoint the Jordan symbolizes the pure River of Life which flows through man's inner spiritual body and which brings to him a realization of the purifying spiritual truths with which he must be baptized; that Divine Stream which separates man from the lower kingdoms as definitely as the Jordan separates the wilderness from the Promised Land.

In the zodiac the Sun is led for its baptism to the River of Heaven or the Milky Way. By reference to our map of the heavens it will be seen that as the Sun enters the sign *Cancer*, the Milky Way is seen overhead at a point where it separates into two streams, between which is revealed the constellation *Cygnus*, the Swan or Dove. Therefore, it is said: "The heavens were opened unto him, and he saw the Spirit of God descending *like* a dove, and lighting upon him."[2] As the sign *Cancer* is at the right hand of Leo—which is called the Throne of the Sun or where the Sun is exalted in the midheaven—naturally the allegory tells us: "I saw the heavens opened, and the Son of Man standing *on the right hand* of God."[3] Also, "Hereafter

---

[2] *St. Matthew, III*, 16.
[3] *Acts, III*, 55.

shall ye see the Son of Man sitting *on the right hand* of power, and coming in the clouds of heaven."[4]

The use of the river Jordan to symbolize purification we have already explained, but it also has another important symbology to which we have alluded above. As we have said before: "One aspect of this mystic river is the great stream of astral force which surrounds mankind as the amniotic waters surround the unborn fetus."[5] "For the astral, being the great reflector, contains all the mud, debris, and offscourings of earth mingled with the pure, clear Waters of Life from the spiritual plane."[6]

"Because in its waters the pure River of Life flowing to humanity from the higher worlds is mingled with the mud and slime and debris from all the lower worlds, it is fittingly symbolized by the river Jordan in Canaan, for its physical features correspond most marvelously with those of this river of astral force. . . . We realize that we have reached the end of the wilderness, yet between us and the Promised Land there flows a swift, deep, turbulent, muddy and treacherous river. For just as the River of Death (Styx) marks a definite boundary between our mortal life and the life beyond, so does the mystical River Jordan mark a definite boundary between the life of a seeker which we have led as wanderers in the wilderness— to which life we must die as we cross the Jordan—and the new life into which we are born when we cross the mystical river and begin the life of a Neophyte. At this step our astral senses begin to unfold and we are confronted with strange happenings and experiences which we do not understand, and which often frighten us. And because these new faculties are beginning to unfold we are subjected to the trials and temptations of that world of insidious desire and delusion. The swift eddies of the astral forces toss us this way and that, often undermining

---

[4] St. Mathew, I 4.
[5] For a fuller symbology of the Jordan see *The Message of Aquaria*, Curtiss, 330-4.
[6] *Realms of the Living Dead*, Curtiss, 31.

our footing and carrying us beyond our depth, just as would happen were we to attempt to wade the physical river Jordan at the season of its flood."[5]

As we enter this stream of astral force when our higher faculties begin to unfold, we can maintain our footing and emerge without being swept away only through the power of the Christ within Who accompanies us, once our intellect (John) has recognized Him and our power is strengthened by the descent of the Holy Ghost. For in ourselves the Jordan symbolizes the swirling, muddy currents of the desires of the flesh which seek to sweep us off our feet (understanding) when we try to make our illumined intellect sustain us in a new and upright life. For there comes a time in our spiritual unfoldment when the newly recognized Christ-power within us must go down to the lowest depths of our nature and bring the purifying and redemptive power of the Christ-love and light into these desires, just as Jesus descended into the muddy waters of the Jordan. But we must not linger there, but "straightway come up" out of those conditions and that state of consciousness.

Just as light and water give new life and growth to all Nature, enabling the pure white lily to rise out of the foul muck of the swamp, so does the Light of the Christ and the Water of Divine Love — the refreshing daily realization of our oneness with the Divine — give life and growth to our spiritual nature and enable the blossoms of spiritual aspiration and attainment to arise out of the lowest mire of our nature.

After we have received our Baptism and have straightway come up out of the stream, our higher centers will be ready to open so that we can see the heavens of the higher consciousness open, can see the Light descend, can hear the Voice and recognize the coming of the Dove. According to the *Gospel* account the events of the Baptism constituted a spectacular, physical demonstration of psychic phenomena, but we have seen that all such phenomena take place within the candidate himself. That "the heavens opened" may not mean that literally the clouds in the sky parted and the Sun shone through and a dove flew down, but that our spiritual consciousness opens or expands so that our understanding is no longer overshadowed by the dark clouds of materialism and doubt, but is able to respond to the higher planes of consciousness and we realize the presence of God within us.

It is this unfoldment or opening of the inner life which brings divine realization: realization of the Presence. This unfoldment enables us to hear the Inner Voice which proclaims that the Divinity within us which we have just recognized is indeed the Christ—"Thou art my beloved Son, in whom I am well pleased"—a Son or a positive manifestation of God. And we are awed by the majesty and are uplifted by the power of that realization.

The Dove is the Christian symbol for the Shekina or Holy Ghost, also for gentleness and purity, as the Swan is in India and the Ibis in Egypt. The Shekina descends in cloven tongues of flame simulating the wings of a dove and brings to the one who has reached this great initiation the dual creative power of the Father-Mother and a full realization of what true spiritual Sonship means, yet it also soothes our sorrow and stills the turmoil of our remorse.

Although this event seems to take place immediately after the Baptism, it must be remembered that the process of purification inaugurated by the Baptism may take months or even years to complete. And it is only after we have completed it so that we can come "up straightway out of the water" that we can expect the heavens to open and the *full* illumination of the Spirit to be given us. Previous to this great event we may have the Inner Guidance of intuition and perhaps many flashes of the Divine Light, but only when the sacred nest in our hearts is fully completed can the Divine Dove descend to remain with us permanently and enable us to manifest *fully* the fact that we are truly Sons of God in whom the Father is well pleased and in whom He can now find expression.

Once we truly realize this in our hearts, we feel and know it is so sacred and so easily lost in the outer wilderness of our own pride and rejoicing that we dare not speak of it to others, but must hide it deep in our hearts, even as we would hide a precious seed in the ground if we wanted it to grow into a great tree that was to bring forth its fruit for all people. For if we proclaim it to the world we dissipate its force and it will wither and die, for the world will not recognize or believe it until we are strong enough to demonstrate it, and will call us hypocrites.

Later on when John sees Jesus coming toward him he cries: "Behold the Lamb of God, which taketh away the sins of the world." The illumined intellect thus recognizes that it requires more than mere thought power, more than a mere change of thought, to transmute the inharmonies and impurities created by us before our awakening, whose vibrations and influence still saturate our minds and life. We must realize therefore that the purification is more than a mental process; that *it cannot be accomplished in our own mortal strength alone*, but that it requires a power higher and greater than our own, the coming of the Christ within; the infusion of the "blood of the Lamb" or the purifying fire of the Christ-force. For it is only the Christ-force, recognized by us and invited to enter and flood our entire being and purify our lives, that can bear and transmute the sins of our world.

Even though the illumined intellect fully recognizes and rejoices at this definite coming of the Christ-consciousness, only too often it is found difficult to hold fast to the realization at first, for the conditions of the outer physical life are like the waves of the sea, tossed by every wind that blows. Clouds and storms are bound to come, and, alas, as we drop down into the trough of routine earthly conditions, so often the memory of our spiritual realization and Soul experience is blotted out and we grow discouraged, and this but adds to the storm. We must therefore learn to impress our spiritual realizations upon our physical brain and write them indelibly upon our hearts so that they will be there at all times to bring peace and joy and realization of the nearness and power of the Christ within, and thus turn the tide of earth conditions and allow the spiritual life to dominate instead.

We must realize that the Christ is forever sending forth His blessings and His help as though from a broadcasting radio station. But only to those who "tune in" with the receiving set within our hearts—a definite work which each must do—can the message of love, understanding and the spiritual power-to-accomplish become a vital part of our daily lives. Then what seemed to be but the daily grind, shutting us away from all our higher ideals, soon gives way to peace, satisfaction, and we are contented to fill our allotted place and do our work in the world.

It is not those who are merely devout who receive the real Baptism, but only the positive and actively striving disciples of the Christ. For while John calls the attention of the multitude thoughts, desires, and emotions of the personality to the need for purification and baptism by water, it is only the Christ who can baptize us with Fire and the Holy Ghost. In other words, if we are to reach the highest state of spiritual consciousness—illumination and union with the Divine (*Buddhi*)—it requires more than intellectual understanding, more than mere passive devotion to the forms of religion we have inherited because we happen to be born in a certain environment and race. For the vast majority do not choose their form of religion after careful study and a comparison with other great religions. They passively *inherit it* with their nationality and their family traditions.

The higher spiritual attainment, therefore, requires more than a clean, good moral life and good citizenship. It requires an active and persistent seeking for the Christ-consciousness as a personal, psychological and spiritual experience, putting aside all ideas of limitation as to the manner in which or the religion through which that realization may come. For in the heart of every true religion the Path of Attainment can be found if searched for diligently. It is this voluntary seeking and recognition of the Christ on our part that is the vital point. Like the first two disciples who followed Jesus we must ask: "Master, where dwellest thou?"[7] And when we are told to "Come and see" we must follow Him and dwell with Him ere we can become His accepted disciples.

The invitation to "Come and see" and enjoy the intimate conscious contact with the Christ *was not given to the multitude*, nor to the mere orthodox follower of the letter of the law (John), but only to those who had repented and been purified and had taken the first steps into the new life, the Kingdom of Christhood; those whose conscious recognition and following of the Christ had both prepared and entitled them to learn the more advanced lessons of the inner life or the "Mystery of the Kingdom of God." "Unto you it is given to know the mystery of the Kingdom of God: but unto them that are without (unpurified and uninitiated) all these things are done in parables."[8]

Therefore, let all who sincerely desire to know the Mysteries of the Kingdom prepare themselves by repentance and purification. Then the heavens of the higher consciousness will surely open and the Dove of spiritual illumination will descend in due season and baptize them with the Holy Ghost

Happy is he who has received his Dove of illumination.

---

[7] *St. John I*, 38-9.
[8] *St. Mark, IV*, 11.

CHAPTER XV

THE TEMPTATION IN THE WILDERNESS

PART I. THE FAST

"Then was Jesus led up of the spirit into the wilderness
to be tempted of the devil. And when he had fasted forty
days and forty nights, he was afterward an hungered."
St. Matthew, iv, 1-2.

"The 30° of *Aquarius*, together with the first 10° of
Pisces, the sign of sacrifice, make up the 40° associated
with the 40 days spent by Jesus in the wilderness where
He is tempted by or has to withstand the trying forces
of Satan, Satar or Saturn, the Tester, the co-ruler of
Aquarius." *Appendix A.*

Since this incident is common to all versions of the
Universal Solar Myth,[1] let us first examine its basic as-

---

[1] *Buddha* was tempted by Mara, the Prince of Evil, not to adopt a religious life,
promising that if he would return to his kingdom he would be given dominion over
all the earth. "In seven days shalt thou become the Emperor of the World, riding
over the four great continents." In the Hindu version the young *"Krishna* plays
in the wilderness and is assaulted by various fiends, and overcame them all. . . .
In the so-called Temptation of *Zarathustra,* the only tempting done is an offer of
Ahriman to the prophet that if he will renounce the good religion of Mazda he shall
have a thousand years' dominion; and Zarathustra refuses; predicting the coming
of his as yet unborn son, the Savior *Saoshyant,* who at the end of time is to destroy
Ahriman and raise the dead." The virgin-born Mexican Savior, *Quetzalcoatle,* was
also tempted by the devil and experienced a 40 day fast. In the Greek version *Pan,*
pictured with the horns, hoofs and tail of the devil, leads the young Sun-god, *Jove*
(Jupiter) to the mountain called the "pillar of heaven," from which he is shown the
lands afar off. In each case the hero passes through a long fast.

tronomical significance. According to one authority: "The whole temptation story is traceable to a Babylonian sculpture of the Goat-God beside the Sun-God, interpreted by the Greeks and Romans successively as an education of Apollo or Jupiter by Pan on a mountain top."[2] Pan, the Goat-god, is usually pictured as the "terror-striker," (pan-ic maker), with horns, hoofs and tail like the Christian devil. Pan is another name for Saturn, the ruler of the sign *Capricorn* in which the Sun begins its climb to the heights of the northern heavens. Thus does Saturn (Satan) test the "climber" up the Mount of Attainment toward heaven (zenith).

But why should this astronomical symbolism be used so universally in all ages and with only minor variations among all peoples? We cannot repeat too often that it is to show that the incidents in the cycle of manifestation of the Sun in the heavens correspond to and illustrate the stages in the manifestation of the Spiritual Sun in the life of every aspirant for Christhood or every candidate for the Sun Initiation or the Initiation into the Christ-consciousness, once that Consciousness has been born in the manger of his heart, as already explained. Neither is a copy of the other, but both are examples of the one universal Law of Manifestation.[3]

In the Christian version of this incident, the use of a name so common among the Jews as that of Jesus, is intended to indicate how common and universal is the human expression of the Godhead or God-in-man; that in the heart of even the most common of mankind there is emplanted a replica of the Divine. Through this Image of God within man the mighty force of the Godhead is poured into the human personality which without it would be but an advanced animal. For it was only when the Soul, the *pneuma*, the "breath of life" or the inner Spiritual Man, was breathed into the nostrils of the human

---

[2] *Pagan Christs*, Robertson, XIII.
[3] See *The Key of Destiny*, Curtiss, 119-122.

animal form that man became more than an animal, "and man became a living Soul."[4]

It is to awaken this Image of God within and to unfold and express its godlike powers in the flesh that is the object of the Soul's incarnation on earth. And the stages in the process of manifesting the Light of this inner Spiritual Man or Sun of God—the Christ within—follow the same stages as the manifestation of the physical Sun during the cycle of the year. Hence, the *Bible* story is but the *Christian version* of the universal allegory and the *spiritual fact* of the manifestation of that "true light, which lighteth every man that cometh into the world."[5]

As in so many other biblical incidents, we have conflicting accounts of the temptation in the different *Gospels*. In *St*. Mark (i, 12), we are told that after the Baptism, "*immediately* the Spirit *driveth* him into the wilderness," while in *St. John (i, 35-9)* we are told that Jesus did not go into the wilderness immediately, for the *next day* John saw Him with two of His disciples who "came and saw where he dwelt, and *abode with him* that day," presumably while Jesus was selecting and testing Andrew and Simon Peter. If Jesus went *immediately* into the wilderness, where He is said to have remained for forty days, He could not have been seen with Andrew and Peter the next day. Nor could He have been seen going on into Galilee "the day following" *(i, 43)*. *St. John* further says *(iv)* that after the Baptism Jesus went out of Judea into Galilee and Samaria, implying that instead of spending forty days[6] in the wilderness Jesus spent the next six weeks in those regions.

St. Luke tells us *(iv, 1)* that it was only after Jesus "returned from Jordan" that He was "*led* (not driven, for the Spirit never drives, only inspires and leads) by the Spirit (not by the devil) into the wilderness." Yet there

---

[4] See *The Truth about Evolution and the Bible*, Curtiss, 56.

[5] *St. John, I,* 9.

[6] Moses fasted for 40 days on Mt. Sinai, and Elijah 40 days on Mt. Horeb. *I Kings, XIX,* 8.

was no wilderness nearer than Peraea or East of Mt. Gilead, into which He could have been *driven immediately*.

In all the Mystery Schools the candidate for Initiation had to be prepared by fasting and meditation to undergo a period of testing, trial and temptation to prove his fitness to take on the added responsibilities of the more advanced steps. In the case of Jesus, His Baptism had conferred on Him certain transcendental powers, and naturally He had to be tested as to whether He would use them for personal and selfish purposes. But who or what is this that tests Him? Why does the *Gospel* story assume that the earth and all the kingdoms thereof belonged to Satan? and that he could give them to whomsoever he pleased? Did he think that Jesus was so simple-minded that He would accept such an offer? And how was Satan able to enter the Holy City at all, much less ascend to the pinnacle of the Temple therein? Also, how did he transport Jesus from one place to another, in one case forty miles and a hundred miles in the other? Did the devil carry Jesus through the air as Faust was carried by Mephistopheles on a broomstick to the Brocken? Or did he *apport* Him from place to place through the fourth dimension, as Philip was *apported* from Gaza in the desert, more than twenty miles North to Azotus in Judea (*Acts, viii, 26, 40*), and as the aged Simeon was *apported* into the temple in Jerusalem so he could meet Jesus before he died, as was promised him by the Lord? (*St. Luke, ii, 26-7*). Only through the symbolic and spiritual interpretation of this incident can the flat contradictions in the accounts be reconciled and such questions as the above be satisfactorily answered. And intellectual honesty cannot ignore them.[7]

---

[7] Thus, they (the literal interpretations) degrade Jesus by showing Him, at the bidding of the Devil, going here and there on foolish and impossible errands; they present a picture of incidents in his life which could never occur in the life of any man. Hence the Temptation does not bring Jesus nearer to humanity, but removes him further away. It has no recorded effect on his later life on earth and therefore is a useless excrescence. . . . If we had to take the story literally, in our day, we should be compelled to think of it as a myth. . . . I take the view that what happened to Jesus took place, solely and only, in the innermost recesses of his soul" *Life of Christ*, Cain, 394-5.

It is because in this biblical version of the Candidate's testing Jesus represents the Neophyte, the spiritual Aspirant, the Climber, in whom the Light of the Spiritual Sun has begun to shine, that he seeks to leave the cities of the plain. He turns away from the attractions of the outer dead-level, physical world, and starts to climb the Mount of Attainment, symbolized by the climbing Goat of *Capricorn*, the tenth sign. This climb begins as soon as the Aspirant has been baptized with spiritual realization and is filled with a fervent desire for spiritual attainment. For few there be among sincere seekers who do not at some time have a Baptism of the Holy Ghost or a realization of oneness with the Divine, even though that heavenly consciousness opens only for a moment, just long enough for the "heavenly dove" to descend. Yet we seldom fully understand that our consciousness has momentarily touched or vibrated in harmony with the Christ within, although we are filled with His great desire to manifest through us.

The Aspirant thus often unknowingly enters upon the mystical "Way of the Cross" upon which he must meet and overcome all kinds of discouragements, obstacles and temptations; for he must be tested as to his sincerity, also as to which shall rule his life henceforth, the lusts of the flesh and the ambitions of the mind or the Inner Guidance of the Spirit.

That this period of testing or temptation is necessary for our spiritual unfoldment and the ultimate attainment of the Christ-consciousness is evidenced by the fact that we are "led *up* of the *Spirit* into the wilderness," not downward by the devil. This statement reveals the fact that the experience is a universal inner spiritual one and not an isolated historical incident. For it is inconceivable that God would tempt us to sin or evil, but that He does lead us up to a high state of consciousness where we can prove our sincerity. It also indicates that the Soul thus tested has reached that stage of unfoldment where it has recognized the Inner Guidance and has learned to be "led up of the Spirit," no matter how dreary or forbidding a wilderness is seen ahead.

After even the brief uplift, joy and ecstasy of the Baptism, the Spirit leads us back into the outer consciousness of our daily life, our duties and physical affairs, and the contrast is so great that life seems but a wilderness, uninviting, pathless and purposeless. We are led there not for the purpose of tempting us to fall and sin, but that we may therein put the new-found power of our realizations into manifestation in our lives. It is not what we merely *think of, assent to and approve of* that counts, but how much of those things *we manifest*. For, "He shall reward every man *according to his works*."[8] Like athletes we must exercise our spiritual muscles—powers of accomplishment—strengthen our minds, develop our wills and prove our ability to face and overcome all obstacles in our Path of Attainment.

As we have said elsewhere: "A wilderness is not a desert, for it may embrace beautiful mountains, forests and streams. It is simply a region that has been left to Nature and is uncultivated."[9] It may contain many treasures intended for us, but which only the determined and fearless Soul can find, he who persistently follows the Inner Guidance and is "led up of the Spirit." In this case we "fast" because we find the "fruits of the Spirit" which nourished our spiritual growth are now lacking, either because we have failed to cultivate them or because they have not yet come to fruition.

The fast lasts forty days because it is composed of four "cycles of completion" in earth conditions, 4 being the number of the earth plane and 10 the number of completion (4 x 10= 40).[9] The same fundamental symbol-

---

[8] *St. Matthew, XVI*, 27. *Romans, II*, 6. *Revelation, XX*, 12.
[9] *The Key to the Universe*, Curtiss 151, 135, 139.

ogy is found in the forty day fasts of Moses and Elias,
who also represented Sun-gods, and in the forty years of
wandering of the Children of Israel in the wilderness.

During these four cycles the Soul seems shut off from
the inflow of the light, life and love which it experienced
during the Baptism and must fast and be "an hungered,"
or subsist upon the spiritual food which it has already received and built into its consciousness and life. It thereby
proves that the Baptism brought an influx of real spiritual
substance and was not merely an emotional experience or
an intellectual conception of its possibility and desirability.

The fast we must endure is not because further spiritual
help is refused us, but because after the exaltation of the
Baptism we fall back into the consciousness of the personality and the chilling fogs of doubt or the skepticism
and ridicule of our family and friends, through which the
Christ-light cannot penetrate. It is much like the cloud of
depression which surrounds a suicide and prevents the
Invisible Helpers from reaching and helping him.[10] As *The
Voice of the Silence*[11] tells us: "Grey mists will overhang
its rough and stony height, and all be dark beyond." All
this creates a dense, heavy oppressive atmosphere—much
like the sudden drop in the barometer just before a storm—
which is very depressing to the Soul, and really tests our
attainment.

During this period of loneliness and hopelessness we
are apt to voice the complaint of St. Paul: "I find then
a law, that, when I would do good, evil is present with
me."[12] This is ever the cry of the newly awakened Soul
that is struggling to cast off the swaddling bands of old
material conceptions and habits which have so hampered
its fuller expression. Apparently the Soul is left alone, yet
just as it is necessary that a babe be weaned and learn
to feed from a nursing bottle, so with the Soul at this

---

[10] See *Realms of the Living Dead*, Curtiss, 152.
[11] Page 56.
[12] *Romans VII*, 21.

stage of its unfoldment. No longer is the spiritual food poured into the Aspirant like a mother's milk. The Divine Mother has prepared plenty of food, but he must now find and imbibe it for himself, yet never forget that the Divine Mother is watching over him, trying to teach him how to feed, and patiently waiting by his cradle for him to learn this lesson.

It is only after this long and seemingly hopeless fast that the temptation comes. Yet we should not be surprised, for it is an experience common to everyone at this stage of unfoldment. And it is consoling to know that: "There hath no temptation taken you but such as is common to man: but God is faithful, who will not suffer you to be tempted above that ye are able,[13] to bear."

As we have already said: "Here we find the Christ-man who has dedicated his life to humanity, driven *by the Spirit* into the wilderness. . . . Thus, they pass 4 cycles of fasting, first trying to feed their spiritual hunger with the joys of the material world, but finding that the mere possession of *things* can never satisfy the Soul-hunger. Then they enter upon a new day in which they realize the greatness of the mind and perhaps are swept away to the extreme of declaring that 'mind is all and all is mind.' They now seek in the intellectual conceptions of the mental realm, in subtle philosophies and metaphysical speculations, to appease the hunger of their Souls. But sooner or later their Souls find that they are still feeding on the husks and still fasting from that true spiritual food which alone can satisfy."

"They then seek satisfaction in the psychic phenomena which their intellectual research has brought to their attention. At first perhaps their hunger is appeased by the phenomena of seances, in messages and platitudes from their departed friends, in anything that will lift their consciousness above the material and mechanistic conception of life. Later this proves to be but a mental diversion, although it is a training which enables them to appreciate

---

[13] *I Corinthians, X*, 13.

the real spiritual Bread of life which must come from the Christ within and not from without, not even from their disembodied friends. Thus they pass the fourth cycle in proving that none of these things bring real Soul satisfaction. By this time they are 'an hungered' and only then do the angels (messengers of God, not disembodied mortals) come and minister unto them."[14] But only after the temptation has been passed and the tempter has left can the angels come and minister unto him. (*St. Matthew, iv*, 11).

Each of these four cycles lasts not merely ten mystical "days," but may continue for years or *until the lesson of each stage is learned* and the cycle (10) is completed. "Many sincere students are to be found in each of these cycles. But if they are all earnestly seeking spiritual food they are not to be condemned or even looked down upon by those who have taken a step higher. Perhaps no one Soul who has reached the fortieth day will pass through all the phases of fasting in one life, but every Soul will pass through either longer or shorter expressions of these periods. The day-periods are those in which enthusiasm fills the Soul and the things it feeds on seem all-satisfying for the time being; the night-periods are those in which the former food no longer satisfies and the Soul is truly hungry and unsatisfied."[14]

As we enter into this new Aquarian dispensation, the force poured out by the Water Bearer of that sign grows stronger and stronger and more nourishing until we feel within us a greater realization of the Christ and the power of love. Even if we do not fully understand it we feel a mighty urge to find God, and a mighty love which cries out for a closer touch with Him. For all those who look within and analyze their inner experiences carefully and without bias, instead of seeking as the materialists do "the living among the dead," will surely find the answering realization. Therefore, instead of seeking the living Christ among the cast-off grave clothes of old ideas and

---

[14] *The Key to the Universe*, Curtiss, 152-4.

former medieval misconceptions with which former ages clothed the Christ, let us seek for Him in our hearts. Then we must listen to His words and obey His guidance, even though it comes, as is so often the case, in a way that may seem but a shadow of spiritual realization passing over our minds or but a half remembered dream and we know not if it be but imagination. Yet we must be sure that it is not mere imagination and that it is the real Inner Guidance. When these vague questionings and chilling doubts arise we should not try to prolong our fast, but should cry out in our hearts: "Lord, what wouldst Thou have me to do? Show me Thy way !"

Although soundless and often wordless, the Inner Voice is always distinct to those who listen believingly and lovingly, since they have learned to know His voice and know that it comes from the Christ within. Some get confused because what seems to come to them in the Silence is simply a corroboration of their own desires.

To really hear the Christ thus speak within and guide us, we must first find Him in a realization of yearning love as the result of constant prayer and meditation upon Him as abiding within our hearts, not as a far-off Deity, but as an ever-present loving Friend, Guide and Counsellor who knows and understands our every need. For not one heart that loves Him and earnestly seeks His guidance shall fail to receive it. This Guidance is not limited to those who have passed "the temptation in the wilderness" and overcome all ordinary temptations and made great attainments, but will be given to *every* heart that opens itself to Him in loving faith and confidence, no matter what its stage of unfoldment and realization. "Him that cometh to me I will in no wise cast out."

Happy is he who has passed through the fast.

(To Be Concluded)

CHAPTER XVI

THE TEMPTATION IN THE WILDERNESS

PART II. THE TEMPTER

"And when the tempter came to him, he said, If thou be the Son of God, command that these stones be made bread. . . . Then the devil taketh him up into the holy city, and setteth him on a pinnacle of the temple, and saith unto him, If thou be the Son of God, cast thyself down. . . . Again the devil taketh him up into an exceeding high mountain, and sheweth him all the kingdoms of the world, and the glory of them; and saith unto him, All these things will I give thee, if thou wilt fall down and worship me." *St. Mathew, iv*, 3-9.

"There hath no temptation taken you but such as is common to man: but God is faithful, who will not suffer you to be tempted above that ye are able." *I Corinthians, x*, 13.

In studying the scriptures most people accept the statements at their face value and as historically accurate, much as children accept the story of Santa Claus and "Jack and the Beanstalk." This is largely due to the strong mental impressions made during childhood and to the fact that in later years they have made no serious study of the story with the analytical faculty of a well trained adult mind. In the story of the Temptation, if we assume it as a physical and historical incident, we unthinkingly assume several other things some of which, when once pointed out, few enlightened minds are willing to accept as literal.

In the first place we rightly assume that the Spirit of man is something apart from and superior to the physical man; that it can direct and guide the latter in all things, even into a desert where he will have to fast for forty days and nights. If we are willing to admit that this is true of Jesus, then the same law applies to us, for He "was in all points tempted like as we are, yet without sin." We therefore have no excuse for not seeking the guidance of the Spirit within and following wherever it leadeth.

Next we find that we have also assumed that there is an objective and physical embodiment or arch spirit of evil called the devil, who had the entrée into the Temple in the Holy City and could lead Jesus up "into an exceeding high mountain." Then we also have to assume that Jesus was willing to follow such a being without question or challenge. Such conceptions few thinkers are ready to accept. For even in the ordinary investigation of psychic phenomena one of the lessons soon learned is that entities in the invisible may be either helpful or harmful, truthful or untruthful; may be the ones they claim to be or they may be imposters who fraudulently impersonate persons whom they think the inquirer will accept.

The *Bible* tells us that Satan himself can impersonate an angel of light.[1] Therefore all experienced scientific investigators are taught to test and discriminate as to the claims of the entity who is manifesting. St. Paul had this same difficulty in contacting those in the unseen. And the rule he laid down still holds good today. "Try the spirits whether they are of God."[2] That is, all should be challenged "In the name of the living Christ,"[3] to answer truthfully as to their identity, as we pointed out in Chapter II.

Why, then, if the story is literal, did not Jesus recognize the devil at once for what he was and refuse to have anything to do with him, much less follow him blindly into a trap? Or if He did recognize the devil, why did He

---

[1] *II Corinthians, XI,* 14.
[2] *St. John, IV,* 1.
[3] For details see *Realms of the Living Dead*, Curtiss, 226-7.

take such a chance in following such a being all alone in the wilderness when He was already weakened by His long fast? If He was the Son of God, *why should He submit Himself to temptation at all?* Why did He not avoid it in the first place by refusing to follow the devil?

None of these simple questions can be answered satisfactorily from the literal interpretation of the story. But once we understand that the whole story is an allegory of *an inner spiritual experience* which every Soul must undergo at a certain stage of its spiritual unfoldment, as explained in *Part I* of this topic, then all the seemingly preposterous incidents fall logically into their natural order.

Nor should these experiences be regarded merely as optical and auditory hallucinations induced by the excitement of the psychic adventure, the darkness, the loneliness and the long fast, as some modern psychologists would have us believe.[4] For they are actual and very real psychical experiences which beset every Soul as its newly awakened or newly realized super-conscious mind or spiritual consciousness is besieged; when all the lower qualities of the animal man are stirred into activity in the subconscious mind and are anxious and determined to retain their mastery over the personality and use its newly acquired gifts for their own gratification.

Although the wilderness referred to is not an objective acreage of ground near Nazareth or Jerusalem—where there is no wilderness—it is nevertheless very real to the consciousness of the Neophyte. For it is a mental state into which his consciousness is plunged as it descends from the exalted condition it experienced during the Baptism. The Soul that has been filled with a divine enthusiasm and is hungering and thirsting after righteousness is plunged into its old habits of thought and life which, by contrast with the illumination of the Baptism, now seem but a moral and spiritual desolation. Then doubt as to the reality of the Baptism arises, and despair

---

[4] *La folie de Jesus,* Binet-Sangle, 356.

of ever being able to manifest in the wilderness of life, the divine realization so recently attained. Then comes the temptation, a wholly subjective, but very real experience. Yet we need not be discouraged if we remember the law, for the law "will not suffer you to be tempted above that ye are able to bear."

As we have said elsewhere: "Until the pupil has cleansed his heart of self-seeking he is open to the attacks from the first mentioned (evil) source. You are never safe if the devil—the power of all that works against God or good—can find a single vibration of personal ambition or selfishness through which he can enter. As the Higher Self can communicate only through vibrations similar to Himself, so the devil can tempt, and can lead astray and deceive, only over vibrations similar to his own. . . . Every Neophyte is led by the Spirit—the Higher Self—into a mental wilderness where, alone in the dreary wastes of physical experience, he is tempted by the devil of his own creation. The fasting for forty days is that period during which he must abstain from his old thoughts and habits, must cease to seek for outward help and learn to seek within; must turn to his Father-in-heaven, listen to the voice of his Higher Self and refuse longer to be guided by physical vibrations. . . . When it sees that no help can reach him. . . . It is always here that the devil meets each Soul and tempts. In other words, long ere he has found that perfect vibration of love through which alone he can hear his Higher Self speak, the evil genius, or those akin to him—the Masters of the Shadow—can speak and tempt over vibrations of selfishness and self-indulgence. This selfishness, indulgence and ambition often require a long time to be transmuted into love and service for others, for they have a way of hiding behind all sorts of sophistries."[5]

"Up to this point the pupil has had to contend with but petty temptations and appetites, but now, having consciously taken an advanced step, through prayer and fast-

---

[5] See *The Voice of Isis*, Curtiss, 290-1-2-3.

ing, he has deliberately entered the wilderness to be tempted."[5]

In the mystery schools the candidate had to pass the tests of the four elements, earth, water, air and fire. And Jesus had to pass the same tests. To assuage His hunger after His long fast He is tempted to use his newly won powers to transmute physical materials—representing *earth* and *water*—to satisfy the elemental urge of hunger. The second test of self-righteousness, also *fear* and safety, was to be passed by invoking the spirits of the *air*, "lest at any time thou dash thy foot against a stone." The third test was that of ambition, which is always associated with *fire*, from chemical oxidation to the generation of steam and electricity. In our interpretation it is the activities of the rational mind of the personality, the desires of the flesh—acting through the subconscious mind—[6]and the destructive emotions, which constitute the Tempter, personified in the *Gospel* story as the devil. In a three-fold manner—body, mind, spirit—it tempts us to enter upon our spiritual inheritance and use our newly found spiritual attainments for the exaltation of the personality without further preparation and growth. It tempts us to satisfy our physical needs and bodily appetites, to court applause and attain dominion, and to presume upon our spiritual protection;

While nearly all religions teach that God manifests as a trinity[7]—Father-Mother-Son or Father, Son and Holy Ghost—we often overlook the fact that the opposite pole from God—called the devil—also manifests as a trinity. This negative or evil trinity is commonly termed "the World, the Flesh and the Devil." And just as the Divine Trinity is embodied within each heart for us to respond and react to, so is the evil trinity. The result in your life depends upon which of these trinities you respond to most frequently. Usually your life is a mixture of reactions to both. With those who are not consciously striving for

---

[6] For further details see *The Voice of Isis*, Curtiss, 167-8.

[7] See lesson on *The Trinity*, also *The Truth About Evolution and the Bible*, Curtiss, 175.

spiritual attainment, the reactions to the lower trinity usually predominate.

In analyzing the lower trinity as we have the higher[7] that which comprises the "World" is made up of those things which the great majority of mankind strive for to attain success in the eyes of the world. Those things include wealth, position, prestige and power: all those things which exalt the personal self.

The second phase of the negative trinity—the "Flesh"— is composed of all those God-given animal functions, appetites, reactions and "conditioned reflexes" which so largely control the animal organism, both for its welfare and its reproduction. Naturally these are not evil in themselves. Like the things of the "World," the things of the "Flesh" are evil only when they are allowed to dominate both body and mind, to the detriment of our spiritual unfoldment.

The third phase of the negative trinity the—"Devil"— is composed of all those negative thoughts, desires, acts and emotions—reinforced by the influx of similar forces from the astral world—which are definitely destructive, and whose results naturally produce a veritable "hell on earth" in our lives. Therein we must "burn" as with fire and brimstone until those disintegrating vibrations have been burned out or else have been neutralized by the constructive vibrations of the Christ-force or "fire of the Lord." Thus are we cleansed by the mystical "blood of the Christ" or His spiritual life-force.

The unspiritualized personality is cynical and pessimistic. It challenges us to demonstrate powers which we have just glimpsed and as yet have scarce realized, much less learned to direct and use. It says to us: "If your inner experience was a reality; if your divine possibilities, your dream of Divinity, has so uplifted you and baptized you with an added influx of spiritual power, let us see you prove it. Command that these 'stones,' these commonplace, everyday duties which are the foundation of your life-activities in the world, be made into bread. Command that they exalt you above your fellow men. Demand that they bring you wealth, position, power, fame or whatever will satisfy your hunger for worldly aggrandizement and attainment in the eyes of the world."

Such things are not evil in themselves, in fact, they are often worthy incentives to progress and the development of our innate talents. They become evil only when they divert us from the further development of the spiritual powers with which we have recently been baptized.

As we have said elsewhere: "The first temptation coming from the side of evil is generally that of Power. The devil says: 'Command and demand all that you need. You are not sick or hungry. You are the Christ. Therefore command that the earth (which karmic law has bereft of Soul-nourishment and spiritual satisfaction) shall be turned into bread to satisfy your physical wants, even though the very eating thereof binds you tighter to the wheel of physical existence.' "[5]

If we are ready to meet this test with the answer that Jesus gave—"Man shall not live by bread alone, but by every word that proceedeth out of the mouth of God"— it will show that our Baptism has revealed to us one of the most essential and fundamental of realizations. It will prove that we have realized that *man is not a mere mortal* but is a *Spiritual Being*, manifesting only temporarily through a body of flesh; that while the body requires physical food—symbolized by bread—our finer bodies require other food, namely, mental and spiritual food. Therefore the mere turning of stones into bread, or the mere attainment of physical things—possessions, honors, position etc.—or even the gratification of all our physical desires, can never fully feed or satisfy us.

Our mind still craves to understand that mystical Word or the manifested Law of God if it is to comprehend what life on earth really means, and what life in the flesh is for.[8] We must realize that ultimately the Spirit must master and purify both body and mind and so uplift every earthly condition as to bring forth and manifest on earth the beauty and joy of heaven. To accomplish this we must

---

[8] For details see *Why Are We Here?*, Curtiss.

learn to tune in on the spiritual vibrations "that proceeded — or are broadcast—out of the mouth of God."

When our illumination has revealed this basic fact, all material things and attainments are seen in their proper place, as merely avenues of expression or useful instruments by means of which the raw materials of earth conditions may be moulded and used to manifest more of the Divine or Spiritual Self who is now gaining greater expression from within. Hence, useful and even necessary as they may be in their proper place until man has manifested his Godhood, they now have no power to tempt us from our allegience to the Divine Guidance within.

The allegorical nature of the second temptation is clearly evident, for, as we have said before, (a) there is no "exceeding high mountain" in the region indicated: and (b) there is no mountain anywhere on earth from which Jesus could be shown "all the kingdoms of the world," or even the various provinces of Palestine; and (c) it would have been impossible for Jesus to have been set upon "a pinnacle of the temple" in the populous city of Jerusalem without having been seen by thousands, and without having been brought down by the authorities. Moreover, there were no pinnacles on the temple at Jerusalem, as it was either dome-shaped or else flat-topped after the Egyptian style.

"The second temptation comes in the form of self-righteousness. The devil takes the hungry Soul up into a high place, up to the very pinnacle of the Temple (body), and there shows how the Soul has conquered the flesh, growing holier than others by the control of the lower appetites; how it has reached the gates of the Holy City and has become a guide and example for many less holy and less pure followers. The devil declares: 'Thou, if thou be the Son of God[9] (or if you be the Christ as you have affirmed), cast thyself down, for you can do what a lesser

---

[9] When we have been purified and blessed by the Baptism, have heard the Voice and experienced the descent of the Heavenly Dove (Holy Ghost), we have reached a pinnacle or our first great initiation, and in the Mystery Schools are technically called a "Son of God."

Soul could not do without sin. That which would be a sin
in one not placed so high on a pinnacle of the Temple is
for you but a certain license earned because of your holiness.' For it is written: 'He shall give his angels charge
concerning thee lest at any time thou shalt dash thy foot
against a stone.' Therefore you can do that which would
be a sin in others."[5]

This temptation is also one of fear to trust the divine
protection of angelic forces promised Him. It is also a
test whether He would presume on such divine protection while violating a physical law. The answer given by
Jesus—"Thou shalt not tempt the Lord thy God"—at once
reveals the fallacies of both aspects of this temptation. No
matter what our advancement or what pinnacle of attainment we may have reached, we must not "tempt" or trifle
with the laws of God; for the angels will not bear us up
from reaping the consequences—dashing our foot against
a stone—when we violate the law.

With this clearly in mind, such temptations to self indulgence lose their power, unless we should be so foolish
as to think that we could give way to them and not have
to pay the price. When once we realize that the Christ
abides within us and that if we trust and follow Him He
will guide us in all the manifestations of the Law of our
Good, no earthly promises of power or allurements of the
flesh can tempt us to "tempt" or trifle with the Law of our
Good. Only then are we safe.

"The third temptation is one of Ambition. This comes
only to the Soul who has climbed the mountains of spiritual understanding. The Neophyte has painfully climbed
the mountain, has entered the Silence, has heard the Voice
and seen with his spiritual eyes. He has gained certain
psychic powers, and lo! all the kingdoms of the world
and the glory thereof are spread before his sight. His evil
genius points out that by his awakened psychic powers
he can gain the whole world; that men will bow down to
him and give him fame and glory because he is a little in
advance of the average; that he can charge large sums for

interviews, psychic readings, courses, etc.; can be heralded from place to place, be interviewed by the newspapers and receive much public acclaim. All this is a very real and terrible temptation, and one understood only by those who have stood upon the 'exceeding high mountain' of attainment, and in their Soul-vision have actually seen the kingdoms of the world at their feet, who have heard the tempter say 'All these things will I give thee if thou wilt fall down and worship me.' For this temptation cannot come until the Neophyte has approached the mountain top."[5]

The reply of Jesus: "Get thee hence, Satan: for it is written, Thou shalt worship the Lord thy God, and Him only shalt thou serve," is a complete protection from this temptation. While at a certain stage of unfoldment we need a certain amount of ambition to spur us on to ever greater attainment, yet that ambition should not be for personal aggrandizement, but ambition to become more nearly perfect instruments through which the Spiritual Man within can serve the Lord God or help to perfect the expression of the Law of Love, Harmony and Co-operation here on earth. "An understanding of these temptations should make each one judge leniently the shortcomings and failures of those who have fallen, and not condemn them. Let everyone cultivate in his own garden the 'fruits of the Spirit,' namely, love, joy, peace, gentleness, goodness, faith, meekness and temperance. . . . The cultivation of the fruits of the Spirit will leave you no time to see the shortcomings of others."[5]

The days of temptation, trial and tests are now upon us, not only as individuals, but as nations and races. The wars due at the close of each Great Age are upon us and the cataclysms are long overdue. They have been held back and held back through the ardent prayers of the Elect[10] that humanity might have a little longer time in which to make the much needed advance in national and

---

[10] See *The Philosophy of War*, Curtiss, 100-106, also *Prayers of the O.C.M.*, Curtiss, 14.

international brotherhood, harmony and cooperation, but they cannot be held back much longer. Any day now may witness exceptionally great storms, quakes, tidal waves or other disasters on land and sea. Therefore we should all pray daily, especially during the coming few months, both the *Prayer for World Harmony*[10] that further wars be avoided, and also that the coming conditions may so awaken the hearts of humanity to a realization of their touch with the Divine and an understanding of their dependence upon God, that the readjustments of physical conditions which are now due shall come as cleansing blessings and not as hopeless disasters.

Pray that those who are ready for realization may be enlightened; that those who are needed to help during the coming conditions shall be placed in circumstances where they can help most effectively, and that those who should learn their needed lessons in the higher realms, those who are a drag on civilization or who retard the reign of peace and brotherhood, may pass on with as little suffering as possible and be prepared to come back as helpers instead of retarders of the public good.

Remember that wars and cataclysms do not come as a punishment, but as an inevitable reaping in exact justice of the conditions sown by those very Souls who are now involved in them. It is a cleansing process which will prepare the better and more advanced conditions which the Aquarian Age must usher in. Those who are on the Lord's (Law's) side; those who pass their "temptation in the wilderness," who correlate through prayer, meditation and service with the constructive currents of reconstruction now being poured out, will be preserved and used as instruments to help adjust subsequent conditions and usher in the reign of peace, harmony, co-operation and righteousness, unless their services are more needed in the higher realms.

Happy is he who has foiled the Tempter.

CHAPTER XVII

THE MARRIAGE FEAST IN CANA

> "And on the third day there was a marriage in Cana
> of Galilee; and the mother of Jesus was there: and both
> Jesus was called and his disciples. . . . And there were
> there six waterpots of stone (for the purification of the
> Jews). . . . Jesus saith unto them, Fill the waterpots with
> water. . . . when the ruler of the feast had tasted the water
> that was made wine,. . . . saith unto him. . . . thou had
> kept the good wine until now." *St. John, ii,* 1-10.

The first miracle performed by Jesus was the turning of
water into wine at the marriage feast in Cana. This marks
the actual beginning of His ministry; It is therefore much
more important than the mere record of a social event in
the life of His neighbors. And the spiritual interpretation of
the event reveals its importance in the spiritual evolution
of man. *Dionysus,* called "lord of the Vine," performed
the same miracle.

This marriage feast symbolizes the union or "marriage"
of the human personality with the overshadowing Spiritual
Self—the Soul-marriage—or the union of the human and
the Divine through the power of the Christ. It also symbolizes the spiritual oneness which results when the Christ
within presides over the marriage of those who are true
spiritual mates.

The unfolding of the spiritual nature of man and his
advance toward Christhood is not achieved by the mere
mechanical process of growth and evolution. Nor is it imposed upon us by God or by superhuman or angelic Beings
or powers in the super-physical worlds. There is an essential part that we ourselves must play.

The most essential step is that we shall consciously seek to unfold, correlate with, and then bring into manifestation in our daily lives, the power of the Christ within to transmute all that is low and common into that which is high and spiritual. And it is only the miracle of the Christ-force in action in the life that can change what were only the Waters of Purification into the Wine of Divine Life. The truth that merely cleansed and clarified is changed into the truth that inspires.

The Lord of the Feast is the Spiritual Self. For it is only he who recognizes that through the power of the Christ within, the water that merely satisfied the animal thirst has been transmuted into the wine of exaltation that now satisfies the spiritual thirst. The wine or spiritual nourishment created by the Christ-force is far more powerful than the ordinary wine of physical satisfaction. It is the spiritual joy that wells up within when the water of outer conditions has been transmuted by the Christ into ecstasy of the Soul. Naturally this wine comes last, after the lesser joys have been experienced and found no longer satisfying.

It is significant that the mother of Jesus and His disciples were present at the feast. The mother is the universal symbol of mother-force of Divine Love, while the disciples symbolize our higher faculties which have acknowledged the leadership and are trying to follow and serve the Christ within. Naturally, only when both these powers are present under the prescribed conditions can the first miracle of the Christ be performed.

But first the six stone waterpots must be filled with fresh water. These represent the six major occult centers of the body. In the unregenerate and animal man these are lacking spiritual fire, cold as stones. They are "dead in sin" and minister only to the animal nature. They are the wells of physical pleasures at which the lower self drinks and makes merry. But there comes a time when their forces no longer satisfy. The thirsty Soul craves something new and truly satisfying. Then the yearning mother-love appeals to the Christ within for help (*St. John, ii, 1*), well-knowing that only His force can transmute the pleasures of the senses and replace them with the wine of spiritual joy that shall fully satisfy the Lord of the Feast.

But in addition to the inner spiritual development there is another important service which the advanced awakened Soul can do for the Christ and the Race, not only spiritually, but to advance the Race in the arts and sciences. That work is to make conditions in the family life so spiritual, harmonious and happy that spiritually advanced Souls, who became experts in the arts and sciences in past incarnations, will be attracted to the family and be given incarnation immaculately or "without spot"[1] or thought of something impure connected with the physical union necessary for their incarnation.

Only when such conditions of purity of thought, peace, love and happiness are provided can the many advanced Souls waiting incarnation return to carry out their mission. In *Revelation (vi,* 9-11) the advanced Souls are represented as the martyrs and saints who have waited for ages "under the altar" for "yet a little season." They cry out, "How long, O Lord, holy and true" before they can be given their "white robes," that is, their pure and immaculately conceived bodies in which to incarnate that they may accomplish their great mission of helping to uplift and redeem mankind and the planet.

Naturally, such immaculate conceptions can be created only between those who are true spiritual complements or mates; those whose marriage was indeed "made in heaven" because they were already one in heaven before they incarnated; those whom "from the beginning of the creation God made them male and female." While any man and woman may conceive a child, unless they are true spiritual mates they will be united only on the physical plane and will give incarnation only to such lesser developed Souls as are willing to incarnate under conditions

---

[1] For details see Chapter III.

that are not immaculate. For the more spiritually advanced Souls or the so-called Saints, will not incarnate unless the conditions they require are provided. These conditions necessitate the blending of both the beliefs and ideals and also the spiritual consciousness of the mates, in addition to the union of their bodies.

Here we must distinguish between the spiritual force of true love and the force of mere animal desire (passion), through which love finds bodily expression. Love is an expression of the Spirit, while lust is a craving of animal organism for unlimited sex gratification. Love is unselfish and kind; lust is selfish and cruel. Lust seeks fulfillment of sensation regardless of the other's happiness. Love attains fulfillment of spirit in the oneness of union. Lust craves excitement; love brings peace and tranquility. Lust seeks to subordinate the Spirit; love exalts it. In lust there is a hopeless dependence on a bodily organism. In love there is dependence on Spirit. Lust leads to domination and unhappy complications; love leads to freedom and joy.

As we have said elsewhere: "But in striving to cultivate this love, care must be taken that the sensation of mere physical attraction or magnetism shall not be cultivated under the false name of love. The love we refer to is a realization of impersonal and all-embracing Divine Love, the purest, most god-like and holy vibration to which the Soul of man can respond."[2]

If this law were more widely understood, and all listened to the Inner Guidance, and only true mates were married, there would be no need for such propositions as "companionate marriages," much less for "trial marriages." These at best are but palliatives, the attempts of well-meaning but unenlightened persons to help to remedy the deplorable conditions that exist between the sexes today because of the false teaching as to sex; because the *essentially spiritual nature of the sex function* when used immaculately, has been overlooked or misunderstood.

---

[2] *The Message of Aquaria*, Curtiss, 154.

As marriage today is so often looked upon as a mere physical union for the unlimited gratification of animal passion, it is no wonder that the Lord of the Feast cries out that they have no wine; that the six waterpots are filled only with water, but made turbid and stagnant by the impurities of mind and body with which man has defiled it.

If at every marriage feast the Christ and His disciples— our higher faculties—were consciously invited guests, and if the twain who are one flesh would follow the injunction of the Divine Mother: "Whatsoever He saith unto you, do it," then the waters of earthly union could be turned into the wine of immortal, Spiritual Love. But first the "six waterpots of stone" must be emptied of their old water—their old conceptions, ideas, and impure thoughts and vibrations concerning the nature of the marriage feast—ere they can be "filled to the brim" by the disciples and be prepared for the first miracle of the Christ to take place in each heart, the miracle of transmutation.

When the two who are one have consumed the wine of gladness poured out in their love and harmony during the early ecstasies of their union, and they begin to cry for more wine; only after they have done their best to cleanse their waterpots, by purifying both their minds and their bodies, and have reached up and contacted the Divine Mother—especially through the sacred process of bringing a Soul into incarnation—only then can they hear the mystical command of the Christ spoken in their hearts: "Draw out now, and bear unto the governor of the feast," the Spiritual Self. Only under such conditions can the Christ-power within them turn the waters into wine that shall satisfy the thirst of the Soul for self-completion through union with the Divine. For the vague memory of the state of oneness in the higher realms still persists and urges the Soul on to the realization of that union in the flesh.

This miracle cannot be accomplished by the human personality alone, for the best it has is its six pots of water, even if that water be pure. The fundamental spiritual thirst for the Divine cannot be satisfied by mere sexual union, but only by the Wine of the Spirit which has been blessed by the Christ. How then are we to satisfy the cry of the guests the—animal desires—for more wine? First by recognizing the power of the Christ to purify and sanctify the water in the pots, which at best can quench the thirst of the animal only. But through His power we can transmute it into the Wine of the Spirit which will not only satisfy the Soul's thirst for spiritual oneness, but will give the animal nature greater satisfaction than it enjoyed before, because it has partaken of a spiritual oneness in addition to the physical.

This realization is, indeed, an advanced step in spiritual attainment, but it is one that is destined to be increasingly frequent during this new Aquarian Age, the age of miracles of the Christ in manifestation. We can begin to prepare ourselves for this miracle by recognizing the *spiritual basis* of the sex relation. For in man its use should transcend its use in animals to as great a degree as the Soul of man transcends the animal.

As we advance in spiritual unfoldment we can reach a point where this miracle of turning the water into wine is possible because God has given to each Soul the inner power of understanding and appreciating the significance and value of those mysteries of God which can be only spiritually discerned.

The instinctive memory of the oneness in the higher realms of real spiritual mates is inherent in every Soul. And it is this memory, even though vague and unrecognized, that is the basis of the instinct—often expressed as jealousy—for the exclusive possession, each of the other, between mates, even among the most primitive people.

Man and woman can learn many lessons and make great progress in spiritual unfoldment while striving alone, but for the supreme accomplishment and final test of the humanity of this globe each must learn the supreme lesson of Unity in Duality, hand in hand with his or her true spiritual mate in some incarnation.

Striving alone through many incarnations, isolated perhaps in a cave, in the forest or in a monastery has brought a few to a high stage of unfoldment, although often clouded by spiritual selfishness and self-righteousness. But even when such a high stage is attained it is but a one-sided development, and the one reaching it must reincarnate in conditions which seem far beneath him in order to learn the lesson of Unity in Duality with his mate. Or else he must wait for many ages in the higher realms until his mate has reached the same stage of unfoldment as himself ere they can go on from there hand in hand to learn the lessons that can be learned only side by side. Such Souls often incarnate alone and with a great distaste for marriage, for they are closely in touch with their true mate who is not in incarnation and so feel little need of a physical mate.

As man absorbs the Water of Life poured out upon him during this Aquarian Age there must be an awakening of thousands of couples whom God hath joined "from the beginning of creation," and a realization of what their Unity in Duality signifies in their lives and the life of humanity as a whole. These couples will constitute those who are called on the first day of the marriage feast. And in that day woe unto those who forget to invite the Divine Mother and the Christ to their feast and join themselves to one who is not their true mate.

If those who are contemplating the momentous step of marriage will go into the inner sanctuary of their hearts and pray to the Father for guidance, shutting out all thought of sex and worldly considerations, they will receive their light and guidance. Or if they wait a little while, events will so shape themselves as clearly to point out the way. Or if they separate from each other for a short time and pray for guidance, if they are mates they will hear the voice of the heart which cannot be stilled, calling for the other, and life will be tasteless and dreary until they are again together.

But if they are not mates the separation will bring a

great feeling of relief, and they will look back upon their association as but a physical attraction, a wild temptation, or a karmic whirlwind due to mistaken relations set up in the past, but whose tendency to repeat they automatically feel, but need not express.

And if they are brave enough to accept the answer when in the negative and determine not to marry, then outer events will soon transpire in such a way as to confirm their decision as correct. But if they are already married to the wrong one, they must also seek in the same way for guidance as to how best to work out the problem in peace and harmony for the best good of all so that never more will they have to go over it again. Thus they will work out the Karma of the mistake here and now and be free all the sooner for the Great Law to join them to their true mates.[3] But if they refuse to do this they will have to repeat it all in another life.

Those who have, not only a mental conception of the law of Unity in Duality, but who have a clear inner realization as to their true mates, are symbolized by those who are called on the second day of the marriage feast, while those called on the third day are those advanced Souls who have reached the awakening of the true spiritual illumination or the opening of the Third Eye.

As Jesus, or the Christ-man, is represented as performing the first miracle at the marriage feast, so He is represented as unrolling before St. John the great panorama of the book of *Revelation*. Therein is described the woman who was "arrayed in purple and scarlet, and decked with gold and precious stones and pearls. . . . That sitteth upon many waters,"[4] and upon whose forehead was written, "The Mother of Harlots and abominations of the earth." To one who reads understandingly, this horrid picture is easily recognized as the synthesized thought-form that is the natural result of the wrong teach-

---

[3] See chapter on "Marriage and Divorce" in *Letters from the Teacher*, Curtiss, Vol. II.

[4] *Revelation*, XVII, 4-1-9-15.

ings and impure and perverted use of sex, even among those mistaken ones who think that for their own salvation they must put it aside and call it evil. The seven mountains on which she sits are the seven centers of the bodies of those whose perverted ideas of sex nourish her and prolong her reign. "The waters which thou sawest, where the woman sitteth, are peoples, and multitudes, and nations, and tongues."[4]

Those who compose these multitudes are all who look up to sex as something evil and vile, as a mere physical union for the gratification of animal passion, or at best a temptation. And as they raise their eyes to the seven hills, or begin to be aware of their higher centers whence should come their strength, they see only the scarlet woman and are appalled. For they begin to realize that the great harlot is indeed "drunken with the blood of the saints" or the life-force which the sincere and saintly, but mistaken, ones themselves have poured out and polluted by their wrong thought concerning it in many incarnations.

The beast, which "was and is not" which carried the scarlet woman and lifted her as on the highest mountains of Earth, is the monstrous thought-form which has been created by the basically mistaken idea taught by many that sex is but a function of the beast and that it cannot be an avenue for the expression of pure love and the equalizing of the magnetic and spiritual forces which shall make the twain one flesh.

Once we have grasped the idea of the *spiritual basis of sex* and learned to look upon it in purity of thought as a sacred feast to which we should invite both the Divine Mother and the Christ, then we can begin to make that old misconception "desolate and naked and shall eat her flesh, and burn her with fire."[5] In other words, our purified ideas shall strip the old false conception of its garments of prudery and sanctimonious self-righteousness and leave it naked or revealed for what it is, a vile and beastly misconception and a parody of God. Then we

[5] *Revelation, XVII*, 16.

shall begin to consume it and burn it with the divine Fire of the Lord.

Those who have grasped this basic idea and by the power of the Christ within have begun to manifest it in their lives, will be among those needed to help purify and redeem the Earth for the New Age. Hence these will be the ones who will pass in safety through the cleansing cataclysms now beginning on Earth. For they are the ones who can say with *St. John*: "I saw a new heaven and a new earth: for the first heaven and the first earth were passed away." And they shall see "the holy city, new Jerusalem, coming down from God out of heaven, prepared as a bride adorned for her husband."[6]

Happy is he who has attended the Marriage Feast.

---

[6] *XXI*, 1-2

CHAPTER XVIII

THE BETRAYAL

"And forthwith he (Judas) came to Jesus and said, Hail, master (Rabbi); and kissed him. . . . Then Judas, which had betrayed him. . . . repenteth himself, and brought again the thirty pieces of silver. . . . and he cast down the pieces of silver in the temple. . . . and went out and hanged himself." *St. Matthew, xxvi, 49, xxvii, 3, 5.*

"When at midnight *Aries*, the Lamb, reaches the nadir or lowest point of the zodiac, the sign *Leo*—the Lion of the tribe of Judah or Judas—is 30° above the horizon. Hence Judas is said to give the Lamb the traitor's kiss for the 30 pieces of silver or its 30° of light. As Leo disappears it is said to have cast down its '30 pieces of silver' or its light and disappeared below the horizon, or is said to have 'hung' itself." *Appendix A.*

Perhaps there is no place in the *Gospels*, except the flight and massacre, where the historical inaccuracies and discrepancies become such actual contradictions as to facts, or are better illustrated, than in the story of Judas, and where the symbolic interpretation is the only completely satisfactory explanation of such contradictions.

In the first place, there was no need for the betrayal, much less for the priests to pay Judas for it. Jesus had gone openly to the synagogue many times (see *Matthew, xii, 9; Luke, vi, 6; xiii, 10; Mark, iii, 1*) and publicly taught therein, as well as in other public places. And only just before the betrayal He had made a triumphal entry into Jerusalem. In view of the above we can hardly imagine Judas having the effrontery to ask payment for the betrayal. Nor can we imagine the priests paying thirty pieces of silver for the betrayal or identification of a well known figure who could easily have been picked up at any of His public appearances. Jesus Himself pointed this out when He said: "When I was daily in the temple with you, ye stretched forth no hands against me: but this is your hour." (*St. Luke, xxii,* 53).

Secondly, there was no need for Jesus' arrest so late at night when He could as easily have been taken at any time during the day. And thirdly, why should Jesus choose such a character as Judas for a disciple when He knew long beforehand that he would become a traitor? (*St. Luke, vi,* 16). Or why should Jesus have given Judas a sop and allowed him to dip into the dish with Himself, when He had already told His disciples that Judas was a devil? (*St. John, vi,* 70). Since Jesus knew of Judas' intention long in advance, why did He do nothing to restrain him from such a traitorous act? It was Jesus' failure to act on His advanced knowledge that permitted Judas to complete the deed, altho Jesus must have known also that Judas would hang himself and thus seemingly forfeit his eternal salvation. In fact, it is difficult to understand why such a treacherous character was introduced into the story.

It is in the description of the event by the two authors (*St. Matthew* and *St. Paul*) that the direct contradiction occurs. In *St. Matthew (xxvii,* 3, 5) we are told that when Judas repented he brought back the thirty pieces of silver and cast them down at the feet of the priests. But in *Acts* (*i, 17*) we are told that Judas did not bring it back, but took the money and "purchased a field with the reward of his iniquity." In *St. Matthew (xxvii,* 5) we are told that Judas "went out and hanged himself," and that the priests took the money and bought "the potter's field, to bury strangers in."

In *Acts (i, 18),* however, we are told that Judas did not hang himself, but died from an abdominal rupture due to a fall. "And falling headlong, he burst asunder in the midst, and all his bowels gushed out. *And it was known to all the dwellers at Jerusalem.*"

These contradictions have caused heated controversies among scholars for generations as to whether Judas was an historical character or was introduced to represent the Jewish people, which were held by the early Christian Church to be responsible for the death of their Savior, Jesus. To reconcile these two versions physically we must assume that if Judas did buy the land with the silver, he must have sold it at once for the same amount of cash, which in an Oriental country is extremely unlikely. Also, if the account of his death given in *Acts* is true we are forced to the gruesome and altogether improbable alternative that his body was allowed to hang until it was so putrified that the neck gave way and allowed the body to "fall headlong," for there is no record of the body's having been cut down. In such a state of disintegration it is quite possible that when the body struck the earth the gas distended abdomen might easily have "burst asunder in the midst, and all his bowels gushed out."

Some apologists for Judas hold that he had seen Jesus perform so many miracles that he thought that Jesus would perform another rather than be captured. Thus Jesus would escape and Judas would still have the silver. The disciples looked to Jesus to fulfill the prophecies as the Messiah. They naturally expected that He would set up a kingdom and reign as a temporal monarch. But Jesus had told them that was not His mission.[1] The disciples were naturally disappointed, especially Peter and Judas. Judas thought that Jesus would easily prove His Messiahship or else His false pretensions would be revealed. Only when the miracle failed to appear did he realize what a terrible thing he had done, and tried to make amends. Nevertheless he has come down to us in history as the incarnation of base ingratitude, avariciousness and treachery.

---

[1] *St. Luke*, IX, 22.

But this apology for Judas and his motives fails to solve the problems of (a) why Jesus chose one whom He knew would be a traitor[2] and whom He had called a devil, to be a disciple; (b) why one author says Judas brought back the silver and another says he used it "to purchase a field[3] and (c) why one says he hung himself and the other says he fell to the ground dead.[3] Evidently the literal interpretation cannot solve these problems, and hence it is untenable to an honest mind.

Astronomically we have shown[4] that Judas (*Leo*) gives the Lamb (*Aries*) the traitor's kiss by bestowing its 30° of light. Also, since *Leo* is the House of the Sun, when Judas plans to betray Jesus he is represented as being with Him in the upper chamber,[5] the home of the Spiritual Sun, and "dipping into the dish" with the Christ, as *Leo* dips into the dish of the zodiac with *Aries*, the Lamb.

If we interpret this incident symbolically and apply it to our personality all becomes clear. Judas symbolizes that tendency of the human personality to grasp everything it can for itself or in some way turn everything to its own advantage. This is a natural and normal instinct of the animal for self-preservation. But when carried to excess and uncontrolled by ideals it becomes greed and avarice. And once we allow greed and avarice to rule our lives they will lead us to betray our ideals of Christhood for their temporary satisfaction. We know they are there, hence must be on our guard.

In His reaction to the betrayal Jesus gave us a perfect example of spiritual courage and fidelity to principle. For Jesus well knew what was in store for Him. "Behold, the hour is at hand, and the Son of man is betrayed.... behold he is at hand that doth betray me." (*Matthew, xxvi*, 45-6).

He proved that "perfect love casteth out fear," for He

---

[2] *St. Matthew, XVIII*, 22. *St. John, VI*, 70-1.

[3] *Acts, I*, 18.

[4] *Appendix A.*

[5] *St. Matthew, XXVI*, 23.

was seemingly overcome by fear three times. First He told the sons of Zebedee: "My soul is exceedingly sorrowful, even unto death" So great was His fear that "he fell to the ground. . . . his sweat was as it were great drops of blood." But His prayer brought "an angel unto him from heaven, strengthening him."

"He went away again the second time and prayed. . . . If this cup may not pass from me, except I drink it, thy will be done." "And he went away again, and prayed a third time, saying the same words." (*St. Matthew, xxvi, 42-4*). Even then He could have left the city and escaped had He so desired. But He returned to face Judas and receive the kiss of infamy that has come down the centuries as the epitome of treachery. This is an example of how our lower nature will "kiss" or appear to accept our higher nature only to betray it to better itself: how avarice and greed will betray our highest ideals.

Jesus' reaction is an inspiring example of how we, when faced with an unavoidable crisis, may also overcome fear by absolute reliance upon the power of the Christ within. He conquered the fear of ignominy and death to prove that we can do likewise.

"All the disciples forsook Him and fled." They did not want to be mixed up in any trouble with the ruling authorities, neither did they wish to be connected with a failure. Thus do our intellect and our pride often repudiate our connection with prayer and the spiritual side of life lest we be pointed out as a religious fanatic. And we are tempted to deny the reality of our spiritual experiences as Peter denied three times any connection with Jesus. Until we have passed the test of fear our lower personality is afraid of public opinion, is sensitive to criticism and greatly desirous of public approval. But once we let the Christ-consciousness rule, we are immune to criticism, humiliation and suffering, even the fear of death itself. We may have recognized the Christ-consciousness as the ideal for us to follow, and we may have followed it as best we could for some time, but if we have not made it

the ruler of our lives in all things, and thus conquered selfishness, fear and greed, when the time of testing comes we
will fail. The Christ within knows that greed and avarice
are treacherous as long as they remain unconquered, but
He does not condemn us until we have been given one
last chance.

We may argue with ourselves that we shouldn't be fanat-
ical, but "play the game" of life the way the unenlightened
rest of the world does, that is, take every advantage for our
self, regardless of its effect on others. But when we realize what suffering our conscience must undergo when we
betray our Inner Guidance, we endeavor to make amends
by trying to return the price. But we find it is too late. The
betrayal has taken place and the Christ in us must suffer
the result of the Karma we have created. And our remorse
is so great that we feel like saying: "Oh! what's the use?
I have failed in my test of character. I have betrayed my
highest ideals. I might as well hang myself."

But if we have truly repented and really learned our lesson, then greed and avarice are eliminated from our life. It
is they that are really "hanged," and so bother us no more.
Our personality, of which we were formerly so proud,
falls forward to the ground and collapses in shame. Our
"bowels of compassion" are released and gush out to all
other sinners in understanding love and compassion. The
only restitution we can make is to form a "potter's field"
wherein to bury both the remembrance of our shortcomings
and those of others who may come to us for comfort, as we
absorb the light of *Leo*, the heart, and allow it to illumine
our lives from within or below the horizon of our outer life.

Happy is he who prevents the Betrayal.

CHAPTER XIX

THE CRUCIFIXION

"And when they were come to the place, which is called Calvary, there they crucified him, and the malefactor; one on the right hand, and the other on the left." *St. Luke, xxiii*, 33.

"The equinoctial point where the ecliptic crosses the equator is called the 'cross,' . . . . The drama of the crucifixion is therefore symbolized in the heavens by the Cardinal Cross of the zodiac, and was recognized and understood countless *ages before the Christian era. . . .* The crucifixion therefore takes place on the day of the autumnal equinox at the exact moment when the Sun sets or dies in the West." *Appendix A.*

The greatest tragedy of the ages for the Western world has been the crucifixion, death and burial of the Lord Christ. The story that has shocked the minds and torn the hearts of all who read of it is the tragic spectacle of the innocent prophet of Galilee being led away to the agony of the crucifixion. Yet through the study of comparative religions we find that the Saviors of many other ages and religions have met the same fate.[1] And since

---

[1] In the south of India at Tanjore, and in the north at Oude, the crucified god, Bal-li, is worshipped as an incarnation of *Vishnu*. *Crishna* was crucified to a tree by the arrows of a hunter. Pictures of Crishna as *Wittoba* show the nail-holes in both feet and hands from his crucifixion. *Indra* was crucified in Nepaul. Lactanius says that *Apollo* of Miletus was nailed to a tree or was crucified. *Tamnuz*, the Syrian *Adonis*, was called "the crucified Savior of mankind". *Prometheus*, the Sun Savior, was crucified by being nailed to the rocks of Mt. Caucasus near the Caspian Straits. *Sarapis* was called the Savior and his cross was found in his temple in Alexandria. The Phyrygian *Attis* was tied to his cross. *Iao* was called the crucified Savior. *Adonis* was crucified as a dove. The Egyptian Savior, *Osiris*, was crucified in the heavens, as was also *Horus*. *Samiramis* was crucified by King Staurobates. The Mexicans and Peruvians worshipped the Savior, *Quetzalcoatle*, crucified for the sins of mankind. The Indians of Cozumal represent their Son of God, *Bacob*, as

this same tragic incident is found in all their lives it must have some general significance and meaning common to all.

The crucifixion of Jesus is a subject which, at least among advanced students, often awakens a feeling almost of resentment or at least impatience; for to those who have even a superficial acquaintance with the laws of Karma and reincarnation the questions arise, If Jesus was in truth the Christ, the Son of God, a Divine and Celestial Being, how could He have had such a terrible Karma to work out? or why should He have brought upon Himself such hopeless ignominy and suffering while trying to enlighten humanity? Why should He have been executed like any common felon and had His career limited to a pitiful three years, a bare beginning? As long as this incident is taken only literally as an historical event, these questions have no logical or satisfactory answer. But if this incident is taken, as are similar incidents in other scriptures, in its spiritual and symbolic meaning, the purpose of the crucifixion is easily understood.

Probably most Christians who have not given the subject special study think that the cross was introduced to the world through the crucifixion of Jesus and was the exclusive symbol of the Christian religion. But this is far from being the case. The *Encyclopaedia Britannica*[2] tells us that: "It has been used as a religious symbol from the dawn of man's civilization. . . . *at least ten centuries before the Christian era*. . . . may probably be regarded as almost universal. . . . It was not until the time of Constantine (288-337 A.D) that the cross was publicly used as a symbol of the Christian religion. Under Constantine it became the acknowledged symbol of Christianity, in the same way in which, long afterward, the

---

dying on a cross. Pindar says that *Ixion* was the Sun at noonday crucified in the heavens on his four-spoked wheel.

[2] 11th Ed. Vol, VII, 506.

crescent was adopted as the symbol of the Mohammedan religion."

From the beginning of humanity the cross, or man with his arms stretched out horizontally, typified his cosmic origin. In fact, it is almost impossible to go back far enough in the world's history to find a period in which this symbol was not known.

"The cross was not first introduced in the Christian Era, but is the most primitive of all symbols, representing the real crucifixion or involution, or the descent of Spirit into matter where it must be crucified upon the mundane cross and pass along the geometrical lines of evolution. The cross, being the fourth geometrical figure, represents the completion of *involution*, the turning point where *evolution* begins."[3]

"The claim that the cross is a purely Christian symbol introduced after our era, is strange indeed, when we find Ezekiel *(ix, 4)* stamping the foreheads of the men of Judah who feared the Lord, with the *signum Thau*, as it is translated in the Vulgate."[4]

As we have already pointed out: "As the vertical line represents the descent of the Spirit, so the horizontal line represents matter, thus forming the cross upon which the Divine is crucified in its efforts to express in the physical world. The cross is, therefore, a cosmic symbol and should not be identified exclusively with any one manifestation of the Divine in human form." It symbolizes "the effort of the Spirit to penetrate matter; the Light to illumine the darkness. . . . the cross upon which the Spiritual Self is crucified in matter until the lower self has been lifted up and indrawn and the cross has been balanced."[5]

"The ancients represented the Divine Man crucified within the circle of the manifested Cosmos; Hence the Cosmic Cross represents the crucifixion which must take

[3] *The Voice of Isis*, Curtiss, 57.
[4] *The Secret Doctrine*, Blavatsky, III, 588.
[5] *The Key to the Universe*, Curtiss, 85, 137-8.

place that the Deity may manifest in His creations. The figure of the cross is, therefore, not an artificial symbol arbitrarily chosen. For it is not only formed naturally by the horizontal line. . . . crossing the vertical axis at right angles, but it is also naturally formed in the heavens by the four bright stars which mark the Cardinal Cross in the heavens. . . . The cross is universally used to symbolize the outpouring of the divine, creative Life-essence—the Cosmic Christ-force—that it may manifest within the world of creation as the creative Christ-force. . . . whether or not the blood (or the life-force poured out) of a crucified man is the picture used to emphasize the more esoteric symbology."[5]

That this symbology was well known in the most ancient times is shown by the "Evangelistic Symbols" found in the "Zodiacal Ring on Earth" in Somerset, England. There the figure in the East is that of the zodiacal Man, *Aquarius*, also identified with St. Matthew. A line projected from the center of the circle passes through the eye of Hercules, due East. In the South is the Lion or *Leo*, identified with St. Mark. In the West is the Bull, *Taurus*, identified with St. Luke, the line passing through the eye of Taurus, due West. In the North is the Eagle, *Scorpio*, identified with St. John, the line passing through the Phoenix, due North. These stone figures are said by some to date back to the early Bronze Age, about 2000 B.C.

Astronomically, the Sun enters the sign *Libra* on September 23rd and is "crucified" upon the cross formed by the ecliptic crossing the equator, and "dies" or passes below the equator into the southern hemisphere as the "spear" of the "Centurian" or the arrow of the Archer— the sign *Sagittarius*—is thrust into its side. The Sun continues its descent into the "nether world" where its career is ended. It is at last overcome by its enemies. The powers of darkness and winter, which had hitherto sought in vain to overcome it, have at length won the victory. The bright and innocent Sun of summer is finally slain, crucified before all mankind in the heavens. "Before he dies, however, he sees all his disciples—his retinue of light, the twelve hours of the day or the twelve months of the year—disappear in the sanguinary melee of the clouds of evening."[6]

The early Church Fathers tell us that for the first few centuries the Christians neither adored crosses nor desired them, although the Pagans adored a cross with a man on it. "The crucifixion was not the subject of early Christianity. . . . The oldest representation of Christ Jesus was a figure of a *Lamb*. . . . This custom subsisted up to the year 680 A.D., until the pontificate of Agathon, during the reign of Constantine Pogonet. By the sixth synod of Constantinople it was ordained that instead of the ancient symbol, which had been the Lamb, *the figure of a man fastened to the cross* (such as the Pagans had adored), should be represented. All this was confirmed by Pope Adrian I."[6]

"Indeed, we are told that the cross was not identified with the crucifixion of Jesus during the early centuries of the Christian era; for no figure of a man appears upon the cross during the *first six or seven centuries*!. . . . The earliest known human figure on a cross is on the crucifix presented by Pope Gregory the Great to Queen Theodelinda of Lombardy (about 590 A.D.), now in the church of St. John at Monza."[7] It was not until the year 692 A.D. that the Quinisext Synod at Trullo forbade the pictures of the lamb and required the representation to be of the Savior's human shape. Thus in the cross we find another of those universal symbols that are connected with the life-story of so many previous Saviors of mankind.

As we have explained in *Appendix A* herein: "The equinoxial point where the ecliptic crosses the equator is called the 'cross.' Naturally there are two such crosses, one in *Aries* in the Spring and one in *Libra* in the Fall. Hence there two places of crucifixion mentioned in the *Gospels*, one at Golgotha or Calvary, corresponding to

---

[6] *Bible Myths*, Doane, 483, 202.
[7] *The Key to the Universe*, Curtiss, 138.

Aries, and one in Egypt (*Revelation, xi, 8*), the Land of
Darkness, corresponding to *Libra*. Under the constellation
Centaurus lies the Southern Cross or *Crux*. The drama
of the Crucifixion is therefore symbolized in the heavens by the Cardinal Cross of the northern hemisphere and
the Southern Cross of the southern hemisphere. . . . The
four brightest stars in *Cygnus* form the Northern Cross.
Thus does the Baptism foreshadow the coming tragedy of
Golgotha, as the cross above casts its shadow below. . . .
All this was recognized and understood for countless *ages
before the Christian era*. . . .

"The events preceding the crossing of the equator or
the 'crucifixion' of the Sun at the Autumnal Equinox are
explained by the decanates of *Leo* and *Virgo*. Following the
Cup, the second decanate of *Leo* reveals the constellation
Centaurus, the mounted soldier, symbol of the Captain
and the soldiers who took Jesus and bound, crucified and
pierced Him. In Greek the meaning of this constellation is
'the pierced' one. Similarly, the light and heat of the Sun
are 'bound' or their forces are limited after the Autumnal
Equinox. . . .

"The Crucifixion takes place on the day of the Autumnal
Equinox at the 'sixth hour' or at the exact moment when
the Sun sets or 'dies' in the West. 'And there was darkness
over all the land until the ninth hour!' The 'sixth hour'
when 'the Sun was darkened, and the veil of the temple
(the zodiac) was rent in the midst,' refers to the sign *Virgo*,
the sixth sign. The veil is rent by the passage of the Sun
from *Virgo* to *Libra* which divides the zodiac exactly in
half. Thus the veil of daylight is rent when the Sun sinks
below the horizon. Then 'the saints that slept,' that is, the
stars that were obscured or 'buried' by the light of the Sun,
'arose and came forth.'

"At the time of the Autumnal Equinox in the sign
Libra, whose symbol is the Balance or Scales, the Sun's
forces and the length of the days and nights are again balanced as they were at the Spring Equinox in *Aries*. But
this time, as the Sun crosses the equator, it is 'crossi-

fled' or crucified and dies to the northern hemisphere—
where it had been giving its forces or 'life-blood' for Nature all summer—for it has entered the next sign, *Scorpio*,
the sign of death."

"In the Mysteries the crucifixion of the Christos represents the self-sacrifice of the higher manas, the Father,
who sends his only begotten Son into the world to take
upon him our sins."[8]

When St. Paul speaks of making known to the Gentiles
"the glory of this mystery. . . . which is *Christ in you*, the
hope of glory," (*Colossians, i, 27*), it is quite evident that
he is not referring to any physical personality however
exalted, but to the mystical Christ principle latent in each
heart.

"In the Mysteries the regenerated man, who by crucifying the man of flesh and his passions on the Procrustean
bed of torture, became reborn as an Immortal."[8] St. Paul
confirms this process when he tells us: "They that are
Christ's have crucified the flesh with the affections (passions) and lusts. . . . But God forbid that I should glory, save
in the cross of our Lord Jesus Christ, by whom the world
is crucified unto me, and I unto the world." (*Galatians, v,
24; vi, 14*). "But to manifest these potentialities the Christ
must be born in your heart, or your spiritual consciousness
must be awakened and unfold the cross upon which the
lower man must hang until spiritualized and redeemed."[9]
"Knowing this, that our old man is crucified with him,
that the body of sin might be destroyed (done away), that
henceforth we should not serve sin." (*Romans, vi, 6*).

"This is the true meaning of redemption through love.
For the world was not redeemed by the crucifixion of one
man in any age, however much that man manifested the
Christ, and however much of the darkness was redeemed
thereby. It is by the daily and hourly crucifixion of the
conscious power of the Godhead (the Christ) in matter,

---

[8] *The Secret Doctrine*, Blavatsky, III, 593; II, 592.
[9] *The Key to the Universe*, Curtiss, 138-140.

the living in the darkness and suffering with it until, atom by atom, the whole is transmuted by His life-force (the symbolic 'blood') that the redemption of the world is accomplished. Every earnest Soul who recognizes this principle and takes upon himself the redemption of his own creations, through the Christ within, thus becomes a redeemer to that extent, and releases the Christ from the cross through the crucifixion of his own personality instead."[10]

"Therefore, if we sacrifice knowingly and willingly, the redemption is accomplished without the suffering which the crucifixion brings about for those who resist and refuse to work with the Law. By thus working with the Law (the Law of Jesus, the Law of Redemption through Sacrifice), the cross is rolled up into the cube, and the Stone of Sacrifice becomes the pure White Stone given 'to him that overcometh'; the Foundation Stone to a newer and higher manifestation; that upon which all must be founded."[9]

Down through the ages and throughout the *Bible*, it has been taught that the sins of man could be redeemed by a blood-sacrifice, either of animals or of a man. "The new interpretation which Jesus presented to His disciples was that, instead of the slaughter of animals and the literal shedding of blood's being used to symbolize the Mystery of Sacrifice, the New Testament should bring a deeper understanding of the world-old truth which the slaughter of animals expressed in a crude and materialized manner. . . . The New Testament which Jesus gave was that while 'It is the blood that maketh atonement for the Soul' (*Leviticus, xvii, 11*) and 'Without shedding of blood is no remission'"[11] (*Hebrews, ix, 22*), nevertheless, "It is not possible that the blood of bulls and goats should take away sins." (*Hebrews, x, 4*).

"What is the meaning of this paradox? What is the sacrifice and what is the blood that must atone? The sac-

---

[10] *The Voice of Isis*, Curtiss, 326.
[11] *The Message of Aquaria*, Curtiss, 439-45.

rifice is indeed that of man, not of Jesus alone, but of the lower man of us all, the animal self, and the personality, to the will of the Divine. The blood that is shed is indeed that of man, yet not the literal physical blood, but the spiritual life-force. The physical blood is the carrier of the physical life-force and is, therefore, used to symbolize the spiritual life-force—the Christ-force—or 'the blood of the Christ' within man."[11]

"This was symbolized in the old days by the blood of animals, and in Jesus' time by the wine of the Eucharist. When Jesus said of the wine: *'This is my blood* of the New Testament, which is shed for many for the remission of sins,' (*St. Matthew, xxvi, 28*) He obviously referred not to His physical blood, *which had not been shed*, but to the great sacrifice of the Christ-force coming down or being 'shed' in the darkness of his outer life; the pouring out of his spiritual life-force (blood) to redeem that which was 'lost' or lacked spiritual life-force."[11]

It is the spiritual significance of the crucifixion, and not the physical fact, to which most of the mystical writings of the early church Fathers refer. St. Paul recognized that it was the inner, mystical Christ within that was meant by the incident of the crucifixion instead of the literal, when he said: "I am crucified with Christ: nevertheless I live; yet not I, but Christ liveth in me." (*Galatians, ii, 20*).

"To symbolize this great Mystery of Sacrifice anew, Jesus took bread and wine instead of the body and blood of animals, and with these symbols summed up His whole life and teaching. . . . the sacrificing of the life of the lower man to the Higher. The whole *Gospel* story is focused in this idea.[11]

"We wonder at the darkness of the minds of men who could make literal the blood sacrifice of the personified outpouring of Divine Love—poured out into the hearts of His ignorant, wilful and misguided children—and believe that such a crime would be an acceptable sacrifice to the heart of Divine Love, especially as it has proved so inadequate to save the world from sin! The Redeemer of man and the universe is indeed the mystical Christ-force which is shed abroad like the physical sunlight that none perish but all have eternal life; that Force whose spiritual pressure for expression enables even the lowest trough of the sea of humanity to gain the power and momentum to rise to its highest expression. For without this Christ-force that is inherent in every Soul, nothing can be accomplished. This is the Way, the Truth and the Life; no man cometh unto the Father but by and through this Cosmic Christ-force.[12]

"The sunlight is the physical redeemer of the Earth, for without it nothing could grow and manifest; nor without it could the dead forms and offscourings be fermented and transmuted into helpful substances for future use. . . . In a similar manner the radiance of the Christos is the redeemer and savior of mankind, for without it the seeds of his spiritual life could not grow and manifest, nor could the noxious weeds of his perverted forces — his selfishness, inharmony, lusts and the offscourings of his mind — be transmuted into good, even though this requires the experiences of fermentation and transmutation. Therefore, the redemption of man and the upliftment of his lower forms of manifestation must come through the upliftment of his mind to a realization of and correlation with the radiance of the Christos or Christ-consciousness."[13]

"We are not to look back to and worship a crucified, dead and buried Jesus, but a risen and ever-present Lord of Light, Life and Love! Not a literal event, past and gone ages ago, but a *living Presence*, who calls us to sup with Him now in the 'upper chamber.'. . . . The risen Lord now gives to the world a New Testament, so that all who are hungry for spiritual food, who are tired of suffering, who are sick of bloodshed, may know the glorious truth of His living Presence. As long as a literal blood-

---

[12] *The Message of Aquaria*, Curtiss, 215.
[13] *The Inner Radiance*, Curtiss, 244.

sacrifice of one man or many, is believed in as a propitiation for sin, man will never wake up to the belief that war can be abolished. For if the physical blood of one man could wipe away the sins of the world, why might not the blood of millions, shed for high ideals on the battle fields, wipe away the sins of the nations? But this has not and never will be accomplished; far from it."[14]

It is within man, then, that the Christ within suffers daily as He is crucified between two thieves. In the cosmic symbology the two thieves are the zodiacal signs *Cancer* and *Capricorn*, on opposite sides of the zodiac. As the Sun is "crucified" as it crosses the equator at the autumnal equinox, each of the signs has "stolen" its light from the Sun. Naturally, as *Capricorn* disappears below the horizon that "thief" dies, while the other "thief"—*Cancer*—rises with the Sun. Hence the promise: "Today shalt thou be with me (the Sun) in paradise," that is, in the summer season of growth and fruition.

In our personality the two thieves may be likened to the past and the future. The past, through the experiences of our self-created suffering and sorrow, has stolen from us the joy that realization of the Christ within could have brought to our consciousness. The future, to which we persistently look forward with dreams of personal success, accomplishment and satisfaction or with gloomy foreboding if not fear, distracts our attention from that which the Christ should accomplish through us in the everpresent, eternal Now. Thus both these "thieves," the past and the future, steal from the Christ His opportunity for recognition and expression, for we are forever looking back to that which is past or anticipating that which the future may bring instead of listening to the Voice that is striving to guide us into accomplishing in the now.

The twelve "stations of the cross" correspond to the twelve months of the Sun's cycle. They mark the twelve major steps on the Path of Attainment, while the seven sentences spoken while on the cross epitomize the qualities

[14] *The Message of Aquaria*, Curtiss, 443-4.

manifested during the seven steps of Solar Initiations. (1) "Father forgive them" reveals the compassion gained. (2) "Today shalt thou be with me in paradise" shows the realization that all that which through faith we have conquered and blessed, we carry with us into the higher life. (3) "Woman, behold thy son" shows the recognition of the feminine influence in the life. (4) "Why hast thou forsaken me?" indicates the inadequacy of life without God and the despair of the personality at being left alone. (5) "I thirst" indicates the power old habits of life still have over even the spiritually advanced. (6) "It is finished" shows the cessation of resistance by the personality. (7) "Into thy hands" indicates the final merging of the personality with the Divine.

Only to the extent that we teach our human personality to follow *The Pattern Life* can the Christ within manifest consciously through us. For, "Like the life-story of Jesus, we must ultimately pass through all phases of that life. We must be the carpenter's son, constructively doing his duty in the lowly station in life in which he finds himself, striving to build his temple by compass and square; yet through the power of the Christ he must learn that all events that come to him are but the carpenter's tools with which he must carve out his temple and accomplish the work of his Father."

"He must remain in the obscurity of Egypt for a season while Herod, who rules the personality, seeks to slay Him who is ultimately to become the ruler of the life. He must heal the sick, cleanse the lepers and feed the multitudes within his own body with spiritual food. He must strive. He must suffer. He must be misunderstood and condemned, yet never must he forget his real mission. He must hang upon the cross of material conditions until, in the very depths of his being, in the agony of the higher consciousness that has been born within him — that consciousness which strives to uncover and reveal the Christ Child to a world that cannot understand — he cries out 'I thirst.'"

"In one aspect this is the thirst of the despairing personality for the old life of the world, and its seeming satisfaction, its happiness and security." Our physical senses (symbolized by the Roman soldiers) which formerly had given us so much pleasure, do their best to satisfy this thirst, but are unable to do so. We may resort to the old habits of life, try to join old friends in the old pleasures, but they no longer satisfy, in fact they are but "vinegar mingled with gall."

"But in another and higher sense it is the cry of the awakened man who thirsts for more wisdom; how best to do the works of his Father; how best to lift up the Christ-light that all men shall be drawn into the radiance of that Light. He realizes the mighty power of the Christhood within him and thirsts for the ability to manifest it without crucifying it. But he finds the task too great and lays down the burden crying: 'It is finished. . . . Father, into thy hands I commend my spirit.'"[15]

As we point out in the *Appendix A* herein: "Astronomically the first decanate of *Leo*—the heart—contains an important constellation called the *Crater* or the *Cup*. Around it many myths and legends are woven. Out of this *Cup* the Sun must 'drink' as it passes through this constellation. Hence Jesus—as the representative of the Sun—is made to say: 'O my father, if it be possible, let this cup pass from me: nevertheless not as I will, but as thou (cyclic law) wilt" (*St. Matthew, xxvi, 39*).

"Only when the awakened personality realizes that it cannot achieve, through its own intellectual powers, the destiny that has been glimpsed, and places all the ardor and enthusiasm of his desire to accomplish, into the hands symbol of the power to accomplish of the Father, the Real Self, and ceases to struggle, is the crucifixion over. . . . He must be willing to be crucified, not rejoicing in the crucifixion as a sign of his superiority over others, but recognizing that it is only a crucifixion of the lower man that the glory of the Christ within might shine forth

---

[15] *The Message of Aquaria*, Curtiss, 180-2-3.

the better. In fact, the Christ could accomplish His work more perfectly without the distraction which the suffering of the personality brings upon Him, *if the personality could learn and respond* without the crucifixion."

"What is it all for? It is to awaken in intellectual man an abiding sense of the indwelling Divinity and its power to overcome all things, once the opposition of the personality has ceased. He must realize that he is something more than man; that there is something his cultured mind cannot grasp, which must come as a *revelation from the heart*; that he must call upon the Christ within; must yield up the sense of his sufficiency and superiority; for his god, the intellect, has forsaken him, cry he never so loud."[15]

"Instead of being regarded as a symbol of the descent of the Christ into matter and the pouring forth of the Cosmic Christ-force, the crucifixion has been so materialized and literally interpreted that it has been used as an excuse for negative submission to suffering and sorrow, so that in time, self-torture was looked upon as meritorious, and a doleful countenance was a mark of sanctity. Yet, because back of the misinterpretation of the symbols there was a divine truth, man realized within himself that there was something there which he had not grasped. As he grew spiritually and expanded intellectually, there were many who looked at the materialized idea and revolted at the thought of allowing another to suffer for their sins, especially as they were told that the propitiation was made centuries before they were born! And being unable to accept the literal interpretation they turned away from all religion and were lost either in a slough of indifference or in a mental labyrinth of speculation which brought neither peace nor satisfaction."[16]

As long as Christendom worships the Christ crucified it is but driving the nails more firmly; for the Christ is crucified by being immersed in matter, not to be forever entombed therein, but that matter may be redeemed. This

---

[16] *The Message of Aquaria*, Curtiss, 442.

is a voluntary cosmic sacrifice to which man's disobedience has added cruelty and suffering.

Remember that the Christ in us is nailed to the cross of matter, is crucified and suffers, by our every failure to recognize and follow His guidance.

The nails symbolize the ridicule, mockery and derision with which the world strikes at those who are striving to live *The Pattern Life*. This often results so as to paralyze our power of accomplishment (hands) and hampers our understanding, symbolized by the feet.

And because the Christ is crucified within us we must continue to suffer until resurrected and our consciousness ascends to be one with the Father. There need be no crucifixion, yet we crucify ourselves as long as our personal will crosses the Divine Will. The Will of God, manifesting as the Christ-force, descends into the material world in perpendicular line. As long as our desires and aspirations ascend to heaven over that spiritual line there can be no cross formed. But as long as our personal will crosses that of the Divine we crucify the Christ within and bring the suffering upon ourselves. For we suffer as we oppose the harmonious working of the Law.

The crucifixion continues until the animal nature is completely controlled by the Christ within, and the wilful personality has also submitted and declared: "It is finished. . . . Father, into thy hands I commend my spirit." (*St. Luke, xxiii, 46*). Christhood is a state of consciousness which is attained through a process of crucifixion of many things we formerly thought necessary. Hence, anyone who tries to live the Christ-life is likely to know what it means to be "despised and rejected of men; a man of sorrows and acquainted with grief." (*Isaiah, liii, 3*).

And the suffering is very real and lasting, until we learn—through recognition of His presence and mission within us—to lift up the cross of materialism on which we have crucified Him and hail Him as the Son of God, henceforth seated forevermore as Ruler upon our throne of life. There He guides us through the outshining of

Divine Love and Wisdom into the path of peace and bless-
edness. We will then no longer suffer and perish hopelessly,
but will live forevermore in Him as He in us, thus fulfilling
both in ourselves and in humanity the many promises given
us by the Father.

We must look then within ourselves and realize that
our Lord Christ is still living on earth in us; still teaching,
healing, resurrecting and seeking to draw us and all our
faculties to a higher and fuller understanding of God's
Truth. We must also realize that as we turn away from Him
we join the rabble who cry, "Crucify Him! Crucify Him!"

"Therefore as we learn to know ourselves and our creations in all our worlds we will end the crucifixion by
saying of our personal reliance on outer conditions and
forces, 'It is finished. . . . Into the hands of my Divine
Self I commit my Spirit.' Then we will begin to open our
consciousness to the angelic forces of the spiritual world
and we will know ourselves as Sons of God in the process
of unfoldment and manifestation. Then we will learn to
manifest the Real Self as wholeheartedly and completely as
we have hitherto manifested the lower self or personality."[17]

The whole earth is running to and fro and staggering
like a drunken man, seeking for some principle which shall
bring a lasting peace and stability into their lives and into
the lives of nations. They are seeking to prevent a return of
pre-war conditions and establish new and more just conditions for all mankind. Therefore this is the day when to all
who love their Lord Christ, all who have the welfare of
humanity at heart, all who will listen and learn and follow,
there comes the call to exemplify and spread the doctrine
of humanity's essential unity, and with sanity and wisdom
inculcate the necessity of peace, brotherhood, co-operation
and harmony, both among individuals and nations. For
only so can the crucifixion of humanity be ended.

---

[17] *The Message of Aquaria*, Curtiss, 183.

We as individuals can do much to end the crucifixion and the cruel suffering by teaching humanity, by the examples of our own lives, the necessity of listening to and following the Voice of the Christ within, by taking our stand firmly on the side of righteousness and high ideals, by helping to bring about a greater understanding of the spiritual truths hidden beneath the mysteries of parable and symbol. For verily unto us who have grasped even a little of the hidden leaven that must in time leaven the whole world, it is given to be active agents in hastening the day when there shall be given to the world a fuller and more comprehensive understanding of the everlasting Truth.

Therefore you can attune your hearts and make of them true receiving instruments and amplifiers of the wonderful message of Divine Truth that is forever broadcast throughout the universe. Reach out your hands in loving trust and accept the living Word that is given you. Proclaim the reality of the indwelling Christ. Make a practice of listening for His Voice and asking for His guidance in every problem and condition that confronts you. Declare that, "This is the great work, the great privilege given unto me, to manifest the Christ in me and in my life. I will try to do my best, knowing that nothing is ever given to God's children to do that the strength to accomplish is not given with it."

Happy is he who has ended the Crucifixion.

CHAPTER XX

THREE DAYS IN THE TOMB

"And very early in the morning the first day of the week, they came unto the sepulchure. . . . ye seek Jesus of Nazareth. . . . he is risen: he is not here." *St. Mark, xvi, 2, 6.*

"For Christ. . . . quickened by the Spirit; by which also he went and preached to the spirits in prison. . . . the gospel preached also to them that are dead." *I Peter, iii 18, 19; iv, 6.*

"After the autumnal crossing—the crucifixion—the Sun enters the lowest point in the northern hemisphere where it apparently remains stationary for three days, hence the "three days in the tomb." *Appendix A.*

The incident of Jesus remaining three days in the tomb is another of those well nigh universal incidents which give us pause, and furnish a subject for deeper meditation. The fact that nearly all the Savior-gods[1] of ancient times,

---

[1] In the Hindu *Soma-deva Bhatta* we are told that *Saktideva* was on a ship when a great storm arose. The ship went to pieces and a great fish swallowed *Saktideva* whole. The fish was caught and when opened *Saktideva* came out alive and unhurt. *Hercules* was swallowed by a whale (Dag) near the same place (Joppa) where Jonah was swallowed, remained in its belly three days and came forth alive. According to the Persians *Jamshid* was devoured by a great monster in the sea, but after three days he arose from the sea unharmed. The Hindu *Krishna* descended into Hades to recover certain persons from the dead. *Mercury* descended into Hell to cause a cessation of suffering there. The Roman *Dionysus* descended into Hades to rescue his mother, Semele, and carry her to Heaven. The Persian *Zoroaster*, the Egyptian *Osiris* and *Horus*, the Greek *Adonis*, the Roman *Bacchus*, the Scandinavian *Baldur*, the Mexican *Quetzacoatl*, etc., all descended into Hell for various unselfish reasons and rose again *on the third day*. All these heroes represented the Sun during the three days and nights of the winter solstice.

long before the Christian era, remained in tombs for exactly three days, during which they "descended into hell," takes the incident out of the realm of coincidence and suggests some common, underlying significance, aside from its obvious connection with the Sun apparently standing still or being "entombed" for three days.

The best known example of many other Lightbringers who were "entombed" in one way or another is the story of Jonah remaining for three days and nights in the "nether regions" or the belly of the "great fish." Obviously this incident was not meant to be taken literally, for Jonah would have been smothered in a few minutes if he was not strangled by the acid juices of the fish's stomach. "That story is an allegory. . . . as is now all but universally admitted by scholars."[2]

That this incident is of symbolic significance is evidenced by the fact that the body of Jesus did not remain in the tomb for three full days and nights. "According to the Jewish reckoning the Sabbath was over at 6 P.M. the night before. This is Sunday morning at sunrise (6 A.M). . . . If Jesus was buried at, say, one hour before sunset on Friday, and this was 6 A.M. on Sunday morning, he had been one full day, and one hour of the preceding day, and about twelve hours of a third day, in the grave—thus about 37 hours altogether,"[3] instead of the full 72 hours.

As we have already pointed out: "All these stories are very similar to that of Jonah, and have precisely the same esoteric meaning, namely, that he was 'swallowed' or retired from the outer life, for the three periods—the three days in the belly of the fish—of the Great Initiation into esoteric wisdom before he was prepared to preach to the people of Nineveh."[4]

---

[2] *Bible Myths*, Doane, 79.
[3] *The Life of Christ*, Caine, 979, 984.
[4] *The Key of Destiny*, Curtiss, 158. See also *Bible Myths*, Doane, 79. *Hebrew Mythology*, Goldhier, 102-3. *Anacalypsis*, Higgins, I, 638. *Primitive Culture*, Taylor, I, 306. "Come, and let us return unto the Lord:. . . . be hath smitten, and he will bind us up. After two days will he revive us: *in the third day* he will raise us up, and we shall live in his sight." *Hosea, VI, 1-2.*

The connection of this incident in the life-story of Jesus with the Sun is easily seen. For as a Lightbringer Jesus naturally represents the Sun, as we have shown repeatedly throughout this study. Therefore His entombment for three days represents the three winter months—January, February, March—during which the Sun descends into the "lower regions" of the southern hemisphere or the zodiacal "hell," the "bowels of the earth" or the "belly of the fish," and is then resurrected to renew its career in the northern hemisphere.

The key to this universal symbology is found in the initiation ceremonies of all the ancient *Mysteries*. Initiation into the *Mysteries* has from the most remote ages been characterized by the symbolic death, burial and resurrection of the Candidate. In those early days, when education and culture were possessed by only the very few outside the priesthood, the mysteries of birth, life and death were outpictured in allegorical ceremonies which were intended to impress the Candidate—and also the multitude which witnessed them—the fundamental laws of both physical and spiritual evolution. And his symbolic death and burial prefigured the spiritual change that was taking place within him, namely, the death and burial of the lower personality or man of flesh, that the Spiritual or Christ-man might arise and rule his life from that time on.

In the mysteries of Isis, Attis, Dionysus, Orpheus, Mithra, Eleusis, etc., the Candidate approached the solemn sacrament of Initiation believing that he thereby became "twice-born," a "new creature," and passed in a real sense from death unto life by being brought into a mysterious intimacy with the deity.[5] In the *Eleusinian Mysteries* Apeuleius says he underwent a "voluntary death" and approached the realm of death in order thereby to attain his spiritual birthday.

---

[5] *The Mystery Religions*, Angus, 96-7.

Among the Egyptians this symbology was enacted by placing the Candidate in a sarcophagus or coffin which was then placed in a dark crypt symbolizing a tomb. His entranced body was either stretched upon a cross or a cross was bound upon his heart. It was so arranged that on the third day the rays of the rising Sun would fall upon the mystic center (*Ajna*) in his forehead and thereby awaken him from his trance.

There he was left, apparently alone in the darkness, in a deep magnetic sleep, as dead to any earthly happenings as though in very truth he were dead and placed within a tomb. While his body was thus entranced, his consciousness was released from its confinement to the body and descended into that sub-conscious region where the elemental forces are confined like spirits in prison. Thus was the Candidate brought face to face with all normal instinctive forces of his animal nature, together with his astral creations and all that went to make up his lower personality.

In this way the Candidate was brought to a realization of himself and what he must do about it. For there passed before him in panoramic view, firstly, all his faults and failings, all his unsuspected tendencies, together with all the previous lusts and unworthy desires which he had created and expressed, as well as those he had suppressed; all those things that must be "preached to" and released from their "prison." Secondly, his consciousness was then expanded to recognize and respond to the glory of his Real or Spiritual Self, the Christ within. Thus were his godlike powers and glorious possibilities and the goal to be reached so indelibly impressed upon his consciousness that when he was released or resurrected on the third day, he would be determined to conquer, and thus would apply the unceasing effort necessary to attain the final victory as a "Son of God." "To them he gave power (the right) to become the sons of God." (*St. John, i, 12*).

Today the seekers for the Christ-consciousness have greatly advanced. Out of the horrors of world-wars and their accumulated experiences, they have learned that it is no longer necessary to be placed in a trance and have their evil creations presented to their psychic vision, and have their Path to Mastery thus revealed. In fact, for the untrained majority such an experience would be called but a fantastic nightmare. Today those who have experienced the crucifixion and are facing the next step may expect to be plunged into the darkness of the "tomb" by life itself. Thus will they have the realization of the hidden traits of their lower self brought home to them by the tests and experiences of daily life so that they cannot fail to recognize them. Then they may "preach unto" them, and release them from their prison in their subconscious minds.

As we have already pointed out: "It is only the Christ-consciousness, manifesting through the heart and crucified by the rational mind and nailed to the cross of materiality, that can descend into the lower regions (the subconscious) and preach to the souls (complexes) imprisoned there, or subjugate and control the forces of the lower mind, and through the consciousness thus illumined, make man, in very truth, the Lord of Creation and the image of God the Father."[6]

And if the Candidate refuses to recognize and "preach unto" these traits or "spirits in prison," they will naturally find expression again and again until he is thoroughly aroused to the necessity of conquering or transmuting them through the power of the Christ within. The medieval mystics called such experiences or plunges into the darkness, the "dark night of the Soul," which caused them great mental suffering. But such periods often alternate with periods of lofty inspiration and visions, the most glorious heights of the Christ-consciousness that can be attained. But, as Candidates for Christhood, if we continue to refuse to face and recognize ourselves exactly as we are; if we turn our backs upon and ignore and refuse to "preach unto them," we will continue to make the same mistakes, have the same unhappy experiences and suffer

---

[6] *The Message of Aquaria*, Curtiss, 220.

from them until we are ready to recognize the cause and let the Christ redeem them; for the Christ in us must lie in the tomb or "hell" of our lower self until we do.

In the Christian Mysteries this inner spiritual experience is symbolized by Jesus spending the usual three days in the tomb while He descended into the lowest or "hell" realms of the astral world.[7] And the symbology differs but little from that found in many other religions for this event. It does not mean that those today who are passing through this same momentous experience will literally die, any more than did the Egyptian Candidate who passed three days in a trance. It simply means that they are passing through three periods of spiritual darkness and deadness comparable to that of a tomb.

Many advanced students who are unfolding some of their higher faculties think that when they have attained the spiritual Baptism and have had some realization of the Christ-consciousness they have conquered all and that life henceforth will be a rapid and uneventful progress toward Christhood. In reality they are but preparing for the great trials of the Crucifixion and the Resurrection.

The three days in the tomb therefore, represent three periods of long or short duration during which the life, light and warmth of the Sun of Rightousness is eclipsed; three distinct steps or awakenings in your spiritual life. They are three periods during which you are conquering the lower elemental powers upon the three planes. The first awakening will come after a period of darkness during which you may find springing up within you desires, traits of character and thoughts of an undesirable nature which you never dreamed were yours or which you thought were long since conquered. These you must recognize as yours and "preach unto them" until you can control, purify, redeem and turn them to good.

You now begin to enter upon the long second day. During the short first day you met your tests largely in matters pertaining to the physical body and the physical

---

[7] For details see *Realms of the Living Dead*, Curtiss.

plane, but this second "day" is a long period of mental darkness, during which you must gain control over your thoughts. If necessary you must reconstruct and set in order your entire mental world. During this day you will be tested by doubts and fears and misunderstandings, both as to any teachings you may be following and as to the reality of the inner experiences through which you may be passing.

You must conquer the tendency to intellectual aggrandizement, particularly the idea that you must make everyone think as you do. You must also conquer the inclination to self-satisfaction, self-righteousness and spiritual pride. This is a natural result of your having taken your lower nature in hand and in a measure conquered at least its physical expression. But the feeling that you are superior to your companions who have not reached your point of attainment, because your ideals are higher than theirs, must be conquered. In other words, you must so "preach to the spirits in prison" that you make your whole mental world bow subservient to the Christ-consciousness, just as you have made your physical expressions. Thus you will no longer allow your life to be ruled by worldly conceptions, the opinions of others, or by the plausible arguments of the intellect, but will follow the Inner Guidance of the resurrected Christ within.

This mental house-cleaning and readjustment will occupy a full long "day," from sunrise down through the blackness of the second night-periods until the Sun of Righteousness rises on the "third day." Then you will realize that there is a divine power consciously ruling and guiding your mental world, even as you now rule and guide the physical. Therefore your intellect does not have to work alone, once it has acknowledged the light of the Christ within, and no longer makes excuses for its mistakes. Only when the intellect has become a clear vehicle for the Christ-consciousness, and will allow no amount of misunderstanding or lack of appreciation to disturb you, have you passed the "second day."

Only when the Sun of Righteousness shines clearly in your mental world and you awaken to the realization that your chief aim must be to fix your attention upon the Christ within and live so close to Him that His radiance will bring forth in you the "fruits of the Spirit," only then have you awakened on the "third day." On the third morning you must awaken to the divine possibilities which must be resurrected within yourself, and within your fellow men.

It is probable that this period will be of short duration, for we read that it was "very early in the morning. . . . when it was yet dark" that the angel rolled away the stone from the tomb. The Angel that rolls away the stone from the tomb is the ray of spiritual light which you invoke as the result of your consecration, devotion and aspiration.

Pray then that it be in the dawning of your third day that the Angel of Inspiration shall roll away the stone of materialism from the tomb of mental darkness and permit the resurrection of the Christ-consciousness within. For you have kept Him there wrapped in the bands of your mental limitations and the grave clothes of literal conceptions. Then when the three women, or the three feminine aspects of the Christ-consciousness—Mary, the Mother of Jesus (love), Mary Magdalene (compassion) and Salome (sympathy)—come "very early in the morning" they will find nothing but the grave clothes of old limitations left behind. And the Angel will proclaim: "He is not here: for He is risen !"

At this point there comes to the Soul a subtle temptation, for the feminine principles have wept so long at the foot of the cross and beside the tomb that they find it difficult to rejoice at the resurrection. They cry: "They have taken away the Lord out of the sepulchre, and we know not where they have laid Him" (*St. Luke xx, 2*). The temptation is one of self-pity which tends to hug to you the suffering of the crucifixion. You imagine that you are bearing the sorrows of the world, whereas you have been reaping only the natural results of your own unconquered faults and lack of understanding. But if you will lift your eyes to heaven, instead of fixing them on yourself, you will see your Guardian Angel and hear Him say: "He is risen!. . . . why seek ye the living among the dead?" You will then realize that the resurrection of the Christ-consciousness within you has really taken place and is not a mere dream or an astral experience. For when that takes place all things are made new, and the Sun of Righteousness will illumine even the empty tomb where the limiting grave clothes have been left behind.

As we have said elsewhere: "It is the force generated by the mystical North Wind that shall roll away the stone from the sepulcher of our lives. And as we find the stone rolled away many of us may start back appalled to find only empty graveclothes where we thought to find the Christ. How many of us have had something we valued above all else, that which seemed to be our Lord of Life; taken from us and we have laid it in a tomb and have sealed it with a great stone! Often this stone is fashioned from our hearts grown hard and bitter because our artificial Lord of Life has been taken from us and we know not where they have laid him.

"There are many, many such: many who are carrying through life the memory of such a death and burial: many whose hearts close the mouth of a sepulcher in which their hopes and dearest wishes lie buried. This may be the physical loss of a loved one who seemed so necessary for us to lean on, but who may have been removed only to teach our Soul to lean upon its own inner touch with Divinity. Or it may be some disappointed hope or some affliction of the body which they have sealed up in a tomb in the mind where they go often to weep and lament or to curse the fate that has willed it so."

"Then comes the great North Wind and sweeps them off their feet, tears from their lives all those things to which they have clung so long. By its force the stone they thought so firm is torn from its foundations and rolled away. Then they find in their sepulcher no cherished idol, no Lord of Life, but only the graveclothes of that which has passed away long since. Moreover, if they come to this sepulcher at dawn after the bitter North Wind has blown all the night long, they will find an angel waiting for them saying: 'He is not here, for he is risen. Why seek ye the living among the dead?'

"What is the meaning of this symbol? It is this, there is no thing that is called out by our true, unselfish love that can rest in the grave. Its essence must rise and become a part of our True Self, for we cannot lose anything that is true and pure. Do not hover over the graves in your life, for nothing can remain in the grave but the mere outward covering which we ourselves have woven about the thing we loved. There are no sepulchers which require the hardening of our hearts to seal up, no dark and dismal caverns where our loved ones rest. No thing that has awakened one living spark of Divine Love and has then apparently been taken away from us is dead. Nor can it rest in a grave, for it is risen, risen into the great and mighty oneness of Divine Love, which includes the little things of life as well as the great.

"When the bitter North Wind blows fiercely and our lives seem chilled and going to pieces: when petty cares, like the dust and debris cast up by the wind, are flying about us on every hand, perhaps blinding us; when the Sun of Righteousness and the Moon of Intuition are darkened and the Star of Initiation seems to have withdrawn its light, then look up to heaven, for behold our redemption draweth nigh. For when we have looked up we will see the lesson from the experience and go fearlessly into the tomb and see for ourselves that our Lord of Life and Love has risen, for the stone of misunderstanding and the hardness of heart has been rolled away by the King of the North Wind."[8]

Every Soul who is passing through the experiences of the three days in the tomb is watched over by a Guardian

---

[8] *The Message of Aquaria*, Curtiss, 135-6.

Angel, the same great Teacher who in former ages sat by the entrance to the initiation crypt and followed the Soul down into the darkness to guide, help and protect it. If, through your sincere efforts to help humanity, you have proven that you have donned the livery of the Christ, you have been recognized by the Elder Brothers of the Race. Henceforth your path will lead ever closer to Them until full realization is the reward of your steady conquering and attainment.

But it must be you who draws closer to Them. The clouds which hide Them from you are all of your own creating. They will dissolve and disappear in the bright beams of the Sun of Righteousness as it arises and floods your life with its radiance and the resurrection is an accomplished fact in your heart and life.

These three periods can be three moments, three years or three incarnations according to your own spiritualization and advancement, as you enter into your divine birthright. So let the stone of personality and materialism be rolled away. Let the grave clothes of old, restricting ideas and misconceptions fall away. Awake! Watch for the dawning of the third day! Arise from the tomb and come forth into the light of a new day!

Happy is he who has arisen from the Tomb.

CHAPTER XXI

THE RESURRECTION

"Why seek ye the living among the dead? He is not here, but is risen." *St. Luke, xxiv, 5,6.*

"After spending three months in the 'tomb' of the southern hemisphere, the Sun continues to rise until it crosses the equator into the northern hemisphere. There it enters the sign *Aries* where it is said to be 'exalted.' This event is called the vernal equinox which ushers in the beginning of Spring, and is celebrated universally by the ceremony of Easter. Thus the Sun pours forth its light, heat and lifeforce—sheds its symbolic 'blood'—that all Nature may be resurrected from the tomb of Winter and have life more abundantly. Therefore this event is called the Resurrection." *Appendix A.*

If the greatest tragedy of the ages for the Western World was the crucifixion, death and entombment of Jesus, certainly His resurrection was the most inspiring miracle of the ages. No wonder biblical authorities tell us that: "The Christian Church would never have come into existence without faith in the Risen Lord. His conquest over death is most frequently appealed to in the apostolic teaching."[1]

The details of the precise manner in which Jesus was resurrected—as there were no witnesses—have been the basis of heated controversy for centuries. The literalists insist that it was Jesus' physical body that arose from the tomb and appeared to various persons and groups some thirteen times. They hold that it was the physical body that then ascended into heaven, in spite of St. Paul's

---

[1] *Encyclopedia Britannica*, XVIII, 572.

explicit statement that: "Flesh and blood cannot inherit the kingdom of God." (*I Corinthians, xv, 50*). Psychic research authorities[2] claim that it must have been Jesus' astral or etheric body that arose and materialized. The mythologists frankly state—as we have already mentioned—that: "Such narratives as those of the rockburial and resurrection of the Savior-God in the Gospels are beyond all doubt simple developments of those mourning rituals which we have seen used in so many ancient rituals."[3] "According to the *Encyclopedia Britannica*, twenty-two contradictions of the most serious character are found. . . . between the four accounts to be found in the *New Testament*."[1]

Since the full details of the resurrection require considerable explanation, we will omit many of them until we take them up in connection with the equally miraculous problem of the Ascension, with which it is so closely connected, in the next Chapter.

Probably most Christians think that the Resurrection of Jesus was a miracle that was unique in the history of the world, and in the Christian religion only, but such is far from being true. That is not the only time that death was conquered by Resurrection and Ascension, as we shall explain in the next Chapter. Our research shows that this same miracle is recorded in the life-story of many previous Lightbringers or Sun-gods centuries before the Christian Era.[4]

---

[2] *The Psychic Stream*, Findlay, 909, 882. *The Psychic Life of Jesus*, Elliott. *Communication with the Spirit World*, Greber, 387.

[3] *Christianity and Mythology*, Robertson, 381.

[4] *The Hindu Savior, Krishna,* rose from the dead as "a great light enveloped the Earth and illumined the whole expanse of heaven, amidst great rejoicing." *Rama* rose from the dead and ascended into heaven to renew his divine essence. The death of *Comodeo* was mourned with such lamentations that Mahadeo was moved to pity and resurrected him into heaven, "to hell's great dread and heaven's eternal admiration." *Adonis or Tammus* rose from the dead during the ceremony of Adonia. His image was carried with great solemnity to the tomb, with great lamentations. After a funeral oration a great shout was raised: "Adonis has risen from the dead!" The followers of *Zoroaster* claim that he rose from the dead and ascended into heaven. *Aesculapius* was called a "Son of God." After his death he arose into heaven. Of him Ovid prophesied: "Then shalt thou die, but from the dark abode shalt arise victorious, and be twice a God." The virgin-born *Lao-Kium* also rose from the dead and rose bodily into heaven. The Egyptian Savior, *Osiris*, arose

Since no exact date is known for the Resurrection, its celebration at Easter is a moveable ceremony, varying every year. And its connection with the Cycles of the Sun and Moon is shown by the fact that it takes its name from *Eastre*, the Anglo-Saxon Goddess of Spring, and is celebrated on the Sunday after the full moon following the Spring equinox or the Sunday which follows the calendar moon which falls upon or next after the 21st of March. As to why this should be so, we are again forced to enquire into its cosmic and spiritual symbology for an explanation.

That man is in some mysterious way akin to Nature not even the most positive materialist will attempt to deny. But he who understands esoteric wisdom recognizes that the thread which binds man to Nature is something more than akinness; that it is the same Divine Principle, differing only in degree, that is manifesting in Nature and in man; the same Divine Principle that moved upon the face of the waters of Chaos, and said: "Let there be light." It is a question of a stage of evolution, or degree of manifestation. That which makes man greater than the flowers of the field is his power, consciously, by his own volition, to obey the Law of Divinity rather than follow it blindly; to permit the Resurrection and the life—which in Nature

---

from the dead and bore the title of "The Resurrected One." The Persian Savior, *Mithras*, whose sufferings were believed to have caused the salvation of his followers, arose from the dead amidst a great burst of light. The Phrygian Savior, *Attys* also rose from the dead. The ressurection of the Greek Savior, *Bacchus*, was celebrated with great rejoicings. The Savior, *Hercules*, arose from a funeral pyre and ascended into paradise. The Scandinavian Savior, *Baldur*, rose from his grave to testify to his immortality. Many other Savior-gods, such as *Memnon, Amphiaraus, Frey, Tien, Quetzalcoatle, Dionysus*, etc., all rose from the dead on the same Sun's day at the vernal equinox, now called Easter.

is the blind obedience of matter to Spirit—to take place in him as a conscious individualization of Deity.

Early in the Spring the mind of man is naturally turned with rejoicing toward the resurrection of the Sun from the southern hemisphere, to take its place as the Lifebringer to the northern hemisphere. Research shows that for ages throughout the ancient world the Resurrection of the god *Sol*, under different names in different ages and among different people, was celebrated on March 25th with elaborate ceremonies of great rejoicing. In Christian countries this event is called Easter, and celebrates the Resurrection of Jesus from the three days in the tomb. In so-called heathen lands the same festival is arranged to celebrate the advent of Spring or the bringing forth of a new creation, the rising from the dead of the creative potencies of Nature.

At this season of the year all Nature is performing before our eyes the mighty miracle of the Resurrection. The cold, icy tomb of Winter—the night-time of the year, during which Nature sleeps and assimilates and consolidates the force of growth and digests the experiences of the Summer—begins to feel the rejuvenating warmth of the creative force in action, the out-breathing of the Great Breath whose power arouses and brings forth the life-force in dormant Nature. For just as the inbreathing of the Great Breath indraws the life-force and produces the deadness of Winter, the unconsciousness of sleep and the death of the physical body, so does its outbreathing bring about the Resurrection from these conditions by sending forth a new cyclic outpouring of the divine life-force—the cosmic Christ-force—which makes all things to live.

This great event most beautifully illustrates for us the great Law of Cyclic Manifestation. This basic Law teaches us the inspiring lesson that out of death cometh the Resurrection of life; out of the dark tomb of Winter cometh the glorious Resurrection of Spring; out of the bondage of snow and ice cometh the Resurrection of light and warmth; out of the darkness of night cometh the Resurrection of dawn; out of the prison house of limitation cometh the Resurrection of freedom; out of the darkness of ignorance cometh the Resurrection of enlightenment and understanding; out of the darkness and inertia of materialism cometh the Resurrection of spiritual realization.

These illustrations should teach us the fundamental lesson of the Resurrection, namely, the necessity for absolute reliance upon Divine Law ultimately to resurrect us in due season from whatever entombing condition of darkness, discouragement and limitation we may be experiencing. As St. Paul so confidently assures us: "Therefore we are buried with him by baptism unto death: that like as Christ was raised up from the dead by the glory of the Father, even so we also should walk in newness of life. For if we have been planted together in the likeness of his death, we shall be also in the likeness of his resurrection." (*Romans, vi, 4, 5*).

For just as the farmer relies absolutely upon the Law of Resurrection to bring forth his seeds from the tomb of the earth and thereby bring forth his crops, so must we rely upon that same universal, immutable, Cosmic Law to resurrect the seeds of spiritual realization and ideals we have planted in the tomb of our material conditions, and bring them forth as crops of righteousness in our lives.

All manifestations of the Divine Creative Force are cyclic. And just as each Easter-time marks a new outpouring of that Creative Force to awaken all Nature and resurrect it from the tomb of Winter, so it is with man. Each Easter-time marks a new cycle or season for us also. It gives us a new opportunity to learn the lessons of the Resurrection of Nature around us. For at this season there is an increased outpouring of spiritual life, light and power which will help to awaken us from our winter of spiritual indifference and inactivity. This will enable us to put forth new buds of aspiration and unfold new blossoms of spiritual realization.

This new wave of Cosmic Life-force makes our Resurrection much more possible than at other seasons. For at this season old atoms are being sloughed off in large numbers, like the husks from the sprouting grain, and new atoms are being rapidly assimilated and built into all our bodies. But just as each plant must correlate with the forces of Spring if it is to grow and bring forth its crop, just so is it personally operative in our lives only to the extent that we recognize and correlate with it.

For with man, unlike Nature, there is a personal responsibility to prepare the soil of his mind and heart, and plant the seed, that the spiritual force that is assimilated shall bring forth only that which has been carefully selected as desirable. For without careful preparation the weeds spring up first and grow through the same force that makes flowers bloom. The snakes and poisonous insects also awaken to activity through the same instinct that brings back the birds and urges them to build their nests and prepare to bring forth new life and to fill the air with their glad songs.

Many earnest seekers cry out: "Why am I still held down in the tomb of my hampering material environment, buried under an avalanche of world conditions? Why do I not rise with Nature and the Christ and manifest His power to overcome ?" For many, one reason is that they are still living within the husk or shell of personality, focusing their attention upon the personalities and faults of others, instead of recognizing and focusing on, and mentioning, their good qualities. Many give their attention to, and almost bury themselves in the negative and sordid conditions of life which they contact or even hear about. Instead of letting all such conditions pass them by *without responding* to them, or if directly in their path of life, instead of stepping over or going around them as they would a mud-puddle, they bury themselves in the mud like frogs and croak out their complaints at the hampering, sordid and evil conditions of life.

There can be no Resurrection for such until they realize

the mental slough in which their consciousness is dwelling, and voluntarily climb out of the mud of criticism and condemnation, purify their minds with the waters of compassion and love and learn to soar like birds in mind and heart above the mud-puddles of life and build their nests high up in the green branches of the Tree of Life. There, above the pestilential miasma of the swamps of the sordid things of life, they can see the good in their fellow men shining through the shortcomings and imperfections of their personalities. Then they can sing glad praises to God for the many beauties and blessings which He provides so abundantly for their recognition, for their acceptance and for them to correlate with and absorb.

Once gain this conception and you can rise with the risen Lord of Life, pushing up the sprouts of your purified and expanding consciousness through the soil of material conditions as the early bulbs do in the Spring, steadily persisting in their unfoldment, even though late frosts and untimely snows may come to delay their flowering. Then you will have passed through the death pangs, will have risen out of the tomb of old conditions, have shaken off the grave clothes (mental limitations) and risen above the husks of old ideas and habits.

No interpretation of the Resurrection would be complete without some reference to the egg, for it is a universal symbol of the resurrection of life from the unmanifested. For the egg is the universal symbol of Easter, and its appropriateness cannot be questioned when we remember that the egg is the greatest mystery of creation; for all things must pass through the egg stage before creation or resurrection can manifest. Thus the egg is one of the greatest mysteries known to man, namely, the mystery that out of that which was unorganized, unconscious, formless, and void, a definite, organized form with its own innate consciousness should appear from out the unseen into the seen. From the earliest times and among all nations the egg has been the universal symbol of creation, of the origin of all things. References to this mystery are

found in all ancient religions, and modern religions unknowingly perpetuate its great truth through the use of
the Easter egg.

Back of and through this mystery a great Cosmic Law
is illustrated, for the egg symbolizes the confines within
which the divine creative or Cosmic Christ-force brings
forth, on whatever plane it may be, the ideal that is to be
manifested there. In the universe the shell of the egg represents the "Circle of Manifestation"[5] or the "Ring Pass
Not," within which are the "waters of the great deep" upon
which the Spirit moves.

The germ within the egg brings forth all that was contained within the egg before fecundation. This may seem
mystical language, yet science has demonstrated that this is
literally true, for that which is mystically spoken of as the
"Mundane Egg" in one sense is none other than the fire-
mist of science, which first is diffuse, then coheres into a
more compact egg-shaped mass, then gradually condenses
until it finally becomes a nebula, a globe or a universe.
This is the law of all creation, be it atom, egg or Cosmos.

For our Earth it was the Mundane Egg in which both
the forces and the materials for manifestation were lying
latent, waiting to be brought forth when the Lord said: "Let
there be light," to fructify that which was in the bosom of
the Divine Mother waiting to be brought forth. The thrill of
that Creative Ray brought the joy of life to the entire planet.
On earth the egg symbolizes the Womb of Nature out of
which all growing things are brought forth. And we all
know the thrill of joy we feel as the Christ-force in Nature,
which has so long been buried in the tomb of Winter, is
resurrected and brings forth in the beauty of Spring.

In each solar system the Solar Egg is the Ring Pass Not
and its contained aura within which the Solar Logos pours
the creative Christ-force that each planet may be born.

---

[5] For details see the chapter on *"The Meaning of the Seal,"* in *The Voice of Isis*,
Curtiss, 413.

At such Cosmic Easters it is said that: "The morning stars sang together" for joy that a new manifestation of the Cosmic Christ was coming into expression. Therefore, let the sight of an egg or the advent of Spring always associate itself in your mind with the thought of joy and a new birth.

As we have said elsewhere: "It is a scientific fact that in Nature all eggs and most seeds, in which the future animal, plant or man is latent, are either globular or more or less modified spheroids in shape. . . . Our word for cell is the Celtic name for Heaven, *Cel*, and this continuous birth from cell to cell was held identical with the manifestation of Deity. While the egg is the true symbol of all physical generation, it is also the symbol of the Christ Seed within each heart; for within the spheroidal aura surrounding each Soul like the shell of an egg, there is a germ-center, the Christ Seed, which like the germ-center in the egg, gradually grows and unfolds until at last the Christ Child emerges. He is then just as much a new and different expression of the Lord as is the chicken different from the egg when it emerges from the shell."[6]

Your personal Easter Egg is your oval aura which has been laid in the nest of earth conditions that out of it there might hatch the ideal Christ Man of perfected humanity. The realization of this Spiritual Self within may be latent or unrecognized at present. But some day the warmth of the Divine Mother-love will bring forth that Christ Seed so long buried in the tomb of your material consciousness, and your resurrection will take place.

As the process is out-pictured in *Genesis*, first there comes the Spirit of God—the Divine Light—which moves over the dark and chaotic conditions of your life and says, "Let there be light." This calls forth the love of your heart, and a great inner urge springs up to bring forth in you a new life and higher conditions; to break through the shell of old limitations, old habits, old ideas, and manifest that which in your heart you know you

---

[6] *The Key to the Universe*, Curtiss, 44, 40.

should. When this is accomplished it marks the birth of your spiritual consciousness from the limiting shell of the world's thought, the Resurrection of the Christ in you from the tomb of materialism. But from this time on you must protect and nourish this new-born realization and allow it to grow in manifestation in your life, for unless you consciously strive to do so you cannot hope for results.

The practical lesson to be learned at the season of Resurrection is not only the real meaning of the symbol of the egg, but also its practical application to our daily lives. To each Child of the Resurrection, *i.e.*, to him who has consciously recognized and permitted the Christ to rise from the deadness of his heart and life, is the opportunity given to lend his force toward vivifying the germ of spiritual life. And the Easter season is a great cyclic opportunity.

Each one must resurrect and bring forth the Christ love in his heart individually, and then must collectively send forth the sparks of Divine Love into the world; for collectively we are creating new conditions for the whole world.

Many of you have been passing through the death throes of the old, throwing off the old husks and crucifying the flesh, but on the Easter morn there comes to you the assurance that "I (the Christ within you) am the resurrection and the life; he that believeth in me (the Divine Life-force), though he were dead, yet shall he live: and whosoever liveth and believeth in me shall never die." (*St. John, ii, 25*). This is the whole secret. It means bringing your consciousness into absolute touch with this force of Resurrection. It is Divine Consciousness or Spiritual Ideality, capable of touching everything with life, making dead matter respond to its living force.

This is the lesson the Easter season should bring to you; that the Church services, the anthems, the prayers should teach you. The budding trees, the songs of the birds building their nests for the new life and preparing to bring forth anew, the flowers, and every voice and activity of Spring should convince you that the force which works through Nature to awaken it from its long sleep is the same Cosmic Christ-force working in and through you. Thus you may consciously bring forth the Christ which has been buried under the mass of mental debris while you have been sleeping through the long nights of your Winter-time, with your vibrations slowed down to the rhythm of the mere physical. All this should teach you that the same force can, and will, fill you with the new pulsating life-force and that you will be able to hear the command of the Christ: "Arise! Come forth from the tomb."

Be determined to obey the Voice. Believe that the stone of misconception and ignorance has been rolled away by the Angel of Truth, and that this same stone, which has for so long been a stone of stumbling, has now, by the power of the risen Christ, become the head-stone of the corner, the head of the great Universal Church of Christ, which is built upon the everlasting Rock of Truth, through the Resurrection of the Christ within.

Look around you in Nature and realize that the time has come for you also to put up new shoots of life, new expressions of your resurrected consciousness, new realizations, new ideas, new joys, new unselfishness, and love for the unfolding beauties you now see in your companions and all mankind, as well as in Nature. Breathe in the aroma of the good earth and the scents of the unfolding flowers and trees, and realize that a higher aspect of the same Christ-force which is manifesting in nature to fill the air with perfume, is also pouring its creative force through you that you may spread abroad the perfume of happiness, the "odor of sanctity," the beauty of holiness, if you will but *stop resisting and permit its expression.*

"If the Spirit of him who raised up Jesus from the dead dwell in you, he that raised up Christ from the dead shall also quicken your mortal bodies by his Spirit that dwelleth in you." (*Romans, viii, 11*). Since the Power of the

Resurrection manifests through all Nature, so can it manifest through you! Meditate upon the above quotation and repeat it again and again until its inner significance is revealed unto you in a glorious realization. Thus will you tune-in to the Power of the Resurrection and allow it to bring about the Resurrection in your life.

Strive to live consciously in the Power of the Resurrection. Whenever confronted by a serious problem, sit quietly by yourself, take a few slow deep breaths and relax. Say to yourself again and again *until you feel it*: "The Power of the Resurrection is now working freely in my body, my mind and in my affairs! And I rejoice and give thanks that it is so! And I will wait patiently for its manifestation in due season." Thus will you receive a Resurrection of health in your body, enlightenment in your mind, and peace and love in your heart.[7]

Breathe in, absorb, respond to and *express* that uprushing Christ-force from within as unresistingly and as gladly as do the trees and flowers, without stopping to argue the why and wherefore or the details of its manifestation, and without mental reservation or fear of imperfection. The trees and flowers do not have to understand the process or be taught any special technique in order to grow. When the time for their Resurrection, their springtime, comes and the Christ-force in Nature is uprushing and seeking expression through all forms of life, they respond at once and do nothing to impede it. They simply correlate with it and absorb it and allow it to express through them and bring forth to perfection their inner pattern.

So should your Resurrection be. Pray daily: "O Christ! from every wild flower by the roadside, from every plant and shrub and tree, help me to learn the great lesson of correlation and unfoldment, that I may experience the inner Resurrection and put forth and blossom and bring forth the 'fruits of the spirit' according to the

---

[7] For meditation on "The Prayer for Light" see *The Inner Radiance*, Curtiss, 184.

inner pattern of my true, Spiritual Self." Then you, too, will partake of the renewed life and joy of the springtime, and experience the Resurrection from the unsatisfying life of materialism and the darkness of spiritual ignorance, and fill the air of your environment with the perfume of your Rose of Life.

In summarizing this chapter we cannot do better than to repeat two stanzas of that well known hymn which we have quoted elsewhere.

"Down from their home on high
Down through the starry sky.
Angels, descending fly,
While the Earth shaketh.

Roll they the stone away
From where the Savior lay.
Out into glorious day
His way He taketh."

"And so may the angels of inspiration and divine guidance, spiritual understanding and illumination descend upon us here and now and roll away the stone of ignorance, of misunderstanding and misconception, the stone of materialism, from our hearts and minds wherein we have kept the divine Christ-consciousness entombed these many years, that He may come forth and take His way with us in our lives. Thus shall we be resurrected from the old life of entombing personality and ascend into the consciousness of that larger life of the Spirit which is our heritage and our real home."[8]

Happy is he who has experienced the Resurrection.

---

[8] From an address delivered by the author, before the Second Parliament of Religions of the World Fellowship of Faiths at the Morrison Hotel in Chicago at 8 P. M., on September 13th, 1933, and now included in *The Mystic Life*, Curtiss, 32-3.

CHAPTER XXII

THE ASCENSION

"And it came to pass, while he blessed them, he was parted from them, and carried up into heaven." *St. Luke, xxiv, 51.*

"And when he had spoken these things, while they beheld, he was taken up; and a cloud received him out of their sight." *Acts, i, 9.*

"The Sun continues to climb until it reaches its highest point in the heavens, in the last decanate of *Gemini*. This is called the ascension or the highest point above the earth." *Appendix A.*

The doctrine of the Ascension is so closely related to that of the Resurrection that it has caused almost as much controversy as the Resurrection itself. Also the Ascension is found in the life-stories of almost as many Sun-gods as the Resurrection, hence it is a universal feature of the Universal Solar Myth.

In spite of St. Paul's statement that: "Flesh and blood cannot inherit the kingdom of God," *(I Corinthians, xv, 50)*, the orthodox teaching is that it was the actual physical body of Jesus that was "carried up into heaven." What, then, happened to that physical body to change it so that it could disappear into thin air in the full sight of the watching disciples as "a cloud received him out of their sight"? *(Acts, i, 9)*. But no explanation is given.

Those who have given serious attention to the results of scientific psychic research know that there are ample physical proofs of the biblical teaching that the human personality survives the loss of its physical body in the

change called death. In its new and higher state the sur-
viving personality lives in a world of finer, etheric matter
which is several octaves of vibration higher than that of the
physical plane. In that higher world the person is clothed
in an astral or etheric body which is withdrawn from the
meshes of the physical body at death. The etheric body
is therefore the exact duplicate of the physical body, but
of a finer and more nearly perfect appearance. Because
of this fact the departed ones are easily recognized when
photographed or when seen materialized under test conditions.[1] Thus Moses and Elias were easily recognized by
the disciples when the two appeared and talked with Jesus
at the time of His transfiguration. (*St. Matthew, xvii, 3*).

It has been demonstrated countless times that the
etheric body can be so densely materialized that it can
be clearly seen and recognized by ordinary physical sight
under scientific test conditions in light sufficient for easy
recognition. Such materializations have been repeatedly
photographed[2] and the picture readily identified as that of
the deceased person named. This is one of several *scientific
physical proofs* of the teaching of nearly all religions that
so-called death applies to the physical body only and not
to the astral or etheric body or to the mind and consciousness of the personality.

Naturally those familiar with such materializations
conclude that it was Jesus' materialized etheric body in
which He arose from the tomb, appeared objectively for
forty days, displaying His wounds to Thomas and others,
and finally ascending into the higher realms. Scientifically
that could have been possible. But that theory fails to account for the disposal of Jesus' physical body. And Jesus
disproved that explanation when He said: "Behold my
hands and my feet, that it is I myself: handle me, and see;
for a spirit hath not flesh and bones, as ye see me have

---

[1] For details *see Realms of the Living Dead*, Curtiss.
[2] See *Photographing the Invisible*, Coats, and *The Phenomena of Materialization*,
Schrenck-Notzing.

. . . . And they gave him a piece of broiled fish, and of an honeycomb. And he took it, and did eat before them." (*St. Luke, xxiv, 39, 42-3*). This incident settles the materialized etheric body theory completely, for materialized forms have never been known to eat material food.

Likewise the claim of the mythologists previously quoted that: "Such narratives as those of the rock-burial and resurrection of the Savior-God in the Gospels are beyond all reasonable doubt simple developments of those mourning rituals which we have seen to be in use in so many ancient systems," must also be abandoned in view of the wealth of testimony presented and the reasonable explanation presented herein.

St Paul definitely promises that some day death will be overcome. "The last enemy that shall be destroyed is death" (*I Corinthians, xv, 26*), but he gives no explanation as to how that miracle shall be accomplished. He does give a hint, however, when he says that: "All flesh is not the same flesh. . . . There are celestial bodies, and bodies terrestrial. . . . It is sown in a natural body; it is raised a spiritual body," that is, when the transmutation is completed. "And as we have borne the image of the earthy, we shall also bear the image of the heavenly. . . . The first man Adam was made a living soul; the last Adam was made a quickening spirit. . . . Howbeit that was not first which is spiritual, but that which is natural: and afterward that which is spiritual. The first man is of the earth, earthy: the second man is the Lord of heaven," when the process of spiritualization is finished. "So when this corruptible shall have put on incorruption, and this *mortal* shall have put on *immortality*, then shall be brought to pass the saying that is written, Death is swallowed up in victory." (*I Corinthians, xv, 39-54*).

Here St. Paul definitely tells us that in some way this mortal body shall be so changed that: "In a moment, in the twinkling of an eye. . . . the dead shall be raised incorruptible, and we shall be changed." Yet there must be a definite process by which this instantaneous change can be made possible. And necessarily this process of the spiritualization of the flesh must take considerable time to complete. Yet the *Gospels* do not tell us how to accomplish this miracle—only the hints quoted above—for all such advanced, esoteric technical teachings were given secretly under the vows of Initiation to the initiated disciples only. As Jesus told them: "Unto you it is given to know the mystery of the kingdom of God: but to them that are without (that is, not initiated), all these things are done in parables." (*St. Mark, iv, 11*). "All these things spake Jesus *unto the multitude* in parables; and without a parable spake he not unto them." (*St. Matthew, xiii, 34*).

As we have pointed out elsewhere: "It is certainly not this imperfect and fallible human personality that is to be raised up at the last day. Still less is it this incompletely evolved and incompletely perfected animal body, but the *perfected manifestation* of our Spiritual Self, that is to be raised up at the last day. . . . And yet *there is a body* that is to be raised up at the last day. That is the *Light Body* which we finally build up by the purification, transmutation and spiritualization of the atoms of our various bodies through 'believing on the Son,' or following and manifesting the Christ within, until at our final incarnation we have built up a spiritualized vehicle or body through which we can manifest on any plane we wish."[3]

But since "flesh and blood cannot inherit the kingdom of God," how can the startling and miraculous phenomenon of the Resurrection and Ascension be brought about? Evidently some radical change must take place in the body of flesh to prepare it to enter the higher spiritual realms "in the twinkling of an eye" without passing through the portal of death. The explanation is both physical and metaphysical. The Path of Attainment may be followed in a general way almost unconsciously by trying to live the Christ-life without technical training, or

---

[3] *Why Are We Here?*, Curtiss, 20-1, 126.

it may be followed consciously by employing a definite, scientific technique in the use of super-physical and spiritual forces. In either case the process involves the mysteries of transmutation and translation. These are profound mysteries which can be dealt with only briefly herein.

It is well known in phychology that every thought and emotion generates a definite current of force in the mental world.[4] These currents are either constructive, destructive or neutral according to the character of the thought held.

Thoughts of discouragement and failure react on the body to depress all its vital functions, while fear can absolutely paralyze them. Thoughts and emotions of anger, lust, jealousy and revenge are actually degenerative and destructive to the bodily tissues. On the other hand, thoughts and emotions of joy, peace, love and goodwill are stimulating, purifying and constructive. If the destructive thoughts predominate the body becomes inharmonious, irritable, toxic, acid and even diseased. But if the constructive thoughts and emotions predominate, the body will be harmonious, pure and full of vitality and radiant health, because it is constantly subjected to currents of high and constructive mental and emotional forces.

In addition to constructive mental and emotional forces, when meditation, aspiration and prayer are consciously used to contact the forces of the higher mental and spiritual realms, then still higher octaves of force are involved, namely, spiritual forces. These forces have been measured with a scientific radionic instrument and proved to nearly double the body's vitality. These spiritual forces not only increase the body's vitality, but they hasten its purification and thus gradually transmute and spiritualize it atom by atom. As we have explained elsewhere: "The true or Spiritual Self—the Ego, a spark from the Infinite—incarnates again and again in the human-animal

---

[4] Dr. Hoagland Howard, of Clark University, has discovered *alpha*, *beta* and *delta* brain-waves. Dr. Hallowell Davis, of Harvard University, has recorded them on an electro-encephalogram.

body for the purpose of gaining experience in matter, and, through its informing the physical atoms of an earthly body, helps to redeem and spiritualize matter. . . . It gains more experience and needs a better body from time to time until, finally, it masters the matter which makes up its physical garments and immortalizes it so that the personality is swallowed up in the Individuality: the mortal puts on immortality and becomes one with the Father-in-heaven"[5] or makes the Ascension.

"This process of transmutation begins from within and works outward from the heart center. From there it sends out radiations or lines of force which gradually set up new sub-centers of radiation in various parts. . . . Just as a cancer sends out slender radiating filaments which insinuate themselves into the surrounding tissues and organs to destroy them, so the fiery lives of the Christ-force, when directed by the consciousness of an enlightened mind, manifest in an analogous way, but in a diametrically opposite and constructive manner. . . . This process of transmutation and purifying goes on through every incarnation. In each life some cells are spiritualized, and these are never lost, but are added to life after life. Every cell which the Christ-force has spiritualized becomes immortal, and at the next earth life is built into the new body around the sacred centers, so that little by little we inhabit a more and more nearly perfect body, until *in some life* we find it possible to complete the purification and spiritualization of all our interblending bodies, mental, etheric and physical."[6]

"Thus we can renew our life-forces, revivify and *recreate our bodies* periodically little by little and not be obliged to re-create an entire new body at a later incarnation. This is the great truth back of the doctrine of Regeneration and Immortality in the flesh."[7]

"To obtain the regenerating, redeeming and illuminat-

---

[5] *Letters from the Teacher*, Curtiss, I, 27.
[6] *The Key of Destiny*, Curtiss, 21-2, 20.
[7] *The Key to the Universe*, Curtiss. 168-9.

ing effects of our Christ within, we must have certain definite periods daily when we *deliberately expose ourselves to
or bathe* in the inner mystical Christ-light. . . . We should
visualize our Spiritual Self not as a finite mortal, but as a
great and glorious immortal *spiritual Being*, overshadowing us and endeavouring to find ever greater and greater
expression through us, according to our recognition of and
response to His divine guidance. . . . We often lose the
memory of our heavenly home and *who we really are* so
that we manifest so little of our Spiritual Self that we seem
to be but mortals instead of immortals."[8]

"Immortality in the flesh is therefore a physical possibility, but its attainment does not mean that the one who has
attained it will have to live on earth forever. But it does
mean that such an one can live on earth in such a body
as long as his work requires a vehicle on the earth plane.
When this is no longer necessary, the vibratory key-note
of such a body can be raised at will until it disappears
from physical sight and manifests on any higher plane
desired. . . . This spiritual or *Nirmanakaya* body is not a
ready-made body which we will some day inhabit after we
leave our poor wornout physical body, but is a spiritual or
'fire-body' that is built slowly and gradually, cell by cell,
within the physical throughout all our incarnations."[6] It is
evidently this spiritualized substance of which the "fire-
body" is built to which St. Paul refers when he tells us that:
"Ye have in heaven a better and more enduring substance."
(*Hebrews, x, 34*). "For we know that if our earthly house
(body) of this tabernacle were dissolved (transmuted), we
have a building (or body) of God, an house not made with
hands, eternal in the heavens." (*II Corinthians, v, 1*).

"A true *Nirmanakaya* body, however, altho manifesting
in the etheric world, is not an etheric or even a psychic
body (*Mayavi Rupa*), but is a *spiritual body* which is born
in the heart of the Adept *while in the flesh*, and which takes

---

[8] *The Inner Radiance*, Curtiss, 8, 9.

the form of the personality by first growing out from the heart through the marrow of the bones, and later extending out beyond them until it permeates the entire body of flesh and ultimately spiritualizes all its atoms. This process requires *many, many incarnations*. But ultimately the body thus spiritualized becomes no longer a mere physical body. . . . but is a redeemed and spiritualized body in which its master can appear and disappear in any realm or any world at will."[9]

Since this process of spiritual transmutation is so slow that it extends over many incarnations, there is little hope of the average student's making his Ascension in this life *unless* this is his last and culminating incarnation. If it is, then he will have lived such a saintly life from childhood that he can complete the process now. But even if this is not his last incarnation, every effort he makes to respond to and radiate the forces of the Christ within will help him step by step toward his ultimate sainthood and finally to his Ascension.

Since this spiritual transmutation of the flesh is such an age-long process, it is very misleading to tell the general public[10] that anyone and everyone who will repeat certain affirmations and make certain so called "decrees," can make the Ascension in this life. It is also most disillusioning and discouraging to find that in spite of all one's faith and sincere and faithful efforts, only one in millions is ready or can be prepared to make the Ascension now. Hence, while all are urged to strive toward their ultimate spiritualization and Ascension, none should be discouraged at his seemingly slow progress.

Just as the Sun's slow climb from the lowest to the highest point in the physical heavens constitutes its Ascension, in like manner the slow climb of the Soul from the

---

[9] *Realms of the Living Dead*, Curtiss, 239.

[10] As certain teachers have taught in recent years, but without the slightest proof or example, the leader himself dying of "arteriosclerotic heart disease, and cardiac cirrhosis of the liver." *Psychic Dictatorship in America*, Bryan, 247.

lowest point of animalism to the highest point in its heaven constitutes its spiritual Ascension.

Such a phenomenal transmutation of the physical body is clearly the teaching of Jesus, for He promised that: "If any man keep my saying (His teachings), he shall never see death." (*St. John, viii, 51*). And St. Paul tells us that: "the law of the spirit of life in Christ Jesus hath made me free from the law of sin and death," (*Romans, viii, 2*), even though Paul did not live to complete the transmutation and make his Ascension. Paul did, however, know a man who did make his Ascension, for he tells us: "I knew a man in Christ above fourteen years ago. . . . such an one caught up to the third heaven. . . . into paradise, and heard unspeakable words, which it is not lawful to utter." (*II Corinthians, xi, 2-4*). It was not only unlawful to utter or repeat such instructions, according to the vows of Initiation, but it is impossible to describe in the language of our three-dimensional world the glories of the higher dimensional worlds.

Jesus plainly indicated that this spiritualized or *Nirmanakaya* body, over which He naturally had perfect control, was the kind of body He possessed when He said: "I lay down my life, that I might take it up again. No man taketh it from me, but I lay it down of myself. I have the power to lay it down, and I have the power to take it up again." (*St. John, x, 17,18*).

The fact that Jesus had this absolute power over His body long before the Crucifixion and Ascension is evidenced by His exercising it publicly on two occasions. Once when a crowd was about to stone Him He "went out through the midst of them." (*St. John, viii, 59*). He used it again when a mob had led Him to the brow of a hill, "that they might cast him down headlong. But he passing through the midst of them went his way." (*St. Luke, iv, 29*).

That Jesus was using such a *Nirmanakaya* body is also evidenced by His suddenly materializing it and walking with two of His disciples on the way to Emmaus. After their arrival, and while He was eating with them at the inn: "He vanished out of their sight." (*St. Luke, xxiv, 31*). Later that same evening after the two disciples had returned to Jerusalem, He astonished them and the others gathered with them by suddenly materializing before them so quickly and unexpectedly that: "They were terrified and affrighted, and supposed they had seen a (materialized) spirit." (*St. Luke, xxiv, 37*).

After proving to Thomas and the others that He was no discarnate spirit nor even a materialized etheric body, as we have already pointed out earlier in this Chapter, and that He was still using the same body that was crucified, while He was on the way to Bethany with His disciples, He suddenly dematerialized His body and "was parted from them, and carried up into heaven." (*St. Luke, xxiv, 51*).

From the above incidents—which can be satisfactorily explained in no other way—it is clear that no other body than a *Nirmanakaya* body could possibly have fulfilled all the varied requirements and permitted the Translation and Ascension to take place.

This brief and necessarily incomplete explanation of the profound mystery of the transmutation and Ascension may sound improbable at first reading, but on further study it will be found to be the only rational and scientific explanation which *solves all the problems* of how "the last great enemy"—the death of the physical body—can be overcome. (*I Corinthians, xv, 26*). "Behold, I shew you a mystery."

If proofs of this explanation of the doctrine of the Ascension are desired, we have only to remind you of several well-known instances of such translation of the spiritualized physical body into the higher invisible realms without leaving it behind through death. In addition to the Ascension of Jesus through this process, you will recall that: "Elijah went up by a whirlwind (of force) into heaven." (*II Kings, ii, 11*). Also "Enoch was translated that he should not see death; and was not found, because

God had *translated* him." (*Hebrews, xi, 5. Genesis, v, 24*).

Then there is the heretofore unexplained strange case of Melchisedec, to whom even Abraham paid tithes, and who was called "the priest of the Most high God. . . . being by interpretation King of Righteousness, and after that also King of Salem, which is King of Peace; without father, without mother, without descent (genealogy), having neither beginning of days, nor end of life; but made like unto the Son of God; abideth a priest continually." (*Hebrews, vii, 1-3*). From the above it is evident that Melchisedec must have manifested in a *Nirmanakaya* body; for that is the only body that could have been "without father, without mother, without descent." It is no wonder then that when Jesus manifested in His *Nirmanakaya* body He was "made an high priest forever *after the order of* Melchisedec." Naturally also Jesus was called the "Prince of Peace," since Melchisedec was called the "King of Peace."

There was also the case of the great Kabalist, Simeon Ben Joachai. "Many are the marvels recorded as having taken place at his death, or we should rather say his translation; for he did not die as others do, but having suddenly disappeared, while a dazzling light filled the cavern with glory."[11]

And this same law holds good in modern times as well. In India, where so much attention is given to the mysterious workings of spiritual forces, there are records of numerous cases of translation and Ascension of the bodies of Hindu saints. For instance, some years ago the Mahatma Sri Rama Linga made the Ascension from his bungalow while his chelas and followers completely surrounded it all night chanting prayers. When they entered it in the morning they found only his loin cloth in the spot where he had been sitting on the floor. As is usual in such cases, he had been a well-known poet, prophet and God-conscious saint of Southern India almost from childhood.

---

[11] *The Secret Doctrine*, Blavatsky, III, 93.

Thus he proved his right to the Ascension by his saintly life and teachings, and the many miracles which he wrought. In other words, *he was ready* for the translation and Ascension. And there are records of many others who have thus made the Ascension. "Great saints of yore have attained at-one-ment with the Divine and made the Ascension by worship of Nataraja with their knowledge. It was before His presence that the Saint *Maniccavacha*, and also Saint *Nanda*, the Pariah Saint, *disappeared bodily* into the Brahmic splendor."[12] These facts are too well attested to permit argument as to their reality. Hence they must be accepted as veridical whether fully understood or not.

Once you have gained this cosmic concept of the Ascension, death has no more dominion over you, for you have died to the mental limitations of materialism and the sordid things of life, and have ascended into the freedom, light and joy of the Christ-consciousness. Then the husks of any old material conditions, thoughts or habits which may still cling around your roots for a while will gradually disintegrate, and their forces of good will be absorbed or act as fertilizer, as you consciously extract their misdirected good and use it toward your ultimate Ascension.

If you are sincere in your desire to live *The Pattern Life*, and wish to apply its teachings to the mastery of your life and the conditions of your environment, and also to your daily steps toward your unfoldment and Ascension, so that you may be "transformed into the same image from glory to glory, even by the spirit of the Lord," there is something you must do toward that great end. The more you strive to fill out the pattern set for your life, the more joy is manifested through you for the greater uplift and happiness of those within the sphere of your influence, the more you advance toward Christhood.

A life based on prayer: a life of faith and worship: of compassionate understanding: of guided usefulness (i.e., encouraging and helping others to help themselves spirit-ward), will help to manifest the pattern which your

---

[12] *The Kalyana-Kalpataru Magazine*, November 1935, page 709.

Spiritual Self incarnated to express. Contemplate your digressions daily from this standpoint in order that you may correct any deviation from your pattern and fill it out wherever it may be lacking. "Be ye doers of the word, and not hearers only, deceiving yourselves. . . . But whoso looketh into the perfect law of liberty, and continueth therein, he being not a forgetful hearer, but a doer of the world, this man shall be blessed in his deed." (*St. James, i, 22*).

Thus will your understanding of *The Pattern Life* of Jesus reveal to you the Way, the Truth and the Life, whereby you also can understand and achieve the Resurrection and make the Ascension, and thus enter into the glory and the satisfying joy of Christhood here and now.

"If ye then be risen with Christ, seek those things which are above, where Christ sitteth on the right hand of God. Set your affections (heart) on things above, not on things on earth. For ye are dead, (to sin) and your life is hid with Christ in God." (*Colossians, iii, 1-3*).

Happy, indeed, is he who makes the Ascension.

APPENDIX A

THE ASTRONOMICAL EVENTS

Astronomically the Sun is said to be "born" into its cycle of the New Year soon after it reaches its lowest point in the southern hemisphere—the Nadir—and starts on its upward journey toward the northern hemisphere where its light, life and warmth will bring all things into a new expression of life in the springtime.

This "birth" takes place when the Sun is in the sign *Capricorn*—the Goat, from the Latin *caper*, a goat, and *cornus*, a horn—symbolizing the universal productive or creative force in Nature, involving the creation or genesis of all forms.

"In ancient Akkadian folklore the Sun was called 'the Goat,' *Uz*, because he was *par excellence* the Climber, the High One; and the same name was given in the usual mythological way to the zodiacal constellation (*Capricorn*) which marks the beginning of the Sun's upward climb in the heavens. . . . The final mythological lesson is that. . . . the God, and the Mountain are all mere variants of the one original idea of the Climbing Sun in *Capricorn*, the High One who rules the world."[1]

The ancients called *Capricorn* the "Gate of Heaven" or the region through which the Light of Heaven (Sun) is manifested on Earth. Hence this event marks the beginning of the new cycle of the Sun as it starts out from the Nadir or lowest point in the southern hemisphere—often called the "pit" or "cave" of the zodiac—on a new era of expression.

---

[1] *Christianity and Mythology*, Robertson, 320-4.

The Moon has its "detriment" in *Capricorn*, hence, as the reflected light of the Moon wanes, the light of the Sun can again begin to shine with more force. The sign *Capricorn* rules shepherds and the stables, hence the lowly birthplace of all Lightbringers; for they are usually represented as being born in a stable in the presence of an ox, ass, goat, etc., and laid in a manger and attended by shepherds.

Astronomically, at the time of the birth of the Sun, the sign *Virgo*, the Virgin, is rising on the eastern angle of the planisphere. Hence all the Sun-gods or Lightbringers are represented as being born of a Virgin. Another remarkable fact is that all the Mothers have names which mean or symbolize the sea, the Great Deep or Divine Love, thus: Mary, Maia, Maria, Meris, Myrrh, Miriam, Maritala, Mariamna, Mariankynium, etc.[2] The names all begin with the letter M, which is also the symbol for the sign *Virgo*, ♍. And the fathers are all artisans of some kind, carpenters, smiths, modellers, etc., indicating the active, creative, fashioning power of the Sun, focussing the ruling aspect of the Divine Will or Father-force of the Godhead upon all Nature. "For by him were all things created." (*Colossians, i, 16*). "All things were made by him; and without him was not anything made that was made." (*St. John, i, 3*).

And since *Virgo* is the sixth sign, the Annunciation is made in the sixth month. The Sun is therefore born of *Virgo*, and naturally without a father, except the overshadowing of the "highest"—the vault of the sky—while the mother still remains a virgin.

In all cases the birth takes place while the mother has been riding upon an ass while on a journey, the journey of the Sun through the zodiac. Astronomically, the great star Spica (Arista) arises in the constellation *Virgo*—which rules Bethlehem, the House of Bread—with her companion, Joseppe, in the constellation Bootes, and travels to a position in the heavens corresponding to the journey from Nazareth southward to Bethlehem. Hence the birth

[2] For details see *The Key of Destiny*, Curtiss, 143-5.

of all Lightbringers is announced by the appearance of a
great star. And they are always sought out by the Wise Men
of their age who accord them divine honors and present
gifts.

The brightest star in the constellation Canis Major is
Sirius, the Dog Star, which symbolizes the Savior himself.
For many years the beautiful *Sirius* has been associated
with the approach of a Savior. In Egypt when this star
appeared the people knew that the annual rise of the Nile
was near, and this increase of water meant renewed life
for them, hence it was their Savior.

Just as kings are preceded by heralds, so is the Savior
star, *Sirius*, preceded by its forerunner, *Procyon*, the brightest star in the constellation Canis Minor. *Procyon* therefore
corresponds to John the Baptist. And *Procyon* is in the
sign *Cancer* at the time of the summer solstice, six months
before the birth of the Sun at the winter solstice. Naturally,
then, since John the Baptist is six months older than Jesus,
he is made to say: "He must increase, but I must decrease."

By many, *Sirius* is called the "Star of Bethlehem" that
led the three Wise Men, the three bright collinear stars of
the second magnitude—*Alnitake, Alnilam, Mintaka*—in
the belt of the mighty hunter, Orion, the middle decanate
of *Taurus*. For on Christmas Eve *Sirius* arises at 7 P.M.
and at midnight is on the meridian and East of the stars in
Orion's belt. Thus the Wise Men see His star in the East.

These stars rise in the East and travel westward to a
point where the great star *Arcturus* rises over the manger
of *Io* in the constellation Bootes, the Great Bear, *Ursa
Major*, as *Virgo* rises in the East. *Io* is called the "cow-
horned maid" because of her identity with Eve, Isis and the
Moon, which are everywhere recognized as the symbols
of passive, generative force of Nature. Hence her natural
connection with the manger. The meaning of Io-seppe is
"the manger of Io."

As the constellation *Draco* or *Ophiucus*—the Dragon,
Hydra, or Herodes—armed with a cudgel naturally arises

up over *Libra* in the East, the constellation *Aries*—the Ram
or Lamb—flees before it in the West and disappears below the horizon towards "Egypt" or the land of darkness,
so that the Dragon of Night (Herod) seems to devour all
the stars in his path. All infant Lightbringers are therefore
represented as being pursued by some vindictive ruler and
fleeing to some far-off place of safety. But in none of the
stories is the child ever caught, so the pursuer orders a
slaughter of the innocents, just as the stars pale and disappear at dawn.

As the Sun leaves the 30° of *Capricorn* it enters upon
the watery period of the year in the succeeding signs of
Aquarius—the Water Bearer—and *Pisces*—the Fishes. The
Christian era marked the entry of the Sun by precession
into the two thousand year cycle of the Piscean or Fish Age.
The symbol of the Fish therefore runs like an illuminating
line of light, not only through the *Gospels*, but through
the whole early Christian mysticism and ecclesiastical art.
As His representative the Pope wears the "Fisherman's
Ring," while the Bishop's mitre represents a fish's head.
"The newly baptised Christians used to be called 'fishes'
(*pisciculi*) by Tertullian, and the baptismal font is still
called the *piscina*, or 'fish-pond.'"[3] Also the first letters
of the Greek words expressing the title of Jesus—*Iesous*,
Christos, *Theo*, *Uios*, *Soter*—(Jesus Christ, Son of God,
Savior)—form an acrostic which spells the word fish—
Ichthus—in Greek.

Many of Jesus' miracles were connected with fish or
the sea, such as the two small fishes used to feed the multitude, and the twelve basketfuls gathered afterward. The
disciples' miraculous draft of fish, the coin found in the
mouth of a fish, the walking on the water, stilling the waves
and so forth, all identify Jesus as the Lightbringer for the
Piscean or Fish Age.

Altho only four of Jesus' disciples were fishermen, they
were all called "Fishers of Men," not because they all made
their living catching and peddling fish, but because they

[3] *The Witnesses to the Historicity of Jesus*, Drews, 190.

were the twelve representatives—one for each sign of the
zodiac—of the Savior of the Piscean or Fish Age. Hence
no zodiacal sign could be more fitting for the Christ and
His disciples than the fish sign, *Pisces*. Also *Pisces* is a sign
that is said to overflow with sympathy, while its association
with the maimed, the distressed and the downtrodden is
well known to all students of astrology.

Astronomically, the "shepherds" refers to a pair of
bright stars, *Alpha Capricornis*, of the third and fourth
magnitude—each of which has a companion of the ninth
magnitude—which are said to "guard the flock" of twenty
nine stars in the constellation *Capricorn*, whose symbol
is the Goat.

When the Sun has completed its circuit through the 12
signs of the zodiac it is said to be 12 years (or cycles) old,
and is ready to be about its Father's business or ready to
start out on a new cyclic round.

The ancients assigned to *Capricorn* the constellation
Cygnus, the Swan. This is a most appropriate assignment,
for like the Sun and the bird, *Cygnus* travels South in the
winter and North in the summer. The river Jordan corresponds to the celestial river Eridanus or the Milky Way.
Hence, when the Sun enters the Milky Way, that celestial
river spreads apart or the "heavens opened" and the constellation *Cygnus* the Swan or heavenly dove, "descends"
or becomes visible directly overhead. At the same time
the Water Bearer of *Aquarius* pours out the water from his
urn in baptism into the mouth of the Southern Fish in the
third decanate of *Capricorn* and thus causes the Baptism.

Since *Pisces* occupies 30° of the zodiac, all Sun-gods
receive a baptism of water at the mystical age of 30. The
four brightest stars of *Cygnus* form the Northern Cross.
Thus does the Baptism foreshadow the coming tragedy
of Golgotha, as the cross above casts its shadow below.

The 30° of *Aquarius*, together with the first 10° of
Pisces,—the sign of sacrifice—make up the 40° associated
with the 40 days spent by Jesus in the wilderness where He

is tempted by or has to withstand the trying forces of Satan, Satar or Saturn, the Tester, who is the co-ruler of Aquarius.

After the autumnal crossing—the crucifixion—the Sun enters the lowest point in the southern hemisphere where it apparently remains stationary for three days, hence the "three days in the tomb."

After spending three months in the "tomb" of the southern hemisphere, the Sun continues to rise until it crosses the equator into the northern hemisphere. There it enters the sign *Aries* where it is said to be "exalted." This event is called the vernal equinox which ushers in the beginning of Spring, and is celebrated universally by the ceremony of Easter. Thus the Sun pours forth its light, heat and life-force—sheds its symbolic "blood"—that all Nature may be resurrected from the tomb of Winter and have life more abundantly. Therefore this event is called the "Resurrection."

In the last decanate of *Aries* is found the constellation *Perseus* with the uplifted sword. This symbolizes the sword with which Peter cut off the ear of the high priest's servant, for this decanate adjoins the sign *Taurus* which rules the ears. This *Sagitarius* decanate is ruled by Jupiter which has dominion over priests and their households.

The Sun then encounters *Gemini,* the Twins (Simon and Andrew), above the horizon, and naturally they follow him as Simon and Andrew did Jesus. The Sun then encounters Argo, the Ship, containing the two fishermen (James and John). Later on it meets *Libra*, or Levi the publican with his scales—the symbol of *Libra*—who also follows, as did Levi.

The Sun continues to climb until it reaches its highest point in the heavens in the last decanate or the last 10° of *Gemini*. This is called the "Ascension" to its highest point above the earth. In the first decanate of *Cancer* the Sun begins to fall. This seemingly backward movement gives to *Cancer* the appropriate symbol of the Crab, which has a sideward or backward motion. This point symbolizes

Jesus' return to Jerusalem after reaching the zenith of His triumphal journey.

After the Sun passes through *Cancer* it enters its home sign, *Leo*, the Lion. It is therefore only natural that Jesus should be called "the Lion of the tribe of Judah." For when Jacob gave the emblems of the twelve signs of the zodiac to his twelve sons as the emblems for the banners of the twelve tribes of Israel, he said that Judah was *Leo*, "the lion's whelp."[4]

The first decanate of *Leo* — the heart — contains an important constellation called the Crater or the Cup. Around it many myths and legends are woven. Out of this Cup the Sun must "drink" as it passes through the constellation. Hence Jesus — as the representative of the Sun — is made to say: "O my father, if it be possible, let this cup pass from me: nevertheless not as I will, but as thou (cyclic law) wilt."[5] Benjamin was detained in Egypt by this cup, and it is also the Heavenly Cup of the legends of the Holy Grail. In the Eucharist it is this Cup of *Leo* that holds the sacrificial wine or the symbolic "blood of the heart."

The zodiac itself forms a magic ring or cup[6] in which all the forces needed for the evolution of this planet and its inhabitants are held like essences or salts in solution in some magic potion from which our Cosmos is refreshed and renewed, each essence being precipitated from the solution when the proper time and conditions vibrate to its "critical point of crystalization" or point of materialization.

The events preceding the crossing of the equator or the "crucifixion" of the Sun at the autumnal equinox are explained by the decanates of *Leo* and *Virgo*. Following the Cup, the second decanate of *Leo* reveals the constellation *Centaurus*, the mounted soldier, symbol of the captain and the soldiers who took Jesus and bound, crucified and pierced Him. In Greek the meaning of this constellation

---

[4] Genesis, XLXIX, 9.
[5] St. Matthew, XXVI, 39.
[6] See "Man and the Zodiac" in *The Inner Radiance*, Curtiss, 36-52.

is "the pierced." Similarly, the light and heat of the Sun are "bound" or their forces are limited after the autumnal equinox. In the third decanate of *Leo* we find the Raven, symbol of the cock that crew when Peter denied the Christ.

When at midnight *Aries*, the Lamb, reaches the Nadir or lowest point of the zodiac, the sign *Leo*, "the Lion of the tribe of Judah" or Judas, is 30° above the horizon. Hence Judas is said to give the Lamb (Jesus) the traitor's kiss for 30 pieces of silver or its 30° of light. As *Leo* disappears from sight it is said to have cast down its 30° pieces of silver, and is said to have "hung" itself.

Passing onward, the Sun enters three closely grouped constellations in the sign *Virgo*. The first decanate is Boötes, the Bear-driver with his whip. The second decanate is *Hercules*, with his club, who died from wearing the robes of the centaur *Nesscus*, pictured by the second decanate of *Leo*. As the soldiers put the purple robe upon Jesus and then removed it "and put his own raiment on him,"[7] so the Sun dons the purple robe of sunrise which fades and disappears as it "puts on its own raiment" of light. The robe is thus connected with the soldiers of the second decanate of *Leo* which rules over the color purple.

The last decanate of *Virgo* is *Corona Borealis* whose rays from above resemble a crown of spikes or thorns. Likewise, "They had platted a crown of thorns, they put it upon his head."[7]

The equinoxial point where the ecliptic crosses the equator is called the "cross." Naturally there are two such crosses, one in *Aries* in the Spring and one in *Libra* in the Fall. Hence there are two places of crucifixion mentioned in the *Gospels*, one at Golgotha or Calvary, corresponding to *Aries*, and one in Egypt (*Revelation, xi, 8*), the Land of Darkness, corresponding to *Libra*. Under the constellation *Centaurus* lies the Southern Cross or *Crux*. The drama of the Crucifixion is therefore symbolized in the heavens by the Cardinal Cross in the northern hemisphere and by the Southern Cross in the southern hemisphere. . . .

[7] *St. Matthew, XXVII*, 28, 31, 29.

The four brightest stars in *Cygnus* form the Northern Cross. Thus does the Baptism foreshadow the coming tragedy of Golgotha, as the cross above casts its shadow below. . . . All this was recognized and understood for countless *ages before the Christian era. Aries* and *Libra* are the Northern and Southern poles at the head and foot of the cross, and *Cancer* and *Capricorn* at the Eastern and Western poles.

The two thieves who are crucified on each side of the cross are symbolized by the two signs (*Cancer* and *Capricorn*) on the left and right arms of the Cross. After the balancing of the cross at the vernal equinox, when the days and nights are of equal length, something is taken off or "stolen" from each sign. Hence these signs are called the two thieves. As *Cancer* rises in the East, this thief is said to ascend into heaven to be with the Christ (Sun) in Paradise, that is, in the summer season of growth and fruition. As *Capricorn* disappears in the West the other thief is said to die or sink into the grave of the nether world of Satan or Saturn, the planet ruling *Capricorn*.

By some writers *Boötes* is identified with Simon of Cyrene, the man who was called upon to carry the cross up the hill—the arc of the heavens—to the place of crossifying or where the "crucifixion" takes place.

The Crucifixion takes place on the day of the autumnal equinox at the "sixth hour" or at the exact moment when the Sun sets or "dies" in the West. "And there was darkness over all the land until the ninth hour." The "sixth hour" when "the Sun was darkened, and the veil of the temple (the zodiac) was rent in the midst," refers to the sign *Virgo*, the sixth sign. The veil is rent by the passage of the Sun from *Virgo* to *Libra* which divides the zodiac exactly in half. Thus the veil of daylight is rent when the Sun sinks below the horizon. Then "the saints that slept," that is, the stars that were obscured or "buried" by the light of the Sun, "arose and came forth."

At the time of the autumnal equinox in the sign *Libra*, whose symbol is the balance or scales, the Sun's forces and the length of the days and nights are again balanced as they were at the spring equinox in *Aries*. But this time as the Sun crosses the Equator it is "crossified" or crucified and dies to the northern hemisphere—where it had been giving its life-blood for Nature all summer—for it has entered the next sign, *Scorpio*, the sign of death. The second decanate of *Scorpio* is called the altar of *Ara*, whereon Judas is said to have hanged himself.

"And many bodies of the saints which slept arose and came out of their graves" as the stars became visible after the veil of daylight was rent by the eclipse of the Sun. Nearby is the constellation called *Berenice's Hair* (Mary Magdalene, the hair-platter). The crucifixion is said to have taken place on Friday, as Venus, the ruler of *Libra*, is also the ruler of Friday.

In the ninth sign, *Sagittarius*, the soldiers divide the garment of the Sun—its outshining—into four parts. This symbolizes the division of the zodiac into the four seasons, spring, summer, autumn and winter. The coat woven without seam that could not be divided refers to the interweaving of the planetary and zodiacal forces that goes on continually.

Since the lower side of *Sagittarius* governs gambling, and since the *Sagittarius* decanate of *Leo* governs soldiers, they naturally gamble or "cast lots" for the coat.

After the autumnal crossing—the crucifixion—the Sun descends to the lowest point of the southern hemisphere where it apparently remains stationary for three days, hence the "three days in the tomb."

Then follows the results of the sacrifice—the redemption—the Sun sacrificing its light and life and pouring out its life-force symbolic blood that all Nature might find "salvation" and express more abundantly. From then onward the Sun ascends to the "throne of David"—the summer solstice—whence it shall "judge the quick and the dead," or the results of the season's assimilation of its life-force, the season's crops, "quick or dead," good or bad.

As the life-force of the Sun matures the grain from which bread is made, and turns the juice of the grape into wine, so does the life-force of the Spiritual Sun transmute our experiences into the "bread of life" and the "wine of the Spirit" for the nourishment of our spiritual life. Hence the spiritual significance of the seemingly cannibalistic statement of Jesus: "Except ye eat the flesh of the Son of Man, and drink His blood, ye have no life in you." (*St. John, vi, 53*).

APPENDIX B

SYMBOLICAL OR METAPHYSICAL INTERPRETATION

The symbolic or mystical interpretation of the *Gospels* explains the allegorical or spiritual sense which underlies the literal significance of persons, places, events, things and sayings. The principle was recognized by St. Paul when he tells us (*Galatians, iv, 24*) that the whole story of Abraham's two sons, one (Ishmael) born of a bondwoman (Hagar) and the other (Isaac) born of a freewoman (Sarah) was only an allegory. He also refers to it when he says: "The natural man receiveth not the things of the Spirit of God: for they are foolishness unto him: neither can he know them, because they are spiritually discerned." (*I Corinthians, ii, 14*).

In the great theological school at Alexandria in the early days of the Christian church, the tendency was to make little of the event itself in comparison with the truth it conveyed. The writings of St. Clement (150-215 A.D.), the head of that great school, are full of the symbolic interpretation of the *Gospels*. Fra. Origen (185-254 A.D.), the successor to St. Clement in the Alexandrian school, with great learning and critical discernment combines the allegorical with the literal interpretation. He defines three classes of interpretation, the literal, the moral and the allegorical or spiritual. He goes beyond St. Clement in teaching that the literal sense of many passages was not to be understood at all. He holds that in most cases the moral and mystical interpretations are used to explain the spiritual meaning of actual facts. But in other cases they are the only interpretations to be accepted.

St. Origen says: "Who that has understanding will suppose that the first and second and third day, and the evening and the morning, were without sun and moon and stars, or that the first day was without sky?. . . . I do not suppose that anyone doubts that these things are said figuratively by means of a history which is external and not literally told. . . . Those who are not wholly blind can collect countless such instances recorded as if they had happened, but which *did not literally happen*." (*De Principiis*, IV, iii, 1).

Another of the great church authorities, St. Augustine (354-430 A.D.), says: "In the narrative of events which have happened, we enquire whether all things are to be accepted only in a figurative sense or whether they are also to be asserted and defended as literal occurrences." (*De Genesis ad Lit.*, xi, 2) St Thomas Aquinas (1226-1274 A.D.) also distinguishes the literal and historical from the allegorical and spiritual interpretation, as do many of the early church authorities.

A modern authority on the subject says: "Modern anthropology finds in crude nature-myths, cosmogonies, and theogonies the germs of philosophy and science. Psychology is busy finding in dreams and myths imaginative symbols of profound rational significance, and interprets them accordingly. . . . When we pause to consider the action of the inspiring Spirit of God, we are faced with the fact that myth and symbol and legend and ceremony have been as truly the subject or vehicle for inspiration as history or prophecy." (*The Mystical Interpretation of the Old Testament*, Harris, 697).

All profound students and logical thinkers must discriminate between those passages which are of literal and historical value and those whose very wording makes their literal and physical interpretation rationally and spiritually impossible.

Elaborating the statement of St. Origen referred to in our *Introduction* (xix), we quote: "Since the chief aim was to announce the spiritual connection in the things that

have been done and that ought to be done. . . . The Scripture
wove into the history an event which did not happen, sometimes that could not have happened, and sometimes that
could have happened and did not." He held that if the right
use of enlightened Christian reason shows that a literal
interpretation would be physically, morally or spiritually
impossible, then that which is repugnant to the enlightened
conscience is not to be accepted. (*De Principiis*, Origen,
IV, ii, 7-9.)

APPENDIX C

BIRTH DATES

Since the Christian Church celebrates December 25th as the birthday of Jesus, most people naturally think—because they have been taught so—that was the day of the month on which Jesus was actually born. But that is far from being true. As a matter of fact, no one knows what the date was.

Cannon Farrar, in his *Life of Christ*, (App. 673) says: "It is *universally admitted* that our received chronology, which is not older than Dionysius Exiguus, in the sixth century, is wrong. But all attempts to discover *the month* and the *day* are useless. *No data whatever exists* to enable us to determine them with even approximate accuracy." The Rev. Dr. Giles, in his *Hebrew and Christian Records* (ii, 189), says: "We have no clue to either the day or the time of year, or even the year itself, in which Christ was born."

The Rev. Dr. Geikie, in his *Life of Christ*, (i, 559), says: "The whole subject is *very uncertain*. Ewald appears to fix the date of the birth at *five years* earlier than our era. Petavius and Usher fix it on December 25th, *five years* before our era. Bengel. . . . Anger and Winer, *four years* before our era, in the spring; Scaliger, *three years* before our era, in October; St. Jerome, *three years* before our era, on December 25th; Eusebius, *two years* before, on January 6th; and Idler, *seven years* before our era, in December."

Albert Barnes, in his *Barnes' Notes*, (ii, 402), says: "God has concealed the time of his birth. *There is no way to ascertain it.* By different learned men it has been fixed at *each month* in the year."

Bishop Thomas J. Thorburn, in his *Mythological Interpretation of the Gospels*, (33), says: "The earliest church commemorated it at various times from September to March, until in 354 A.D. Pope Julius I assimilated the festival with that of the birth of Mithra (Dec. 25th) in order to facilitate the more complete Christianisation of the empire. . . . There is a great deal of evidence to indicate that he was born in the month of October."

"The institution of the festival of the Nativity of Christ Jesus being held on the 25th of December, among the Christians, is attributed to Telesphorus, who flourished during the rule of Antonius Pius (A.D. 138-161), but the first *certain* traces of it are found about the time of the Emperor Commodus (A.D. 180-192)."

"If the writer of the *Gospel according to St. Luke* is correct, Jesus was not born until about A.D.10, for he explicitly tells us (ii, 1-7) that the event did not happen until Cyrenius was governor of Syria. . . . Cyrenius was not appointed. . . . until long after the death of Herod. . . . therefore about 10 A.D. . . . conjectures and traditions. . . . led one to the 20th of May, another to the 19th of April, and a third to the 5th of January. . . . It was not until the fifth century that this day (Dec. 25th) was generally agreed upon. . . . Eusebius, the first ecclesiastical historian, placed his birth at the time that Cyrenius was governor of Syria, and therefore about 10 A.D."

On the first moment after midnight of the 24th of December (i.e. on the morning of the 25th), nearly all the nations of the earth, as if by common consent, celebrated the accouchement of the *'Queen of Heaven,'* of the *'Celestial Virgin'* of the sphere, and the god *Sol.* . . . On this account the Christians *adopted it* as the time of the birth of their virgin-born God. . . . in order that whilst the heathen were busy with their *profane* ceremonies, the Christians might perform their *holy* rites undisturbed."[1]

"It was not until the year A.D. 530 or so—five centuries

---

[1] *Bible Myths*, Doane, 361-7.

after the supposed birth of Christ—that a Scythian monk, Dionysius Exiguus, an Abbot and astronomer of Rome, was commissioned to fix the day and year of that birth. A nice problem, considering the historical science of the period! For the year he assigns the date we now adopt, and for the day and month he adopted the 25th of December. . . . the very date, within a day or two, of the supposed birth of previous Sungods. . . . In fact, the dates of the main pagan religious festivals had by that time become so popular that Christianity was obliged to accommodate itself to them. . . . It was not until 534 A.D. that Christmas day and Epiphany were reckoned by the law courts as *dies non.*[2] Since the Christian system of reckoning was by the short cycle of the 19 year Epact, the dates were difficult to determine. But the dates were finally determined, not from any historical facts or mathematical data, but by the mere opinion of the clergymen concerned, as determined by their votes.

The researches of Dr. Albert T. Ohlmstead, of the University of Chicago's *Oriental Institute*, into the Babylonian records preserved on recently discovered clay tablets, shows that Jesus must have been at least 50 years old instead of 33 at the time of His crucifixion. "What is not so well known today," says Dr. Ohlmstead, "is that, thanks to astronomical tablets, we can establish a calendar for events in the late Babylonian period with rarely a probable error of a day. For the period from 367 to 11 B.C., our table is exact to a day."

Fitting this Babylonian calendar to the Passover dates of the year of the crucifixion, Dr. Ohlmstead declares that he has clinched the evidence that the crucifixion was on April 7th, 30 A.D. He says confidently: "The date of the crucifixion is as certain as any in ancient history and is more exact than the majority."[3]

"Since the dawn of astrological wisdom, astrologers

---

[2] *Pagan and Christian Creeds*, Carpenter, 26.
[3] *Science News Letter*, April 12th, 1941.

have attached paramount importance to the conjunctions of the major planets, Jupiter and Saturn. It was on these conjunctions that the Sages and Magi of such world-old civilizations as Chaldea, Babylonia, Assyria, Egypt, Persia and India based all their major and minor prophetic keys. For these conjunctions were held to coincide with the genesis of new kingdoms, new dynasties. . . . and the establishment of new religions, laws and social orders. . . . Consequently the Magi were fully aware that any work undertaken, or doctrine promulgated under the joint auspices of Jupiter and Saturn was likely to endure and become consolidated in time. . . . gradually grow to immense proportions, getting impetus and accretion in the passage of years, becoming firmly implanted in the minds and hearts of the people from generation to generation."

"In November, 662 B.C., Saturn and Jupiter formed their conjunction in the fiery sign *Sagittarius*, and was coincident with the birth of Zoroaster. . . . In October, 563 B.C., the same planets formed their conjunction in 5° of the practical, earthy sign *Taurus*, and this period saw the birth of Gatama Buddha. . . . In June of 384 B.C., Saturn and Jupiter formed their conjunction in the second degree of the intellectual and scientific sign *Gemini*. And this year witnessed the birth of the great Aristotle, the father of the analytical method. . . . At the birth of Mohamet, in A.D. 570, we again find these two planets together."[4]

"Jupiter and Saturn form a conjunction every 20 years, but in 240 year cycles, they form a conjunction in a given astrological quadruplicity, such as in a Fire, Earth, Air or Water sign. The following period of 240 years each of the 20-year conjunctions are in the same quadruplicity. The beginning of one of these cycles, or the first conjunction in a new quadruplicity is called a *Great Mutation*. There has been such a *Great Mutation* at the birth of every one of the great Teachers. It was in B.C. 7 that such a *Great Mutation* occurred in the sign *Pisces*, and it was on the basis of this conjunction of Saturn and Jupiter that

---

[4] Cyril Fagers, in *American Journal of Astrology*, Winter, 1937.

astrologers of Persia specifically predicted the birth of the Christ. And we believe that is the correct birth date."[5]

In a recent letter to the author, Mr. Robert L Ripley of "Believe It or Not" fame, corroborated the above quotations. He says: "Christ was not born December 25th, 1943 years ago! Most church authorities admit that our present calendar is based on the erroneous calculations of the sixth century monk, Dionysius Exiguus.

"According to Josephus (*Ant. xvii, 8, 1*) King Herod died in April of the year 4 B.C. Jesus' birth must have been prior to that time. The best conclusion is supplied by the Gospel, telling of the massacre of the babes ordered by Herod, that all children born within two years should be killed in order to include the Messiah. That would bring Christ's birth back to 6 B.C. (*Luke, ii, 1, 2. Matth. ii, 1, 16*).

"Kepler calculated that 'the Star of Bethlehem'—a conjunction of Jupiter and Saturn—was visible over Palestine about 7 B.C. The Jewish calendar of the olden days was very difficult to calculate for the reason that they used a strictly lunar year.

"Quirinius—under whose governorship of Syria the census which brought the family to Palestine is said to have been ordered—was Consul of Syria about 8 A.D. But Prof. W. M. Ramsay has discovered an authentic inscription—known as the Inscription of Pisidia—which makes it certain that Quirinius was Governor-Proconsul of Syria between 10 and 8 B.C. This can be reconciled almost wholly with the account of St. Luke, who claims that the census was ordered during the Consulship of Quirinius. That census brought the family to Bethlehem where later Jesus was born.

"But the results of the latest research—astronomical by Kepler and Weiseler; religious by Koenig; and historical by Prof. Ramsay, documentary—make it certain that

---

[5] Extract from a personal letter from Mr. Ernest A. Grant, the first President of the American Federation of Scientific Astrologers.

Jesus was born in August of the year 6 B.C. Therefore this is the year 1949 instead of 1943. BELIEVE IT OR NOT !"

During our visit to a certain Coptic temple in Egypt in 1938 we were told that the Coptic Church possesses detailed records, in actual physical documents, rescued from the great Library at Alexandria when it was pillaged and burned by Bishop Theopholis in 389 A.D., which give the details of Jesus' *three* sojourns in Egypt. Having had foreknowledge of the pillage and burning of the library, the Church secured the records and placed them where they would be secure from the ravages of insects, fanatics and the passage of the ages.

In one temple we were present at a ceremony held in the very cave or grotto in which the Holy Family are said to have lived when they first visited Egypt. After their return to Nazareth, between the ages of seven and twelve, Jesus' precocious wisdom refuted many of the doctrines of the learned Rabbis. He also denounced their alliance with Rome. This aroused such antagonism that He was again forced to flee into Egypt. There He was initiated into the Essenes of the Great White Brotherhood, and took the name of "Issa" and later was known as Saint Issa. There He studied in the temple schools for a number of years as a young man until He was ready to travel to the Far East. While the Masters of the Brotherhood could not add anything to His spiritual illumination, they did give Him much instruction as to the scientific technique concerning the mastery of His mind and His physical and finer bodies. They also stored His mind with the cosmic philosophy which had been handed down by the Brotherhood since the days of Atlantis.

After visiting Ethiopia, Arabia, India and Thibet, the Copts claim that Jesus returned to Palestine to take up His life's mission. Because of these travels He was well known in those countries, where the visit of any great man, and especially a great Initiate, was carefully recorded. Hence the name of the great Initiate and Master "Issa" appears in the Mohammedan *Koran* and in the ancient records of both Hindus and Thibetans.

In one of the temples we were shown the very bench on which it is claimed that Jesus sat at the temple services during the many years of His sojourn there. During His stay He trained seven Masters of the higher degrees of the Brotherhood to act as Custodians to preserve and transmit the whole truth of His doctrines — induding Karma and Reincarnation — unchanged by exoteric misinterpretations and translations, to succeeding ages until the cosmic cycle for His second coming should arrive. It is claimed that that time is now at hand, and that the prophecy of *Hosea* (xi, 1): "Out of Egypt have I called my Son," will again be fulfilled at the proper moment. But it will not be until the world is so sick of strife and war that it will realize the essential unity of all mankind, and that *brotherhood and co-operation* on all planes are the *basic laws of life*. Only then will it be ready to listen to and follow Him into the New Age of world unity, peace and happiness

Appendix D

INACCURACIES, CONTRADICTIONS AND PHENOMENA

No doubt many persons have heard it said that there were many inaccuracies and contradictions in the *Gospels*, but when we come to list them the number is astonishing. And this list does not include the many more which involve hair-splitting details of philology, grammar and punctuation. They have to do, not with mere details, but with scientific facts of astronomy, physics, meteorology, and the accepted facts of history. These the literalists, fundamentalists, and those who hold that the whole *Bible* is the word for word, God-inspired and inerrant word of God, will find it impossible to explain. Yet all are satisfactorily explained by the symbolical and metaphysical interpretation which we have endeavored to present in this volume.

1. *St. Luke* tells us (i, 26) that the angel Gabriel was sent to "a city in Galilee, named Nazareth," where he would find Joseph and Mary. History records no such village in Galilee either before or after the Christian era until after the third century A.D. Probably the first reference to it was made by St. Epiphanius (315-402 A.D.).), and St. Jerome (340-420 A.D.) toward the middle of the fourth century by which time such a village may have been established.

2. *St. Luke* says (ii, 1,2) that Joseph and Mary were on their way from Galilee to Bethlehem in Judea (about 100 miles) to be taxed when "Cyrenius was governor of Syria." History shows that Quintus Sentius Saturninus

was governor of Syria at the time of Jesus' birth, not Cyrenius. And even though Cyrenius later did make a register of the inhabitants of Judea and Samaria, it did not include Galilee. Hence Joseph would not have been affected and would not have had to make the journey. Also, in the Roman censuses the residents were registered at the towns and villages where they lived, not where they were born. So here are two reasons why such a journey was unnecessary, even ten years after Jesus' birth.

As opposed to this it is claimed that because of the discovery of an edict issued by Gaius Vibius Maximus, Eparch of Egypt, in the 7th year of the reign of Trajan, (about 104 A.D.), requiring all persons residing out of their *nomes* to return to their homes for the coming census, it can be *assumed* that a similar custom was in vogue in Palestine 104 years previous! It is, of course, pure assumption to say that because such an edict was issued in *Egypt*, it must have been the custom in *Palestine* 104 years previously! and without the slightest corroboration.[1]

Roman history, as recorded on the ruins of the *Monumentum Ancyranum* at Angora, Turkey, shows that Emperor Augustus had three "lustrums" or censuses of the Roman Empire taken in 28 B.C., 8 A.D. and 14 A.D., but none near the reputed date of Jesus' birth in 4 B.C.

3. The geneology of Jesus is given through Joseph to make Him a descendant of the House of David. Yet we are distinctly told (*St. Luke, i, 34*) that Joseph was not his father, for Mary told the angel Gabriel that she was still a virgin. "How can this be, seeing I know not a man?" Gabriel then told her that a physical father would not be necessary since, "The Holy Ghost shall come upon thee, and the power of the Highest shall overshadow thee:" Thus the only geneology Jesus could have would come through His mother, Mary. But she, like her cousin, Elizabeth, was of the House of Levi, not of David.

4. *St. Luke (i, 35)* tells us that He was miraculously

---

[1] *Mythical Interpretation of the Gospels*, Thorburn, 332.

conceived by "the power of the Highest." But St Paul states definitely (*Romans, i, 3*) that He "was made after the seed of David *according to the flesh.*"

5. St Luke implies that Jesus was born in a *stable* (*ii, 7*), while St. Matthew tells us that the Wise Men found Him in a *house* (*ii, 11*). Yet the early Church historians (Tertullian, Eusebius, etc.) say that He was born in a cave.

6. The fact that the Angel Gabriel both *appeared* to and *spoke* to Joseph, Zacharius and Mary assumes either that all three of them were *clairvoyant* and also *clairaudient*, or that Gabriel materialized before them—or at least materialized his larynx and vocal cords, a psychic phenomenon which has been photographed repeatedly in modern psychic research—and spoke in an audible voice.

7. For over eighteen centuries (until 1854) the Christian Church could not make up its mind as to the truth of the Immaculate Conception.

8. We are told that the Wise Men followed a certain special Star which altho they saw it in the East, it led them West to Jerusalem. It not only led them, but it actually *stopped*, not only at an obscure village, but actually "*stood* over where the young child was." (*St. Matthew, i, 9*). It is self-evident that it is a physical impossibility for a star to stop, and especially over any designated place.

9. The Magi told Herod that they had seen His star in the East (*St. Matthew, ii, 2*), yet they travelled West! i.e., "*from* the East to Jerusalem" (*ii, 1*) as the star went before them. The star then changed its course and *went South* to Bethlehem! This is an astronomical impossibility.

10. We are told that the shepherds were watching their flocks on the hillside at night (*St. Luke, ii, 8*) on December 25th. That would be during the coldest of the winter months in Palestine. During that period the sheep were never left out in the fields, but are either kept in or at least driven back to the sheep-fold at night. Hence there were neither sheep nor shepherds out on the hillside that night

11. We are told that Herod. "slew all the children that

were in Bethlehem, and in all the coasts thereof, from two years old and under." (*St. Matthew, ii, 16*). The number is variously estimated at from 14 to 20,000. But there is no record of any such slaughter, either in the carefully compiled Jewish or Roman history.

12. St. Matthew says *(ii, 13, 14)* that as soon as the Wise Men left Joseph: "he arose, he took the young child and his mother by night, and departed in to Egypt." Yet *St. Luke* tells us (*ii, 21-2*) that instead of fleeing into Egypt that same night, the family *remained right there* in Bethlehem for *eight days*, had Jesus circumcized, and *remained there over a month* longer until Mary's 40 days of purification were over. Even then they did not go to Egypt, but presented Jesus at the temple in Jerusalem, and then returned to their home in Galilee. Furthermore, "his parents went to Jerusalem *every year* at the Feast of the Passover." (*ii, 39,41*).

13. In *St. Mark, i, 12* we are told that after the baptism, "*Immediately* the Spirit *driveth* him into the wilderness." But in *St. Luke, iv, 1* we are told that it was only after Jesus "returned from the Jordan, and was *led* (not driven) by the Spirit into the wilderness." And in *St. John, i, 35-9* he tells us that "the *next day* after John stood, and two of his disciples," saw Jesus "and abode with him that day. . . . The day *following* Jesus would go forth into Galilee," instead of into the wilderness. Besides, there was no wilderness near either place.

14. *St. Matthew*, (*ii, 5,6*) makes Bethlehem the home of Joseph and Mary. They go to Nazareth only after their return from Egypt. But *St. Luke* (*ii, 4*) tells us that Nazareth was their home and that they went to Bethlehem only to be taxed.

15. In *St. Matthew, iv, 5* we are told that the Devil took Jesus "into the holy city, and setteth him on a pinnacle of the temple." In the first place, how could so foul a fiend as the Devil have access to so consecrated a sanctuary as the holy temple? And in the second place, the temple had no pinnacles. Its top was dome-shaped. Also the story

assumes that all the kingdoms of the world belonged to the Devil to give away to anyone he chose. And there was no "exceeding high mountain" near Jerusalem from which all the kingdoms of the world could be seen.

16. In one place (*St. Matthew, xxvi, 20,49*) we are told that Jesus' betrayal took place after the last supper on the night of the Passover, but in *St. Luke, xxii, 66* we are told that it took place the *next day*, "As soon as it was day."

17. In *St. Matthew, xxvii, 3-5* we are told that Judas repented his betrayal of Jesus and brought back the 30 pieces of silver to the chief priests, "and went and hanged himself." And the chief priests "bought with them the potter's field." But in *Acts, i, 18* we are told that Judas did not bring back the silver to the chief priests, but instead "purchased a field with the reward of his iniquity."

18. Instead of Judas's hanging himself, the same passage says that he died from a fall "Falling headlong, he burst asunder in the midst, and all his bowels gushed out. . . . And it was known unto all the dwellers of Jerusalem."

19. *St. Mark, xvi, 2* says that when *three* women visited the tomb of Jesus "they saw a young man sitting on the right side, clothed in a long white garment." *St. Luke, xxiv, 4* says that *several* women visited the tomb and "behold, *two men* stood by them in shining garments." But *St. John, xx, 11* says that Mary Magdalene at first went to the tomb *alone*, but saw no one. Then she called Peter and John and they both went into the sepulchre but saw only the grave clothes. After they had gone away Mary again "looked into the sepulchre, and seeth *two angels* in white."

20. *St. Mark, xvi, 9* says that the angels told the women to go and tell Jesus' disciples that He had arisen, but they were afraid and "neither said anything to any man." But *St. Luke, xxiv, 9* says that they "returned from the sepulchre, and *told all* those things unto the eleven, and to all the rest."

21. *St. John, xxi, 12,13* says that after His resurrection Jesus took bread and fish and gave them to His disciples, but without eating them Himself. *St. Luke, xxiv, 41,43,*

on the other hand say that it was Jesus who asked for meat. "And they gave him a piece of broiled fish, and of an honeycomb. And he took it, and did eat before them."

22. In *St. Luke, xxiii, 43* Jesus promises the thief on the cross: "Today shalt thou be with me in paradise," yet Jesus did not make His ascension for forty days.

23. Since the grave clothes were found in the tomb by Peter (*St. Luke, xxiv, 12*), Where did Jesus get the clothes which made Mary Magdalene mistake Him for a gardener? (*St. John, xx, 15*).

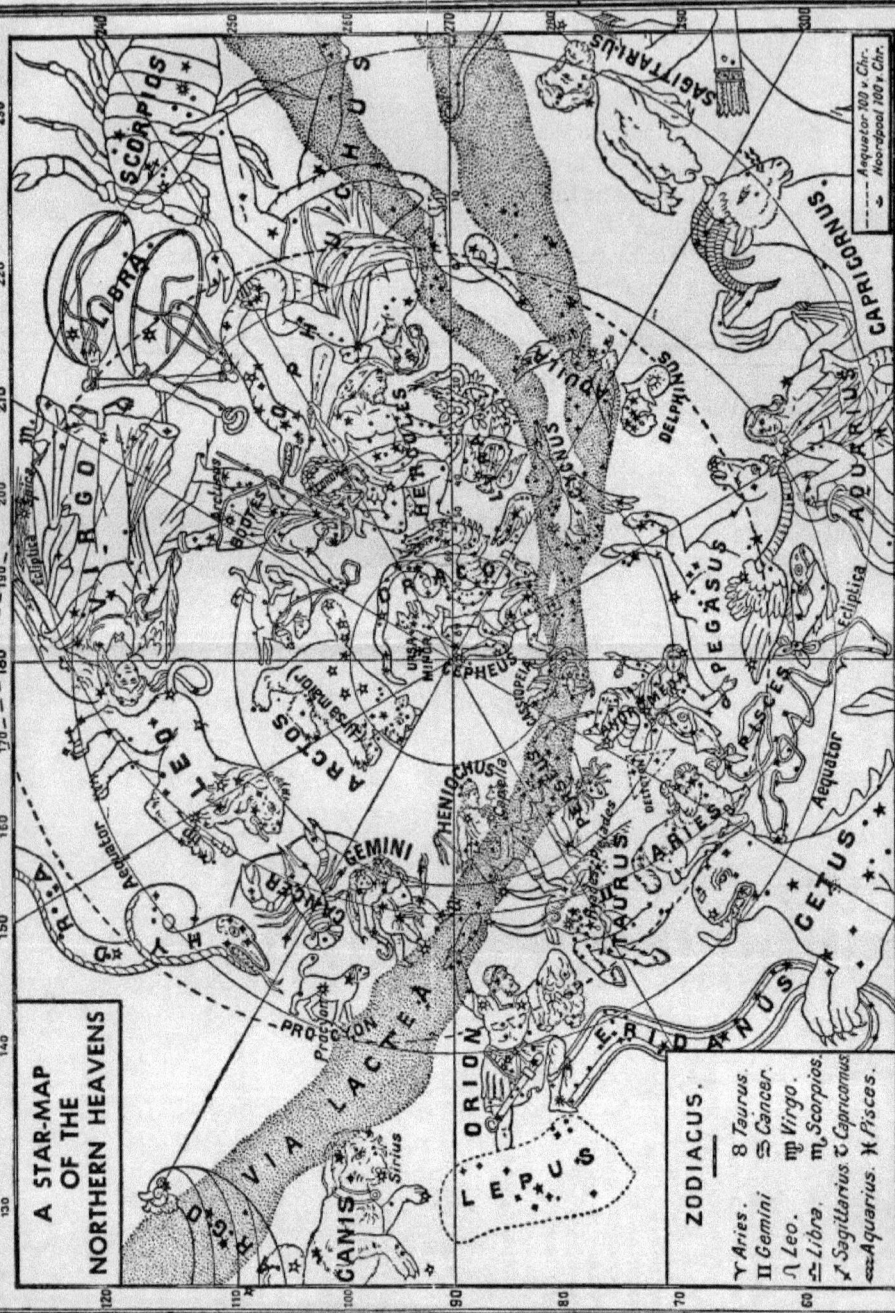

A STAR-MAP
OF THE
NORTHERN HEAVENS

ZODIACUS.

♈ Aries.   ♉ Taurus.
♊ Gemini   ♋ Cancer.
♌ Leo.   ♍ Virgo.
♎ Libra.   ♏ Scorpios.
♐ Sagittarius ♑ Capricornus.
♒ Aquarius. ♓ Pisces.

SCORPIUS
LIBRA
VIRGO
BOOTES
HERCULES
DRACO
CEPHEUS
ARCTOS
Ursa minor
Ursa major
HENIOCHUS
GEMINI
CANCER
HYDRA
VIA LACTEA
CANIS
Sirius
PROCYON
ORION
LEPUS
ERIDANUS
CETUS
TAURUS
ARIES
PISCES
ANDROMEDA
PEGASUS
AQUARIUS
CAPRICORNUS
SAGITTARIUS
DELPHINUS
AQUILA
CASSIOPEIA
OPHIUCHUS

Aequator 300 v. Chr.
Noordpool 100 v. Chr.

INDEX

www.ingramcontent.com/pod-product-compliance
Lightning Source LLC
LaVergne TN
LVHW051110080426
835510LV00018B/1985